TEACHING AND LEARNING

FORMAL METHODS

AN

Academic Press

International Series in Formal Methods

Series editor: Michael G. Hinchey

TEACHING AND LEARNING
FORMAL METHODS

edited by

C. Neville Dean

School of Applied Sciences
Anglia Polytechnic University
Cambridge, UK

and

Michael G. Hinchey

Department of Computer and Information Science
New Jersey Institute of Technology
Newark, NJ 07102, USA

ACADEMIC PRESS
Harcourt Brace & Company, Publishers
London, San Diego, New York, Boston, Tokyo, Toronto

ACADEMIC PRESS LIMITED
24–28 Oval Road
LONDON NW1 7DX

U.S. Edition Published by
ACADEMIC PRESS INC.
San Diego, CA 92101

This book is printed on acid free paper

A catalogue record for this book is available from the British Libarary

ISBN 0–12–349040–5

Printed in Great Britain by WBC Book Manufacturers Ltd,
Bridgend, Mid Glamorgan

Table of contents

Foreword

So-called "natural language" is wonderful for the purposes it was created for, such as to be rude in, to tell jokes in, to cheat or to make love in (and Theorists of Literary Criticism can even be content–free in it), but it is hopelessly inadequate when we have to deal unambiguously with situations of great intricacy, situations which unavoidably arise in such activities as legislation, arbitration, mathematics or programming. To this perplexing dilemma we can observe three main reactions.

The first reaction is to stick to those activities where unrefined natural language (kind of) suffices (*vide* the educationalist telling the future social worker to include in her reports no sentences of more than 17 words).

The second reaction is to bend the natural language to one's special purpose, as we can observe in the practice of government, but the resulting language is only superficially "natural", for it is in fact so unnatural that even the educated layman needs a lawyer or tax consultant to decipher it.

The third reaction is the most drastic one: a completely new language is designed, geared to its purpose and without pretence to being "natural", as we can see in formal mathematics and programming.

The last approach is, of course, the one with the greatest potential: unfettered by compatibility requirements, freed from the shackles of our native tongues, the new formalism can be designed to facilitate the major manipulations, and can thus become a highly effective, powerful and reliable tool, but experience has shown that it cannot avoid becoming controversial as well. All its technical merits fail to address the social problem that the smooth mastery that enables one to use a calculus with confidence and advantage is not reached without an intellectual investment of exercise and training for which most people are just too lazy: it is much simpler to declare that the formalism is no good and that learning how to use its calculus is not worth the trouble. The majority of people — even in mathematics and computing! — prefer the comfort of a fuzzy language in which cruel precision is impossible.

In this field of tension, on the cross–roads of incompatible tendencies, "Teaching and Learning Formal Methods" is a valuable anthology. Most of its authors are seasoned scientists with considerable educational experience. In some of the essays one can read between the lines the sad combination (which is only to be expected) of high expectation of the technology and low expectation of the student body's willingness to turn dream into reality. The book as a whole contains a wealth of technical and educational material that convinces me that in this area my academic colleagues are doing exactly what they should do: developing and propagating an indispensable technology so that it will be available when "the world out there" undeniably needs it.

Austin, 12 May 1996   Edsger W. Dijkstra

Series Foreword

As early as 1949, computer pioneers realized that writing a program that executed as planned was no simple task. Turing even saw the need to address the issues of program correctness and termination, foretelling groundbreaking work of Edsger Dijkstra, Bob Floyd and Tony Hoare, and Sue Owicki and David Gries two and three decades later.

The term *formal methods* refers to the application of mathematical techniques for the specification, analysis, design, implementation and subsequent maintenance of complex computer software and hardware. These techniques have proven themselves, when correctly and appropriately applied, to result in systems of the highest quality, which are well documented, more easy to maintain, and which promote software reuse.

With emerging legislation, and increasing emphasis in standards and university curricula, formal methods are set to become even more important in system development. The *Academic Press International Series in Formal Methods* aims to present results from the cutting edge of formal methods research and practice.

Books in the series will address the use of formal methods in both hardware and software development, and the role of formal methods in the development of safety-critical and real-time systems, hardware–software co-design, testing, simulation and prototyping, software quality assurance, software reuse, security, and many other areas. The series aims to include both basic and advanced textbooks, monographs, reference books and collections of high quality papers which will address managerial issues, the development process, requirements engineering, tool support, methods integration, metrics, reverse engineering, and issues relating to formal methods education.

It is our aim that, in due course, the *Academic Press International Series in Formal Methods* will provide a rich source of information for students, teachers, academic researchers and industrial practitioners alike. And I hope that, for many, it will be a first port-of-call for relevant texts and literature.

Professor Mike Hinchey

Preface

After over a quarter of a century of research and development, formal methods are now identified as one of the most promising techniques for the development of quality hardware and software systems.

Their use, though currently far from commonplace, in large-scale industrial practice — and particularly some highly-publicized success stories — has indicated that projects involving the application of formal methods can come in on-time, within budget, and yet produce high quality software and hardware systems that satisfy the requirements and constraints of users, procurers, and regulatory bodies.

A number of issues still need to be addressed for the successful and widespread uptake of formal methods in day-to-day industrial development. Such issues include the need for greater emphasis on the methodological aspects of formal development methods, the development of standards for the application of formal methods, and the need for industrial-strength toolkits.

Most of all, the need arises for an appropriately educated and trained workforce that can apply the results of existing and future academic research to the practical problems real-world. This means that graduating engineers, mathematicians and computer scientists must have a sufficient background in the relevant mathematics, as well as hands-on experience in applying formal methods.

This collection aims to present the issues that are relevant to the education of our future formal methods practitioners, and to the continued training and retraining of industrial users.

The latter is addressed by John Wordsworth in his paper *An industrial perspective on educational issues relating to formal methods*. He identifies the differing roles that an industrial practitioner must play, and the ramifications that this has for education and training.

In *Effective formal methods education for professional engineers*, David Garlan describes experiences of teaching formal methods on a professional Master of Software Engineering course at Carnegie Mellon University, where formal methods are integrated into each module, and whereby students are exposed to several different notations. The results have been remarkable, and the course is widely-cited as exemplary of the sort of professional training course that we should be striving for.

Based on his considerable experience in both education and industrial practice, David Lorge Parnas presents his views on the necessary educational background that we must provide our future graduates with in his first paper, *Education for computing professionals.* In his second paper, *Teaching programming as engineering*, he continues his emphasis on the need to address engineering issues in system development.

Jeannette Wing describes typical errors of novice specifiers in her contribution, *Hints to specifiers*, and offers advice for beginners and experienced developers alike that should help them to improve the quality and readability of their specifications.

Michael Barnett and James Foster in their chapter, *Moore formal methods in the classroom*, describe their experiences with using the Moore method to teach formal methods, giving their students hands-on experience with proof and proof techniques.

Neville Dean and Mike Hinchey (i.e., ourselves!) report, by contrast, on experiences with emphasizing hands-on experience with modeling, in the chapter *Formal methods and modeling in context*, the belief being that modeling skills are best learned through practice. A role-playing approach was used to give students the necessary experience, and is reported in detail in our chapter.

Kate Finney and Alex Fedorec describe the application of quantitative, educational research in their chapter, *An empirical study of specification readability*. Their study has produced interesting results and findings on the factors affecting the readability of Z specifications, and the success with which their students took to formal specification. It also demonstrates the value of quantitative research, to supplement the more anecdotal and purely qualitative research that is often reported both in this volume and elsewhere. A further, and quite extensive, example of the great value of this quantitative approach is presented by Vicki Almstrum who describes significant results on her study of the problems that students encounter when introduced to logic. Her chapter, *Student difficulties with logic*, describes experiments conducted to identify problem areas, and describes some very interesting results.

Joseph Goguen and Grant Malcolm describe their experiences of providing students with tool support (in the guise of OBJ) to prove the correctness of programs written in an imperative programming language. Their course, and their experiences, are described in their chapter, *An executable course in algebraic semantics*.

David Gries, another highly-respected educator, considers the teaching of equational logic in his chapter *Improving the curriculum through the teaching of calculation and discrimination*. His view is that an emphasis on calculation in the curriculum can offer great benefits in the overall mathematical education of our students, and to making discrete mathematics and logic seem more relevant to computing and software engineering students.

Wim Feijen and Netty van Gasteren's chapter, *Programming, proving, and calculation*, introduces a number of notes and examples emphasizing the relationship between programming, proof, and the calculation of programs, and the benefits to students of emphasizing such a relationship.

The relevance of formal methods to hardware development is considered by Mike Gordon in the final chapter, *Teaching hardware and software verification in a uniform framework*. This chapter describes a module taught at University of

Cambridge, which provides students with experience of various techniques for the verification of both software and hardware systems.

The collection addresses a wide-range of issues, and we trust that at least some of these will be of significant interest to the reader.

We would like to express our sincerest thanks to Professor Edsger W. Dijkstra for kindly agreeing to write an introduction to the collection, and for suggestions for suitable contributions. We are grateful to several colleagues who suggested topics for inclusion, and who made suggestions for improvements. Most of all, we are grateful to everyone who contributed to this collection.

Our grateful thanks also go to Kate Brewin and Heather Burroughs of Academic Press, for their faith in us, their continuing support, and their patience when things went wrong.

C.N.D.   M.G.H.
Cambridge, England   May 1996   *Limerick, Ireland*

List of contributors

Dr. Vicki L. Almstrum, University of Texas–Austin, Department of Computer Science, Austin, TX, USA.

Dr. Michael Barnett, Microsoft Corporation, Redmond, WA, USA

Dr. C. Neville Dean, Anglia Polytechnic University, School of Applied Sciences, Cambridge, UK.

Professor Edsger W. Dijkstra, University of Texas–Austin, Department of Computer Science, Austin, TX, USA.

Alex M. Fedorec, The University of Greenwich, School of Computing and Mathematical Sciences, Woolwich, London, UK.

Dr. Wim Feijen, Eindhoven University of Technology, Department of Computer Science, Eindhoven, The Netherlands.

Kate M. Finney, The University of Greenwich, School of Computing and Mathematical Sciences, Woolwich, London, UK.

Professor James Foster, University of Idaho, Department of Computer Science, Moscow, IO, USA.

Professor David Garlan, Carnegie Mellon University, School of Computer Science, Pittsburgh, PA, USA.

Dr. Netty van Gasteren, Eindhoven University of Technology, Department of Computer Science, Eindhoven, The Netherlands.

Professor Joseph A. Goguen, Oxford University Computing Laboratory, Oxford, UK.

Professor Michael J.C. Gordon, University of Cambridge Computer Laboratory, Cambridge, UK.

Professor David Gries, Cornell University, Department of Computer Science, Ithaca, NY, USA.

Professor Michael G. Hinchey, New Jersey Institute of Technology, Department of Computer and Information Science, Newark, NJ, USA.

Dr. Grant Malcolm, Oxford University Computing Laboratory, Oxford, UK.

Professor David Lorge Parnas, McMaster University, Communications Research Laboratory, Hamilton, Ontario, Canada.

Professor Jeannette M. Wing, Carnegie Mellon University, School of Computer Science, Pittsburgh, PA, USA.

John B. Wordsworth, IBM UK Laboratories, Hursley Park, Winchester, UK.

An industrial perspective on educational issues relating to formal methods

1.1 Introduction

By *formal methods* of software development I mean methods that exploit the power of discrete mathematics (set theory and predicate calculus). The value of discrete mathematics is that it allows developers to make a precise record of some things that are, in traditional development practice, left vague. In formal methods of software development, mathematical notations are most often applied to the specification of functional requirements (what the software will do). They are less frequently applied to recording design (how the components of the software system will be organized). The formal methods on which the following remarks are based are state-based methods. These methods support the construction of an abstract model of the software system in which state components have values that are modified by operations.

- Vienna Development Method (VDM) is a specification and design notation. It is the oldest of the formal methods, and probably the one most widely used. See Jones (1986).

- Z is a specification notation that can be used in many parts of software development. It is a notation rather than a method, and can be used in conjunction with traditional software development methods. See Wordsworth (1992).

- The B-Method is a complete development method. It uses abstract machine notation (AMN) for constructing specifications and designs, and it supports the use of code generators to produce compilable source code from formal designs. See Wordsworth (1996).

There are other formal methods that are not considered here.

My involvement with formal methods of software development has been as a student, teacher, and practitioner in an industrial software development environment. I have been largely concerned with training, the transfer of job-related skills and attitudes, rather than with education. But it is clear to me that the problems that face formal methods today are in education, the transfer of cultural values, rather than in training. The problems are not how to train people to use formal methods, but how to educate industry and society to use the trained people effectively. My concerns about the difficulties that face education in formal methods can be summarized in four questions:

1. Is formal methods education worth the effort?

2. How are we to teach industry the proper roles for software development using formal methods?

3. How are we to convince our professional institutions of the proper place of formal methods in our profession?

4. How are we to get our universities to teach mathematics as the basis of all software engineering activity?

1.2   Progress so far

Over the last few years, formal methods have taken a growing share of academic education and industrial training in software development. The output of the Software Engineering Institute at Carnegie Mellon university, and the introduction of formal methods courses, especially Z-related courses, in UK universities are indicators of this growth. The initial trickle of books on this subject has become a respectable stream that is an effective tributary to software engineering education.

1.3   The fundamental question

But the first real question that we must face in formal methods education is this: "Is it worth the effort?" As an industrial student and teacher of formal methods I know how easy it is to be enthused with the application of mathematics to software development, but how difficult it is to make this application in the workplace. Though most industrial courses are courses of training that transfer specific skills, the use of mathematics in software development is sufficiently surprising to existing programmers that there is a significant education content in the courses. The preparation and delivery of courses in formal methods suitable for industrial students demands a lot from instructors, even those for whom instruction is a career, and too often instructors see their achievements in the classroom come to nothing in the work-place.

Industrial use of formal methods is under constant attack. Even where there is adequate training and enthusiasm, users of formal methods are continually surrounded by a desert of incomprehension, and by pressure to omit the essential in favour of the expedient. A patient professional response to these pressures is hard to find. The provision of training in formal methods needs to be guided by certain principles formulated in Wordsworth (1987) and I should like to elaborate these principles here.

Academic teachers are better placed to see their labour bear fruit in graduate and undergraduate courses. A well-chosen case study can allow students to explore the influence of mathematics on many stages of the software development process. In a later section of this chapter I outline the kinds of roles that software engineering graduates might fill in an industrial software engineering organisation. There should be no difficulty in the academic environment in including appropriate mathematics in a well-balanced software engineering or computer science degree course, in spite of the lukewarm attitudes of our leading professional institutions. But even well-educated graduates can find it difficult to apply their formal methods skills in an industrial environment.

1.4 Industrial training

If we are to train people to fill roles, we need to know what the roles are, and what activities, skills, and attitudes are appropriate to them. When formal methods were beginning to be used in industrial contexts, these roles were not well understood, and developers of industrial training courses had to invent them. It could hardly have been otherwise then, but now things should be different, as we have over ten years experience of success and failure in using formal methods in industrial contexts. However, I think that the bulk of industry, even the bulk of that part that has invested in formal methods, does not know what the proper roles are. So here is another question: How are we to teach industry the proper roles for software development using formal methods?

1.5 Software engineering roles

In Wordsworth (1993), I outlined the main roles to be filled in software development using formal methods, and here I should like to characterize those roles in more detail. The providers of education in formal methods need to understand these roles because the education provided needs to underpin the training that students will later receive in an industrial context. The roles are as follows:

- Specification engineer

- Design engineer

- Programmer

- Documentation engineer

- Test engineer

- Service engineer

1.5.1   Specification engineer

The work of the *specification engineer* is part of the requirements-gathering process. The specification engineer is skilled in formalizing the informal, and of interpreting the formal in informal terms. He or she is the salesperson of formal methods, because customers of software are part of the great desert of incomprehension I mentioned earlier. "Customers don't understand mathematics, and never will" is the enemy's slogan here. The specification engineer must make them eager to learn. Being a front for the development organization, the specification engineer needs to have a good idea of what the development organization can achieve in the time the customer is prepared to wait and for a price that the customer can afford to pay. The specification engineer's skills are wide-ranging, and the job is an exacting but exciting one. The specification engineer must establish proper formal and informal communications between customers and the development organization. The informal communication takes place in a natural language like English, and uses a technical vocabulary approved by the customer and understood by customer and developers. It is important that this vocabulary is customer-centered, related to the customer's perceptions of the problem that the software is to solve, rather than programmer-centered, related to the proposed technical solution. Deciding the technical vocabulary can be done with the help of the documentation engineer (see below). The formal communication is the mathematics that makes the informal vocabulary precise. Each of the informal concepts of the vocabulary needs to be formalized using an appropriate mathematical notation.

In current software development practice, part of the work of the specification engineer is done during requirements gathering and analysis, and the rest is not done at all. Although a technical vocabulary is established, it is usually programmer-centered, and is not made precise. In this way the distinction between specification (what the software must do) and design (how it will do it) is blurred.

1.5.2   Design engineer

The second role is that of the *design engineer*. The design engineer's job is to decide what components will be used to build the system, and how they will be organized to provide what the specification promises. One of the things the design engineer does not have to do is to worry about the functional requirements, because these have been sorted out by the specification engineer and the customer to their mutual satisfaction. This will come as a great surprise to those used to traditional software development activity, since arguing about the requirements, usually without any reference to the customer, is a continual accompaniment to the whole process — design, coding, testing, and service — and can even continue beyond the death of the product. However, it is possible for the design engineer to discover aspects of the specification that are difficult or impossible to implement, and to wish to change the specification. The design engineer must recognize when a specification change is required, and confirm it with the parties to the specification, namely the specification engineer and the customer. If any role in software development has the right to be considered engineering, it is this one. More technical vocabulary is developed in the design phase, and the documentation engineer should be involved here.

In current software development practice, the role of design engineer is usually combined with that of programmer, or programming team leader. Because a clear distinction has not been made between specification and design, this part of the process is really filling in the details of the design already begun when the requirements were gathered. Unfortunately the details being filled in turn out to be specification details as well as design details, so the specification is changed, often without consultation with the customer.

1.5.3 Programmer

The third role is that of the *programmer*. This role is like the design engineer's in that it involves working from precise specifications and organizing things to implement them, but in the programmer's case the specifications are the output of the design process, and the things to be organized are program data structures and program statements. This also is very much an engineering activity. Again it should be said that worrying about the functional requirements must be no part of the programmer's duties. Nevertheless I have been at code reviews at which the behavior of the external interface of a piece of code was entirely disrupted by a sudden feeling that to do X in circumstance Y was quite the wrong thing. Although the predicates of the specification had been reviewed and approved long before, the appearance of IF Y THEN X caused a reaction previously absent. At last we were talking about something real, and we felt it deserved some real attention. However, it is possible for the programmer to discover aspects of the design that are difficult or impossible to implement. The programmer must recognize when a design change is required, and confirm it with the parties to the design, namely the design engineer and the specification engineer. It will occasionally happen that programming activity will require a specification change, but if such a change is necessary it must be reworked through the specification and the design before being implemented in the programming.

In current software development practice, it is the programmer who is first faced with the problem of attributing a precise meaning to the requirements. The programmer is often required to make specification changes without consulting the customer.

1.5.4 Documentation engineer

The *documentation engineer* will ensure that the internal documentation of specifications, designs, and code are of a high standard, and that external publications present the different classes of user of a product with clear information about the product and their relation to it. Professional writers are usually employed to write *publications*, manuals for the use of customers of the product. In Wordsworth (1993) I suggested that *documentation*, retained by the development organization, should be seen by software manufacturers as a valuable business asset, but professional writers are seldom, perhaps never, used for this. I believe that the idea that professional writers should have a hand in writing documentation is novel, and perhaps revolutionary. Formal specifications written in VDM, Z, or B, part of product documentation, form an excellent basis for understanding interfaces and communicating them to users, which is the purpose of publications. I suggested above that the documentation engineer could be involved in establishing the customer-centered technical vocabulary for the product, and the programmer-centered vocabulary for the design. This is because the some of the publications will rely heavily on these two vocabularies, so the documentation engineer needs to be involved in auditing them. Stylistic and grammatical concerns need to be dealt with as soon as the vocabulary is assembled.

In current software development practice, technical writers are often not used until product development is well advanced, and hewing a sensible customer-centered vocabulary out of the common parlance of the developers is often a mammoth task.

1.5.5   Test engineer

In software development using formal methods, the role of the *test engineer* is not so much to detect errors of function as to confirm the soundness of the design decisions with respect to the non-functional requirements, and the clarity of the external publications. A precise specification tells the testers what to test, and how to judge whether the outcome of a test is correct. Since testers view the product from the customer's point of view, they can test the technical vocabulary of the specification, and the use of that vocabulary in the publications.

In current development practice, software testing can degenerate into a struggle between two different views of what the requirements mean. The first view is that of the programmers, who have embodied their view in the program code. The other view is that of the testers, who have only the informal requirements to guide them, and have embodied their view in the test cases and the interpretation of the outcomes of the tests.

1.5.6   Service engineer

The *service engineer* will use the documentation and publications produced by the development process to determine whether a reported behavior is erroneous, and what changes to specification, design, code, documentation, and publications are necessary to correct it. The amount of work for the service engineer will depend on what risks have been accepted during the development.

In traditional software development practice, the service engineer is in the centre of the continuing battle to determine the functional requirements of the software system. The users advise the service organization of problems, and the service engineer must resolve them. The only precise documentation the engineer has is the program code, which expresses only the programmer's view of the requirements, and expresses them in a very user-unfriendly language.

These are, I think, the principal roles we should be creating through our training of software engineers in industry. They are the kinds of roles in which new graduates can develop into software engineering professionals. But what is the attitude of professional institutions to the use of formal methods?

1.6 Professional institutions

I hinted earlier that I was dissatisfied with the attitudes of the professional institutions to formal methods, and I should like to say a little bit more about this. In November 1989 I attended a meeting in London to discuss a draft of BCS/IEE (1990), a report on undergraduate software engineering education produced by a joint committee of the two professional associations for software engineers. At this meeting, one of my colleagues and I were the only representatives of British Industry, apart from a few of the university teachers there who also represented their companies. As far as speakers were concerned, I was the voice of Industry in the groves of Academe. Professional institutions are not the places where revolutions are made, and although the report wished to emphasize that software engineering was not just another name for advanced programming, the curricula it recommended suggested that it was. Part of the trouble seems to be that the professional institutions reflect the confusions of their members with an amazing degree of accuracy. Nobody seems to have a very clear idea of what software engineering is, but everyone is sure that what they do must be part of it. Consensus seems preferable to clarification, evolution to revolution. I was put on near the end of the afternoon, and I attempted to explain why I thought that a revolution in attitudes to software development was necessary if any substantial improvements were to be made. A few of the earlier speakers had expressed some misgivings about the concentration on programming and testing in the proposals, and the lack of attention to the earlier stages of software development, but others had expressed the opinion that the earlier stages were too difficult for young minds, and that prospective employers were more likely to be looking for programmers than requirements analysts. This attitude seems to betray a misunderstanding of the difference between university education and industrial training.

This reflection brings me to my last question: How are we to get our universities to teach mathematics as the basis of all software engineering activity?

1.7   University education in software development

Universities need to acknowledge that software is an important part of the computer industry, and that software engineering is not just an advanced kind of programming. In my earlier remarks I have tried to make it plain that programming is an essential activity whose skills have a mathematical foundation that every programmer should know, but programming is not the whole story, and it is a mistake to think that programming skills will solve problems in other parts of the development process. Perhaps university teachers lack an appreciation of software development as a process with different phases needing different skills. I hope that my clarification of software development roles will help to improve this situation. In Wordsworth (1992) and Wordsworth (1996) I have tried to indicate some of the ways that the theoretical and practical aspects of software development can illuminate one another. To those whose primary interest is mathematical, I should like to point out that software development is an excellent field for the application of mathematics. Hardly anything that the software engineer does has not got a mathematical theory that can explain and illuminate it. In a brief review (Wordsworth, 1990) of the BCS/IEE report I identified certain aspects of software engineering, neglected in the report, in which mathematics could be used. They were the study and formalization of customer requirements (part of the work of the specification engineer), process modelling and quality control, and reverse engineering. For those whose primary interest is in the practical development of large-scale software, the help that mathematics can give in controlling and understanding the software is immense. It is of course a revolution to suggest that mathematics should be made the basis of an entire education program in software development, but one that I feel obliged to propose.

Of course you may object that the espousal of mathematics as a teaching medium makes the courses more difficult to understand, because we are not good at teaching mathematics, and our students are not good at understanding it. It seems to me that this, if it is true, is a significant issue. We have to find ways of improving our teaching and enthusing our undergraduates, or of selecting them better.

1.8   Conclusion

I have raised and discussed four significant issues of education in formal methods affecting industrial software developers, professional societies and universities. The paper suggests that universities have a critical part to play in fomenting a software engineering revolution based on the use of formal methods.

Acknowledgements

I am grateful to Mark Ardis of AT&T Research and Neville Dean of Anglia Polytechnic University for several useful comments that encouraged me to improve the paper in various ways.

References

BCS/IEE (1990) *The BCS/IEE Joint Report on Undergraduate Curricula in Software Engineering*, British Computer Society and Institution of Electrical Engineers.

Jones, C. B. (1986) *Systematic Software Development Using VDM*, Prentice Hall International Series in Computer Science, Hemel Hempstead.

Wordsworth, J.B. (1987) Education in formal methods for software engineering. *Information and Software Technology*, **29**(1), January/February.

Wordsworth , J.B. (1990) *The BCS/IEE Joint Report on Undergraduate Curricula in Software Engineering: a Personal View by a Practising Software Engineer.* Unpublished report solicited by the BCS after the November 1989 meeting.

Wordsworth, J.B. (1992) *Software Development with Z*, Addison-Wesley, Reading, MA.

Wordsworth, J.B. (1993) Formal methods and product documentation. In *Formal methods of systems engineering*, Springer-Verlag, Berlin.

Wordsworth, J.B. (1996) *Software Engineering with B*, Addison-Wesley, Reading, MA (to appear).

Effective formal methods education for professional software engineers

2.1 Introduction

At the core of any engineering discipline is a collection of formal techniques for development and analysis of the artifacts produced by engineers. For example, civil engineers use structural analysis based on formalisms for characterizing strength of materials, and chemical engineers use formalisms based on unit operations.

Unfortunately, software engineering has had relatively little success in applying formal techniques to real systems. There is little in the way of routine formalism that is applied throughout the industry. By and large, software engineers develop systems using informal methods and procedures based on accumulated experience building similar systems.

One explanation for this is that the state of the science underlying large-scale, commercial software development is relatively immature (Shaw, 1990). While there are many proposals for formal software development methods, (such as program verification (Hoare, 1972), rigorous program development (Gries, 1981; Jones, 1986), abstract specifications of modules (Guttag and Horning, 1980), and modeling of concurrency (Hoare, 1978) there is as yet no well-established body of formal foundations that are uniformly recognized as fundamental to industrial software development. While there are some notable successes of formal methods in industry (such as Barrett, 1989; Nix and Collins, 1988; Delisle and Garlan, 1990), the fact remains that the primary proponents of systematic application of formal development have been academicians and those working in the areas of secure and safety-critical systems.

But a lack of widely accepted, scientific underpinnings is (at best) only partly the reason. Indeed, the emerging examples of successful development and the application of special-purpose formalisms (e.g., in areas such as protocol verification (McMillan and Schwalbe, 1991), testing, and real-time scheduling (Sha and Goodenough, 1990)) indicate that benefits of existing formal methods are simply not being exploited.

For educators this presents both a problem and an opportunity. It is a problem because the lack of a coherent body of widely-applicable, formal methods makes it difficult for educators to know what and how to teach existing techniques. It is an opportunity because it allows educators to advance the state of practice by helping to produce fresh practitioners who are equipped with a new set of practical, formal skills, and who can speed the broader dissemination and adoption of formal methods in industry.

In response to this situation, the typical approach to introducing formal methods in software engineering curricula is to provide a special course in which a variety of formal techniques are surveyed, and perhaps partially mastered by the students. Such a course satisfies the need to make students aware of some formal approaches to software development. But it also has a number of problems, detailed later, the most serious of which is that it tends to isolate the use of formal methods from the mainstream activities of software development emphasized in the rest of the curriculum.

In this chapter we describe a different approach. Rather than segregating the instruction of formal methods, we attempt to integrate it across the curriculum. To illustrate this approach we describe the role of formal methods in the Master of Software Engineering curriculum at Carnegie Mellon University, and evaluate our experience in using it over the past three years.

2.2   Current approaches

Professional software engineering curricula generally incorporate formal methods into their curricula in one of three ways.

The first way avoids teaching formal methods at all. The rationale for this approach is that formal methods are not sufficiently mature to be useful to the practicing software engineer. Programs that adopt this approach are often those that serve a population of local software firms that send their technicians to school for "refresher" classes on a part-time basis. These students are usually motivated by the pressures of current software development projects and the need to acquire skills that are directly applicable to their immediate predicaments.

The second way bases an entire curriculum around a specific formal method, such as VDM or Z. In such a program students learn about that method in their first term and are expected to apply those formal skills to all of their software development activities and all of their other courses. This approach is often used in an academic master's program, where students frequently go on to an more advanced degree in computer science.

The advantage of such a program is that students learn to use one, or perhaps several, formal methods well and to apply them uniformly in their practice of software development. However, there are also disadvantages. First, by focusing on a small number of specific methods, students may not be exposed to the broader spectrum of formal approaches. Second, while it would be wonderful if commercial software were developed in a formal, systematic way, as noted above, the state of the practice is far from this goal. Consequently, students who emerge from such programs will usually find that their formal skills cannot be directly applied, since the gap between practice and what they have learned is too great.

The third, and most widespread, approach adopts a single course specifically devoted to formal methods. In such a course students are usually exposed to a number of different formal techniques. (See Ford, 1991 or Garlan, 1992 for examples.) This has the advantage that exposure can be broad, and the course can be tailored to the kinds of formal skills that are most directly applicable to practicing software engineers.

But it also has a number of serious drawbacks. First, such courses tend to emphasize notations over underlying principles. This is almost inevitable, since the breadth of coverage makes it difficult to deal adequately with the fundamental underlying principles. Second, the isolation of formal methods into a single course tends to lead students to segregate this knowledge from their other courses and software development activities. Students often feel that the formal methods course is a token gesture towards the way we would like things to be — i.e., development based on formal principles and notations — but that this has very little to do with the "practical" activities of producing industrial-scale software. Third, students taking such a course rarely become skilled users of *any* of the methods treated.

Recently we have been experimenting with a fourth approach in which formal methods are integrated across the entire curriculum. Unlike the second approach outlined above, a number of formal techniques are introduced over the span of five core courses. But also, unlike the third approach, those techniques are taught in enough depth that students gain some facility in applying them to realistic problems. In the remainder of this paper we describe this approach.

2.3 The CMU Master of Software Engineering Program

The Carnegie Mellon University Master of Software Engineering Program (MSE) was founded in 1989 as a joint program between the School of Computer Science and the Software Engineering Institute. It is a four-semester, intensive program for professional software engineers, and leads to a terminal masters degree. The goal of the program is to develop technical leaders in industrial software engineering. These people should be able to act as agents of change in their respective organizations, and be able to apply to software development both the best of current practice and emerging technologies. Consequently, students who are accepted in the program must have both a strong background in computer science and two years industrial software development experience that indicates strong potential for leadership.

The incoming class size for the program is usually about 20 students. In the past these students have had an average of about 5 years industrial experience. About half of the students come from large corporations (Digital Equipment, HP, Westinghouse, General Motors, etc.), while the others represent a variety of smaller software development firms. Many of the students are supported by their employers, who expect them to return to the company after finishing their degree.

The MSE program has three basic components: a Core Curriculum, a number of elective tracks, and a Software Development Studio. The Core Curriculum develops foundational skills in the fundamentals of software engineering, with an emphasis on design, analysis, and management of large-scale software systems (Garlan *et al.*, 1992). The elective tracks provide an opportunity for students to develop deeper expertise in one of several specialties, such as real time systems, human–computer interfaces, or the organizational environment of software systems. In the Software Development Studio students plan and implement a significant software project for an external client over the full duration of the program. Students work in a team environment under the guidance of faculty advisors to analyze a problem, plan a software development project, execute a solution, and evaluate their work. In that respect, the Studio is similar to the design studios that characterize architectural degree programs.

2.4   The Core Curriculum

The MSE Core Curriculum consists of five semester courses:

1. **Models of Software Systems:** This course treats foundations for software engineering based on the use of precise, abstract models and logics for characterizing and reasoning about properties of software systems. Specific notations are not emphasized, although some are introduced for concreteness. The main topics include state machines, algebraic models, process algebras, trace models, compositional mechanisms, abstraction relations, temporal logic. Illustrative examples are drawn from software applications.

2. **Methods of Software Development:** This course addresses the practical development of software using methods that help bridge the gap between a problem to be solved and a working software system. The intent of the course is to introduce students to comprehensive approaches to requirements analysis, design, creation, and maintenance. Representative methods and notations include: object-oriented methods, JSD/JSP, VDM, Z, Larch, Structured Analysis/Design, Cleanroom development, and prototype-oriented development. In particular, students gain in-depth experience with three specific design methods, and are expected to understand the scope of applicability of each method. The course also introduces students to the use of supporting tools.

3. **Management of Software Development:** This course focuses on the management and organization of resources – both human and computational – for large-scale, long-lived software development projects. It treats the management of individual software development efforts and long-term capability improvement, including life cycle models, project management, process management, capability maturity models, product control (e.g., version and configuration management, change control), documentation standards, risk management, people management skills, organizational structures, product management, and requirements elicitation.

Table 2.1: The Core Curriculum.

FALL 1	SPRING	SUMMER	FALL 2
Studio	*Studio*	*Studio*	*Studio*
Directive	*Electives*		
Models			*Electives*
Methods	**Analysis**		
Management	**Architectures**	*Elective*	

4. **Analysis of Software Artifacts:** This course focuses on the analysis of software development products including delivered code, specifications, designs, documentation, prototypes, test suites. It treats both static and dynamic analyses, such as type checking, verification, testing, performance analysis, hazard analysis, reverse engineering, and program slicing. Tools for analysis are used where appropriate.

5. **Architectures of Software Systems:** This course is concerned with the design of complex software systems at an architectural level of abstraction. It treats organization of complex software based on system structure and assignment of functionality to design components. The main topics include common patterns of architectural design, tradeoff analysis at architectural level, domain-specific architectures, automated support for architectural design, and formal models of software architecture.

As illustrated in Table 2.1, the Management, Models, and Methods core courses are offered in the Fall semester. The Analysis and Architecture courses are offered in the Spring semester. Studio participation occurs throughout the program, although it is most pervasive during the Summer semester. The rest of a student's curriculum consists of electives and a directive. As detailed later, electives are drawn from a broad menu of courses across the university in areas such as business management, real-time systems, human–computer interaction, and distributed systems. The *Directive* is a required course that is used to balance the core content in an individualized way for each student. Typically the directive will be a course that fills gaps in an entering student's computer science background. Typical directives include algorithms, operating systems, and compilers.

2.5 The role of formal methods in the Core Curriculum

The Core was designed to allow us to integrate the use of formal methods throughout the curriculum.

Models of Software Systems is based on the conviction that it is essential that software engineers have a coherent understanding of the fundamental mathematical models that underlie most of the good abstractions of software systems. It is in this course that students learn the basic ideas of applying mathematics to software systems. Thus the Models course provides a "scientific" basis that can be exploited by the other courses in the program.

In this respect, the course fills the role of formal methods courses in most other curricula. But unlike courses in formal methods found in other programs, Models focuses less on specific notations than on the pervasive mathematical models on which those notations rest. Moreover, unlike many formal methods courses, it considers not only the use of mathematical models for software specification, but also models that apply to testing, analysis, process modeling, and design selection.

Methods of Software Development was designed to help students gain in-depth experience with a small number of techniques that span the gulf between a problem to be solved and a successful implementation. This course coalesces material often distributed across a number of distinct courses in other curricula: requirements specification, design, creation, maintenance. Among other things, Methods builds on the notations and concepts introduced in the Models course and demonstrates their practicality to real software systems development. In particular, among the methods treated in depth by the methods course, at least one focuses on the use of formal methods of software development. In addition, the methods course uses formal models to make distinctions between methods that are not themselves formal.

The Models and Methods courses have an important symbiotic relationship: Methods puts the use of formal models into perspective and builds skills in using particular formal notations. Hence, while Models might introduce a specific notation, such as Z or Larch, to illustrate a kind of formal model, Methods shows how those notations are used in the context of a complete software development project. It accomplishes this, in part, through the presentation of a number of case studies and by requiring students to carry out a project in which they gain experience at using a formal method to solve a non-trivial problem. (Appendix B contains a description of a project used recently in this course.)

Analysis of Software Artifacts integrates various techniques for understanding the things produced by software engineers. It adopts a broad view of analysis, including topics often divided into separate courses, such as testing, formal verification, and techniques of static analysis. The analysis course builds strongly on the models course by assuming that students have already learned the basic mathematical concepts that form the basis of many of the analytical techniques. Typical kinds of formal analysis considered in this course include topics such as precondition calculation for Z schemas, analysis of state machines using tools such as Statemate (Harel, 1987) and model checking (McMillan, 1992), and fault tree analysis using Petri-Nets (Bowman *et al.*, 1991).

Architectures of Software Systems tackles head-on the problem of structuring large-scale software systems. It is concerned with system composition in terms of high-level components and interactions between them, rather than the data structures and algorithms that lie below module boundaries (Garlan *et al.*, 1992).

Formal methods are used in the architectures course in several ways (Garlan, 1993). First, they are used to illustrate how to formally model the architectures of a specific system (Delisle and Garlan, 1990). Second, they are used to illustrate how to capture the essence of an architectural family or style (Garlan, 1991; Allen and Garlan, 1992; Abowd *et al.*, 1993). Third, they are used to explore the a theory of architectural "connection" (Allen and Garlan, 1994). To drive these points home, students are asked to extend a formal architectural model as a homework assignment. (Appendix A contains the text of the most recent assignment of this sort.)

2.6   The role of formal methods in the Studio

The Studio runs throughout the four-semester program. It is patterned after the "studio" courses in many professional architecture degree programs: students work closely with instructors and other students to carry out a significant development project and evaluate the results of that effort.

In the first semester students interact with a "customer" to elicit requirements for the system that they will be constructing. In the second semester students produce a design for that system. In the third semester (typically during the summer) students implement the system. In the fourth semester, students maintain the system and reflect on their experience to try to understand in retrospect what they could have done better. (Cf., the phasing chart in Section 2.4.)

As a representative example, a recent Studio was responsible for constructing significant portions of a mobile robot project for NASA. In particular, when finished, the robot will automate critical aspects of the NASA Space Shuttle maintenance that is performed after each shuttle flight. This development was done as part of larger NASA-funded project involving Boeing, Rockwell, SRI, and the CMU Field Robotics Center.

In addition to being a challenging and realistic software development exercise in its own right, the Software Development Studio also provides a context in which students can apply the techniques they have learned in their courses. However, the extent to which students use specific material from the core courses is left up to them. This forces them to consider which of the many techniques that they have learned can be most appropriately applied to a specific problem. In particular, the use of formal methods is entirely optional.

Our experience has been that students have chosen to apply formal methods in different, but appropriate ways. While none of the teams has yet attempted to produce a full, formally developed software product, each has found specific points of leverage for which formal methods have been useful. In studio work associated with the NASA project mentioned above, for instance, students used formalism in the following ways:

1. The system architect for the master control subsystem produced a Z specification of the central control functions of the system. This helped identify a key design flaw in an earlier design for the system.

2. The student responsible for the arm motion of the robot developed a formal kinematic model and associated tool for analyzing the arm movements.

3. Another student analyzed the arm base control algorithm (designed by the Field Robotics Center) and discovered a substantially improved algorithm that minimized the need for gross repositioning of the arm.

4. Several students used finite state machine models to argue the satisfaction of certain safety-critical properties.

5. Students used CSP to model the control portion of a high-performance switch whose software was being built in the studio.

6. Several projects modelled certain aspects of their design using SMV (Burch *et al.*, 1990) and applied model checking technology to test for system invariants.

2.7   The role of formal methods in the elective tracks

The elective tracks allow students to specialize in a particular subarea of software engineering, such as real-time systems. They also allow students to design independent study courses to pursue interests not otherwise covered by regular courses.

The real-time track makes use of formal modelling in two significant ways. First, students are introduced to real-time scheduling theory, and, in particular, they are expected to be able to apply rate-monotonic analysis to appropriate real-time problems. This allows them to determine schedulability for suites of periodic tasks, and to adjust various task parameters to improve processor utilization. Second, students learn various formal techniques for performance analysis. This permits them to reduce performance monitoring data to understandable results and to track down performance bottlenecks.

Several students have also developed independent study courses to explore formal methods in greater detail. For example, one student used Z to model a portion of the proposed POSIX real-time distributed systems communications standard. Although the student had little experience either with that domain or with the standards body, he was able to produce a specification that identified a number of ambiguities, inconsistencies, and points of incompleteness (Reizer *et al.*, 1994). He then presented his findings to the POSIX working group (Working Group P1003.21), which plans to incorporate a version of his specification as an appendix to their final report. More recently a student from General Motors has used an independent study course to model the system architecture of GM audio system product families.

Another student recently completed a study to see whether the use of Z in specifying a set of requirements could lead to more accurate function point estimates than is typically found with informal requirements documents.

Recently two students have started working with the SEI to develop a formal architectural model of the Simplex framework, an architectural design for real-time, fault-tolerant computing. They started with a model in CSP, against which they checked a number of assertions using the FDR (Formal Systems Europe, 1992). They are now in the process of developing a corresponding architectural model in the Wright specification language (Allen and Garlan, 1994).

2.8 Some observations

Overall, our experience has been quite positive. We find that students learn to approach the use of formal methods with an open mind and a willingness to discover ways to exploit them on practical problems. By and large, they appear to have a realistic view as to the benefits and costs associated with the use of formal methods. This permits them to make judicious, cost-effective choice of formalisms. They appear receptive to new techniques and theories, but they hold those theories up to fairly high standards in terms of their ability to have an impact on industrial software development.

As an instructor in the program I have found this integrated approach to formal methods challenging but rewarding. The challenge comes from the need to identify the key underlying principles that will equip students with the ability to learn and apply a variety of formalisms. The reward comes from having had some success in doing this.

Perhaps the most encouraging aspect of the use of formal methods is the fact that students are increasingly finding ways to use formalisms in cost-effective ways. This comes about in two ways. First, students have developed a formal vocabulary that informs their software development on a daily basis, permitting them to use good mathematical abstractions for developing and communicating their ideas. To illustrate, the following note was recently sent to me by one of our students.

> . . .
>
> It's no secret that I am a somewhat outspoken critic about the usefulness of the Z notation for formal specification. If fact I have been a little outspoken about a lot of the formalization methods I have learned so far.
>
> I guess I am a little industry hardened: skeptical, critical, practical, realistic, and sometimes cranky! Most of these formal methods have been very difficult for me to understand (I have just been out of school too damn long!).
>
> I am taking Doug Tygar's distributed systems class (and already having a tough time, I might add). We were assigned a project to create a name server using RPC. Our group met last night to begin to analyze the requirements for the project. Someone in the group said, "I don't understand what we are supposed to keep track of in the name server . . . ". And that started it all . . .

I replied to the question by saying, "we are mapping a name to an IP address and port tuple ... ". I froze for a second and thought, did I say that? Then I continued by drawing the state space out on the white board. Then I said out loud, " ... what the hell am I doing, I just used Z for a real problem!". It just came out that way! My group is composed of all MSE students and they were more that astonished that I (of all people in the solar system) wrote Z spec (and it made sense).

In a very short time we had about a half-a-dozen Z schemas that completely described our solution, ... and I understood it, ... and I helped write it without anyone twisting my arm or using a hand-gun. Most importantly, we were able to identify several items that were side effects that we needed to consider at a very early stage. It reduced our fully understand and design a solution. I just never would have guessed it! We fUZZ-ed, and LATEX-ed our solution and plan to turn it in with our project.

I was always taught that when you think something is not right, say so. But by the same token, if its right, ... say so. So since I often question the usefulness of Z (and other formal reasoning), I honestly felt obligated to tell you about this experience that happened last night. while I don't believe that I am a complete convert, I must admit that there are times and places where formalism (in the form of Z) can really help!

> ...

Second, students are able to identify key areas in which detailed formal treatment would be useful. Thus formalism becomes a useful tool that can be applied where appropriate, without a dogmatic instance on using it being formal at all times. As an example, last semester students were discussing on the Studio electronic bulletin board what should be their process for change management. Midway through the discussion one of the students proposed a model characterized in CSP. Other students then responded suggesting modifications to the formal model.

2.9   Conclusion and agenda for future development

To summarize, our primary goal in introducing formal methods into the MSE curriculum has been to give students the intellectual tools that will enable them to make concrete use of formalisms in their practice of software engineering. To do this we have adopted a two-pronged approach towards integrating the study of formal methods into the curriculum. First, we provide a foundational course that identifies common underlying themes and techniques that are the basis of many existing formal methods. Second, we integrate the use of formalisms into the other courses by introducing specific techniques for formal specification and analysis with which students can gain deeper experience.

While this approach has been quite successful it is not without pitfalls and risks that should be kept in mind by others wishing to apply these ideas.

♦ **Lack of Textbooks:** Most texts on formal methods are organized around single notations and methods. While some do a good job in laying foundations in terms of logic, set theory, and even formal, symbolic systems, none that we have found concentrate primarily on the broader underlying principles. This makes it harder to teach what we would like in the Models course without making it seem like a series of units on specific notations.

♦ **Lack of Tools:** Although we would love to expose students to practical tools that support the use of formal methods, we have not found it cost-effective to introduce many of the existing ones. The main problem is that each tool typically involves a large initial investment of time to get to the point where the tool is useful. A secondary problem is that few tools work together or share common interface designs. Consequently, each tool must be learned from scratch and operated in isolation.

♦ **Inter-course Coordination:** To make our approach successful it is important that the courses coordinate their content. In particular, since the Models course lays the foundation for the other courses the designer of that course must take into consideration the needs of the other courses. Similarly, the other courses must know the material in the Models course well enough to build on it in introducing their specific notations and methods. In our program, which is relatively small, this was not a problem, but it could be for a much larger or widely distributed program.

♦ **Able Students:** The students in our program are expected to develop concrete skills in using a number of formal methods and to be able to apply these to real problems in the Studio. Our experience has been that this requires students with a good background both in basic computer science and industrial software development.

♦ **Use of Studio:** A critical component of our approach is the use of the Studio as a test-bed in which students can experiment with the application of formal techniques on realistic problems. Many software engineering programs include a small version of this as a software development project course that lasts a single semester. In such a short time frame it could be more difficult for students to try out different formalisms and evaluate their effectiveness.

Several of these items suggest promising lines of educational development and further research. In particular, we would like to see new textbooks emerge that make it easier for students to quickly learn and use new formalisms. An important step in that direction would be to find a neutral, core, formal language that would allow many of the basic ideas of formal modelling, axiomatic specification, etc. to be explained without having to buy into a specific, complete formal specification method. Additionally, we would like to see further development of tools so that they are both more appropriate for student use and also more integrated with respect to each other. Finally, we would like to find more realistic case studies that we could use to introduce formal methods to students. Too many of the published examples are toy problems, and do not expose the more difficult issues of scalability and expressiveness for industrial software.

Acknowledgements

The CMU MSE Core Curriculum was designed by Alan Brown, Daniel Jackson, James Tomayko, Jeannette Wing, and myself. Mary Shaw and Nancy Mead also provided useful input during the curriculum design process. Gregory Abowd contributed substantially to the Methods course. Much of the success of the current curriculum is due to their course designs and delivery. The opinions and conclusions of this paper are, however, mine alone. This paper is an expanded version of a paper that appeared under the title "Making Formal Methods Education Effective for Professional Software Engineers" in *Information and Software Technology*, May–June 1995 (Garlan, 1995). That paper in turn was a revision of "Integrating Formal Methods into a Professional Master of Software Engineering Program" which appeared at the 1994 Z User Meeting (Garlan, 1994).

References

Abowd, G., Allen, R. and Garlan, D. (1993) Using style to give meaning to software architecture. In *Proceedings of SIGSOFT'93: Foundations of Software Engineering*, Software Engineering Notes 118(3):9–20. ACM Press, New York, December.

Allen, R. and Garlan, D. (1992) A formal approach to software architectures. In J. van Leeuwen, editor, *Proceedings of IFIP'92*, Elsevier Science Publishers B.V., September; an expanded version appears as *Towards Formalized Software Architectures*, Technical Report CMU-CS-92-163, School of Computer Science, Carnegie Mellon University.

Allen, R. and Garlan, D. (1994) Formalizing architectural connection. In *Proceedings of the Sixteenth International Conference on Software Engineering*, IEEE Computer Society Press, Los Alamitos, May.

Barrett, G. (1989) Formal methods applied to a floating-point number system. *IEEE Transactions on Software Engineering*, 15(5):611–621, May.

Bowman, W.C., Archinoff, G.H., Raina, V.M., Tremaine, D.R. and Leveson, N.G. (1991) An application of fault tree analysis to safety critical software at Ontario Hydro. In *Conference on Probabilistic Safety Assessment and Management (PSAM)*, 1991.

Burch, J.R., Clarke, E.M., McMillan, K.L., Dill, D.L. and Hwang, J. (1990) Symbolic model checking: 10^{20} states and beyond. In *Proceedings of the Fifth Annual IEEE Symposium on Logic in Computer Science*, IEEE Press, Washington D.C., June.

Delisle, N. and Garlan, D. (1990) Applying formal specification to industrial problems: A specification of an oscilloscope. *IEEE Software*, 7(5):29–37, September.

Formal Systems Europe (1992) *Failures Divergence Refinement: User Manual and Tutorial.* Formal Systems (Europe) Ltd., Oxford, England, October.

Ford, G. (1991) *SEI report on graduate software engineering education.* Technical Report CMU/SEI-91-TR-2, CMU Software Engineering Institute, April.

Garlan, D. (1991) Preconditions for understanding. In *Proceedings of the Fourth International Workshop on Software Specification and Design*, pages 242–245, IEEE Computer Society Press, October.

Garlan, D. (1992) Formal methods for software engineers: Tradeoffs in curriculum design. In *Proceedings of the Sixth SEI Conference on Software Engineering Education*, Springer-Verlag, October.

Garlan, D. (1993) Formal approaches to software architecture. In D.A. Lamb and S. Crocker, editors, *Proceedings of the Workshop on Studies of Software Design*, External Technical Report, ISSN-0836-0227-93-352, Department of Computing and Information Science, Queen's University, Kingston, Ontario, Canada, May.

Garlan, D. (1994) Integrating formal methods into a professional master of software engineering program. In J.P. Bowen and J.A. Hall, editors, *Z User Workshop*, Workshops in Computing, Springer Verlag, London.

Garlan, D. (1995) Making formal methods education effective for professional Software Engineers. *Information and Software Technology*, **37**(5–6):261-268, May–June.

Garlan, D., Brown, A., Jackson, D., Tomayko, J. and Wing, J. (1993) *The CMU Masters in Software Engineering core curriculum*, Technical Report CMU-CS-93-180, Carnegie Mellon University, August.

Guttag, J.V. and Horning, J.J. (1980) Formal specification as a design tool. In *Proc. Seventh POPL*, ACM Press.

Garlan, D. and Notkin, D. (1991) Formalizing design spaces: Implicit invocation mechanisms. In *VDM'91: Formal Software Development Methods*, pages 31–44. Springer-Verlag Lecture Notes in Computer Science, Volume 551, October.

Gries, D. (1981) *The Science of Programming*, Springer-Verlag, New York.

Garlan, D., Shaw, M., Okasaki, C., Scott, C. and Swonger, R. (1992) Experience with a course on architectures for software systems. In *Proceedings of the Sixth SEI Conference on Software Engineering Education*, Springer-Verlag Lecture Notes in Computer Science, Volume 376, October.

Harel, D. (1987) Statecharts: A visual formalism for complex systems. *Science of Computer Programming*, **8**:231–274.

Hoare, C.A.R. (1972) Proof of correctness of data representations. *Acta Informatica*, **1**:271–281.

Hoare, C.A.R. (1978) Communicating sequential processes. *Communications of the ACM*, **21**(8):666–677, August.

Jones, C.B. (1986) Systematic program development. In *Proceedings of the Symposium on Mathematics and Computer Science*.

McMillan, K.L. (1992) The SMV system, draft, February.

McMillan, K.L. and Schwalbe, J. (1991) Formal verification of the Encore Gigamax cache consistency protocol. In *Proc. International Symposium on Shared Memory Multiprocessors*.

Nix, C.J. and Collins, B.P. (1988) The use of software engineering, including the Z notation, in the development of CICS. *Quality Assurance*, **14**(3):103–110, September.

Nii, H.P. (1986a) Blackboard systems Part 1: The blackboard model of problem solving and the evolution of blackboard architectures. *AI Magazine*, **7**(3):38–53, Summer.

Nii, H.P. (1986b) Blackboard systems Part 2: Blackboard application systems and a knowledge engineering perspective. *AI Magazine*, **7**(4):82–107, August.

Reizer, N.R., Abowd, G.D., Meyers, B.C. and Place, P.R.H. (1994) Using formal methods for requirements specification of a proposed POSIX standard. In *Proceedings of the International Conference on Requirements Engineering*.

Sha, L. and Goodenough, J.B. (1990) Real-time scheduling theory and Ada∗. *IEEE Computer*, **23**(4):53–62, April.

Shaw, M. (1990) Prospects for an engineering discipline of software. *IEEE Software*, **7**(6):15–24, November.

Appendix A
Formal modelling assignment for software architectures

Formal Modelling of Architectural Styles
Architectures for Systems
Spring 93 (Garlan & Shaw)

This assignment is intended to help you develop some experience in manipulating a formal model of a software architecture. In this case you will be using the formal model of event systems presented in class. Following the pattern of specialization in (Garlan and Notkin, 1991) you are to formally characterize as event systems the two architectural idioms described below.

Blackboard Systems

Drawing on Nii's description (Nii, 1986a,b) describe a blackboard system as a formal specialization of *EventSystem*. You may find it helpful to make the following simplifying assumptions:

- There are two kinds of components in a blackboard system: *BBdata* and *ksources*.

- The *BBdata* in the blackboard system are partitioned into a collection of *layers*.

- Each *ksource* is associated with some set of these layers.

- Each *ksource* has a method *UpdateBB*, which allows it to update the blackboard when it is invoked.

- When the data in a blackboard changes, for each layer that is changed the system announces the *ChangedLayer* event to each of the knowledge sources that are associated with that layer.

You need not say anything about the run time mechanisms involved in carrying out the updates. In particular, you don't have to say how the knowledge sources update the blackboard, or how new data is added to the blackboard.

Blackboard Systems

Formally characterize a spreadsheet system as an event system. For the purposes of this assignment you can consider a spreadsheet to be an $N \times M$ matrix. Some of the entries in this matrix will have a *VALUE*. Some of the entries will also have an associated *Equation* that describes the value of that entry as a function over other entries in the spreadsheet. When spreadsheet entries are changed the equations that depend on those entries are implicitly reevaluated.

You might find the following definitions to be a useful starting point:

$[VALUE, EQN]$

$Pos == \mathbb{N} \times \mathbb{N}$

$Params : EQN \rightarrow \mathbb{P}\,Pos$
$Eval : (EQN \times \text{seq } VALUE) \rightarrow VALUE$

$\forall e : EQN;\ vs : \text{seq } VALUE \bullet (e, vs) \in \text{dom } Eval \Rightarrow \#vs = \#(Params\,e)$

In other words, we take *VALUE* and *EQN* to be primitive types, and a matrix position, *Pos*, to be a pair of natural numbers. We assume (axiomatically) that we can determine for each equation what its parameters are and also how to evaluate it for actual values. (The invariant guarantees that the number of formal parameters must match the number of actual parameters.)

With this as a basis you can then define a spreadsheet along the following lines:

_SpreadSheet_____
EventSystem
$height, width : \mathbb{N}$
$boxes : Pos \nrightarrowtail Component$
$eqns : Pos \nrightarrow Eqn$
$vals : Pos \nrightarrow VALUE$
$\ldots$
_____
$\ldots$

The symbol $\nrightarrowtail$ indicates that each position is associated with a unique component.

You may assume that each Component in a spreadsheet (associated with a box via *boxes*) can update its value using the method *Update* whenever it gets the *Revaluate* event. Your task is to add any appropriate additional state and the state invariants. In particular, the state invariant should explain how the event-method bindings are determined by the other parts of the spreadsheet.

What to hand in

You should hand in:

♦ A description of the two formal models outlined above. Ideally this should be formatted and checked using Fuzz, but it need not be. As with all Z documents, the formalism should be accompanied by enough prose to explain what is going on. You may work in groups to produce this document.

♦ As individuals you should also turn in commentary addressing the following questions:

   1. What important aspects of the modelled architectures are (intentionally) left out of the model?

2. For the blackboard system, would it be possible to model some notion of "non-interference"? (You need not model it, but you should explain why or why not you answered the question in the way you did.)

3. For the spreadsheet system, does it make sense to check for absence of circularities, as outlined in the paper on the events model? Why or why not?

4. Based on the formal models, briefly compare each of the two new systems with the other ones that were formally modelled. For example, you might explain which of the other systems are they most similar to?

We will mail to you a copy of the Z description for the event system described in (Garlan and Notkin, 1991).

Grading criteria

Your solutions and commentary will be graded by the following criteria:

♦ Whether or not you are able to model the requested specializations.

♦ Your ability to understand and explain the formalisms in the accompanying prose.

♦ Your reflective commentary.

Appendix B
Formal methods project for the methods course

CMU MSE 15-772
Case Study
Methods of Software Development Fall 1993
Fall 93 (Daniel Jackson)

Terminator 3: A toy air traffic control system

Controlled airspace is divided into regions. Aircraft fly along corridors called airways that connect terminal control areas (TMAs). Each TMA contains one or more airports. The airways meet the TMA at gateways. From a gateway, an aircraft travels along a glide path to a landing strip. So that planes can land against the wind, there may be several glide paths from a gateway to a strip.

The job of the controllers is to ensure that planes land safely by keeping minimal separations on glide paths and by scheduling landings into slots of fixed time width. The minimal separation of two aircraft depends on their relative speed. If the flow of aircraft into a gateway is too great, the controllers may delay aircraft by holding them in the gateway's stack.

A plane entering the gateway is handed-off between the region controllers and the TMA controllers. The pilot requests clearance to enter a glide path. He may instead be given clearance to enter the stack at some level. As aircraft at the bottom of the stack are cleared to glide, aircraft above are moved down the stack, one level at a time.

The Terminator system helps control landings in a single TMA with one airport and one landing strip. It reads radar messages giving positions of aircraft and maintains for each aircraft a flight strip containing a log of the clearances it has been given and its progress through airspace. It answers queries about aircraft positions and the holding patterns of stacks. It does not issue clearances, but determines whether a requested clearance is safe. It also warns controllers if aircraft deviate from their clearances.

The system thus receives four kinds of input: radar messages, clearance requests, clearance notifications and status enquiries. It produces three kinds of output: responses to clearance requests, deviation warnings and reports. There are four kinds of clearance: to enter a stack at some level, to descend in a stack, to enter a glide path from a stack and to enter a glide path from a gateway. Radar information arrives already processed in a single stream of messages. There are two kinds of messages: that an aircraft is holding at some level in a stack, and that the aircraft is at some point along a glide path.

Complications and elaborations

♦ Separation rules dependent on weather and aircraft type.

- ◆ Priority for air ambulances allows aircraft to enter glide path when stack is non-empty.

- ◆ Support function to change landing slots.

- ◆ Maintain information about controllers: who gives which clearances.

- ◆ Increase flow by reducing aircraft speed as well as by stacking.

- ◆ Allow intersecting glide paths.

- ◆ Generate clearances automatically.

- ◆ Filter out planes that are detected by radar but are overflying TMA or not in controlled airspace.

- ◆ More than one airport/TMA.

Education for computing professionals

3.1 A "back door" to engineering

Engineering is often defined to be the use of scientific knowledge and principles for practical purposes. While the original usage restricted the work to the building of roads, bridges, and objects of military use, today's usage is more general and includes chemical, electronic, and even mathematical engineering. All use science and technology to solve practical problems, usually by designing useful products.

Most engineers today have a university-level education. Government and professional societies enforce standards by accrediting educational programs and examining those people who seek the title "professional engineer". Certification is intended to protect public safety by making certain that engineers have a solid grounding in fundamental science and mathematics, are aware of their professional responsibilities, and are trained to be thorough and complete in their analysis. In each of these aspects, engineers differ sharply from technicians, who are trained to follow established procedures but do not take responsibility for the correctness of those procedures.

Engineering education differs from traditional "liberal arts" education as well. Engineering students are much more restricted in his choice of courses; this ensures that all graduate engineers have had exposure to those fields that are fundamental to their profession. Engineering education also stresses finding good, as contrasted to workable, designs. Where a scientist may be happy with a device that validates his theory, an engineer is taught to make sure that the device is efficient, reliable, safe, easy to use, and robust. Finally, engineers learn that even the most intellectually challenging assignments require a great deal of boring "dog work".

It has been a quarter century since universities began to establish academic programs in computing science. Graduates of these programs are usually employed by industry and government to build useful objects, often computer programs. Their products control aircraft, automobile components, power plants, and telephone circuits. Their programs keep banking records and assist in the control of air traffic. Software helps engineers design buildings, bridges, trucks, etc.. In other words, these nonengineering graduates of CS programs produce useful artifacts;

Reprinted, with permission, from *IEEE Computer Magazine*, Vol. 23, No. 1, pp 17–22, January 1990.
TEACHING AND LEARNING FORMAL METHODS   ISBN 0-12-349040-5

their work is engineering. It is time to ask whether this back door to engineering is in the best interests of the students, their employers, and society.

I have written this article to discuss a trend, not to single out any particular department's curriculum or any particular committee report. Each new curriculum proposal includes more "new" computer science and, unavoidably, less "classical" material. In this article I reject that trend and propose a program whose starting point is programs that were in place when computing science began.

3.2   An historical debate

In the early 1960s, those of us who were interested in computing began to press for the establishment of computing science departments. Much to my surprise, there was strong opposition, based in part on the argument that graduates of a program specializing in such a new (and, consequently, shallow) field would not learn the fundamental mathematical and engineering principals that should form its basis. Both mathematicians and electrical engineers argued that computing science was an integral part of their own fields. They felt that students should major in one of those fields and take some computing courses near the end of their academic careers, rather than get an education in computing science as such. They predicted that graduates of CS programs would understand neither mathematics nor engineering; consequently, they would not be prepared to apply mathematical and engineering fundamentals to the design of computing systems.

My colleagues and I argued that computing science was rapidly gaining importance and that computing majors would be able to study the older fields with emphasis on those areas that were relevant to computing. Our intent was to build a program incorporating many mathematics and engineering courses along with a few CS courses. Unfortunately, most departments abandoned such approaches rather early. Both faculty and students were impatient to get to the "good stuff". The fundamentals were compressed into quick, shallow courses that taught only those results deemed immediately relevant to computing theory.

3.3   The state of graduate CS education

Nearly 25 years later, I have reluctantly concluded that our opponents were right. As I look at CS departments around the world, I am appalled at what my younger colleagues — those with their education in computing science — don't know. Those who work in theoretical computing science seem to lack an appreciation for the simplicity and elegance of mature mathematics. They build complex models more reminiscent of the programs written by bad programmers than the elegant models I saw in my mathematics courses. Computing scientists often invent new mathematics where old mathematics would suffice. They repeatedly patch their models rather than rethink them when new problems arise.

Further, many of those who work in the more practical areas of computing science seem to lack an appreciation for the routine systematic analysis that is essential to professional engineering. They are attracted to flashy topics that promise revolutionary changes and are impatient with evolutionary developments. They eschew engineering's systematic planning, documentation, and validation. In violation of the most fundamental precepts of engineering design, some "practical" computing scientists advocate that implementors begin programming before the problem is understood. Discussions of documentation and practical issues of testing are considered inappropriate in most CS departments.

Traditional engineering fosters cooperation between theory and practice. The theory learned in mathematics and science classes is applied in engineering classes. In computing science, though, theory and practice have diverged. While classical mathematical topics, such as graph theory, continue to have applications in computing, most of the material in CS courses is not relevant in practice. Much theory concentrates on machines with infinite capacity, although such machines are not, and never will be, available. Academic departments and large conferences are often battlegrounds for the "theoretical" and "applied" groups. Such battles are a sure sign that something is wrong.

As the opponents of computing science predicted, most CS PhDs are not scientists; they neither understand nor apply the methods of experimental science. They are neither mathematicians nor engineers. There are exceptions, of course, but they stand out so clearly that they "prove the rule".

3.4   The state of undergraduate CS education

The preparation of CS undergraduates is even worse than that of graduates. CS graduates are very weak on fundamental science; their knowledge of technology is focused on the very narrow areas of programming, programming languages, compilers, and operating systems. Most importantly, they are never exposed to the discipline associated with engineering. They confuse existence proofs with products, toys with useful tools. They accept the bizarre inconsistencies and unpredictable behavior of current tools as normal. They build systems of great complexity without systematic analysis. They don't understand how to design a product to make such analysis possible. Whereas most engineers have had a course in engineering drawing (also known as engineering graphics), few CS graduates have had any introduction to design documentation.

Most CS graduates are involved in the construction of information and communications systems. These systems are highly dependent on information representation and transmission, but the graduates working on them are almost completely ignorant of information theory. For example, CS graduates are not conscious of the difference between the information unit "bit" and the storage unit, which is properly called a "binary digit". As a result, conversations on important practical issues, such as the design of data representations, proceed on an intuitive *ad hoc* level that engineers would consider unprofessional.

Although most CS graduates have been exposed to logic, the topic's treatment is usually quite shallow. The students are familiar with the symbol manipulation rules of the predicate calculus but are usually unable to apply logic in practical circumstances. For example, most cannot use quantifiers properly to "translate" informal statements into formal ones, perhaps because their instructors prefer inventing new logics to applying conventional ones. Mathematicians can successfully invent formalisms, but engineers usually succeed by finding new ways to use existing formalisms.

Because they lack knowledge of logic and communications concepts, CS graduates use fuzzy words like "knowledge" without the vaguest idea of how to define such a term or distinguish it from older concepts like "data" and "information". They talk of building "reasoning" systems without being able to distinguish reasoning from mechanical deduction or simple search techniques. The use of such fuzzy terms is not merely sloppy wording; it prevents the graduate from doing the systematic analyses made possible by precise definitions.

Reliability requirements are forcing the introduction of redundancy in computer systems. Unfortunately, current CS graduates are usually unfamiliar with all but the most naïve approaches to redundancy. They often build systems that are needlessly expensive but allow common mode failures. Many CS graduates have not been taught the fundamentals needed to perform reliability analyses on the systems they design. Few of them understand concepts such as "single error correction/double error detection". Familiarity with such concepts is essential to the design of reliable computing systems.

Public safety is seriously affected by the fact that many CS graduates program parts of such control systems as those that run nuclear plants or adjust flight surfaces on aircraft. Unfortunately, I do not know of a single CS program that requires its students to take a course in control theory. The basic concepts of feedback and stability are understood only on an intuitive level at best. Neither the gradutes nor most of their teachers know of the work in control theory that is applicable to the design of real-time systems.

Some graduates work in the production of signal processing systems. Unfortunately, signal processing is not offered in most CS programs; in fact, many departments will not allow a student to take such a course for CS credit. Signal processing deals with issues that are fundamental to the science and application of computing, but it is neglected in most programs.

Although many CS programs began with numerical analysis, most of our graduates have no understanding of the problems of arithmetic with finite representations of real numbers. Numerical analysis is, at best, an option in most CS programs.

3.5   What went wrong?

Most CS departments were formed by multidisciplinary teams comprising mathematicians interested in computing, electrical engineers who had built or used computers, and physicists who had been computer users. Each had favorite topics for inclusion in the educational program, but not everything could be included. So, the set of topics that was included was often the intersection of what the founders knew, not the union. Often, several topics were combined into a single course that forced shallow treatment of each.

The research interests of the founding scientists distorted the educational programs. At the time computing became an academic discipline, researchers were preoccupied with language design, language definition, and compiler construction. One insightful paper speculated that the next 1700 Ph.D. thesis would introduce the next 1700 computer programming languages. It might have been more accurate to predict 700 computer languages, 500 theories of computer language semantics, and 500 compiler-compilers.

So, "artificial intelligence" became a popular buzzword with American funding agencies, and the CS field expanded to include a variety of esoteric topics described by anthropomorphic buzzwords. Cut off from the departments of mathematics and electrical engineering by the usual university divisions, CS graduates came to view their field as consisting primarily of those topics that were research interests in their department. The breadth that would have come from being in one of the older, broader departments was missing.

Today, it is clear that CS departments were formed too soon. Computing science focuses too heavily on the narrow research interests of its founding fathers. Very little computing science is of such fundamental importance that it should be taught to undergraduates. Most CS programs have replaced fundamental engineering and mathematics with newer material that quickly becomes obsolete.

CS programs have become so inbred that the separation between academic computing science and the way computers are actually used has become too great. CS programs do not provide graduates with the fundamental knowledge needed for long-term professional growth.

3.6 What is the result?

In recent years, I have talked to a number of top industry researchers and implementors who are reluctant to hire CS graduates at any level. They prefer to take engineers or mathematicians, even history majors, and teach them programming. The manager of one safety-critical programming project stated with evident pride that his product was produced by engineers, "not just computer scientists". The rapid growth of the industry assures that our graduates get jobs, but experienced managers are very doubtful about the usefulness of their education.

As engineers in other fields are becoming more dependent on computing devices in their own professional practice, they are also becoming more concerned about the lack of professionalism in the products that they use. They would rather write their own programs than trust the programs of our graduates.

As an awareness of the inadequacies of CS education grows, as people begin to realize that programming languages and compiler technology are not relevant background for the people they hire, our students may have trouble getting jobs.

The main problem now is that their education has not prepared them for the work they actually do.

3.7   A new program for computing professionals

While the critics of the original CS programs were quite accurate in their predictions, I still believe that a special educational program for computing professionals is needed. When we look at the programs produced by engineers and scientists who did not have such an education, we see that they are quite naïve about many of the things we have learned in 25 years of computing science. For example, new programs in the defense industry are written in the same unsystematic style that was found in programs written in the 1950s and 1960s. Our graduates should be able to do better.

I believe the program proposed below would provide a good education for computing professionals. It is designed to draw heavily on the offerings of other departments, and it emphasizes mature fundamentals to prepare our graduates for a life of learning in a dynamic field. Wherever possible, the courses should be existing courses that can be shared with mathematicians and engineers. Students should meet the strict requirements of engineering schools, and the programs should be as rigid as those in other engineering disciplines.

3.7.1   Basic mathematics

The products of most computing professionals are so abstract that the field could well be called "mathematical engineering". In fact, this is the title used at some Dutch Universities. Computing professionals need to know how to use mathematics, although they rarely need to invent it. Some computer scientists have suggested that their students need only discrete mathematics, not the mathematics of continuous functions. However, while discrete mathematics is the mathematics used in theoretical computing science, many practical computing applications use computers to approximate piecewise continuous functions. Computer professionals need a full introduction to mathematics; they should not be restricted to those items taught as theoretical computing science.

Calculus
All computing professionals should take the standard two- or four-semester calculus sequence taken by other engineers. This is the basic preparation for understanding how to deal with dynamic systems in the continuous domain. Many computer system applications are best understood as approximations or improvements of dynamic analogue systems. Computer professionals require the full sequence.

Discrete mathematics
CS students should join mathematics students in a course on such fundamentals as set theory, functions, relations, graphs, and combinatorics. In current computing courses, students view these as notations for describing computations and do not understand mathematics as an independent deductive system.

Logic
Logic is fundamental to many of the notations and concepts in computing science. Students should have a deeper understanding than that usually provided by CS logic courses or a few lectures on logic in some other course. I propose a two-semester sequence, taken with mathematics students, covering such advanced topics as decision procedures and higher order logics. The relationship between logic, set theory, lambda calculus, etc. should be thoroughly explored. Applications to computing should not be discussed.

Linear algebra
This should be covered in the standard one-semester course for engineers offered by the mathematics department.

Graph theory
Graphs offer useful representations of a wide variety of computing problems. Students who understand graph theoretic algorithms will find them useful in a variety of fields. An optional second course could deal with the application of this theory in computing practice.

Differential equations
This also should be covered in the usual one-semester course offered by mathematics departments for engineers. Many modern computer systems are approximations to analogue circuits, for which this analysis is essential.

Probability and applied statistics
The reliability and adequacy of testing is a major concern in modern computing applications. Probability theory is also a fundamental tool in situations where random noise is present in communications. Everyone who works as an engineer should have at least a one-semester course on this topic; a two-semester sequence would be better for many.

Optimization
Linear and non-linear programming are major applications for large computers. A course in this area would make students aware of the complexity of search spaces and the need to precisely define objective functions. One need not look very far into the class of programs known as "expert systems" to find areas where optimization concepts should have been applied.

Numerical analysis
This topic could be taught as either computing science or mathematics. (It is described below under "Computing science".)

3.7.2   Basic science

Computing professionals need the same knowledge of basic science as engineers. A basic course in chemistry and a two-semester sequence in physics should be the minimal requirement for all technical students.

3.7.3   Engineering Topics

Computing professionals are engineers and should be educated as such. Computers and software are now replacing more conventional technologies, but the people who design the new systems need to understand fundamental engineering systems just as well as did the engineers who designed the old systems.

Engineering electricity and magnetism
This topic should be covered in the standard one-semester course taken by electrical engineers.

Electric circuits
This also should be covered in the standard one-semester course for electrical engineers.

Mechanics
An understanding of mechanics is essential to a study of practical robotics, automated manufacturing, etc. This topic, too, should be covered in the standard, one-semester, electrical engineering course.

Systems and control theory
This standard two-semester sequence for electrical engineers should emphasizes the use of differential equations, transforms, and complex analyses to predict the behavior of control systems. The course should also discuss the discrete analogues of the methods for dealing with continuous functions.

Information theory
This is one of the most fundamental and important areas for computing professionals. In addition to the standard one-semester course for electrical engineers, a second course on the applications in computer system design would be useful as an elective.

Digital system principles/logic design
This topic could be covered under either computing science or electrical engineering. (It is described below under "Computing science".)

Signal processing
This area should be examined in a one-semester course introducing the concepts of noise, filters, signal recognition, frequency response, digital approximations, highly parallel algorithms, and specialized processors.

3.7.4 Computing science

Before the advent of CS departments, engineering and science students were expected to be able to learn programming and programming languages on their own or through noncredit courses. Computers were compared to slide rules and calculators: tools that university students could learn to use. Engineering and science faculties felt that courses in programming and programming languages would not have the deep intellectual content of mathematics or physics courses. We responded that we would teach computing science, not programming or specific languages.

Unfortunately, many of today's courses prove the critics correct. The content of many courses would change dramatically if the programming language being used underwent a major change. The courses proposed below assume that students are capable programmers and avoid discussions of programming languages.

Systematic programming
This would be taught in a two-semester sequence covering finite-state machines, formal languages and their application, program state spaces, the nature of programs, program structures, partitioning the state space, program composition, iteration, program organization, program design documentation, systematic verification, etc. Students should be competent programmers as a prerequisite to this course.

Computer system documentation
This one-semester course would teach formal methods to document computer system design, with emphasis on methods that apply to both digital and integrated digital/analogue systems.

Design and analysis of algorithms and data structures
This course would discuss comparative analysis of algorithms and data structures as well as theoretical models of problem complexity and computability. Students would learn to predict the performance of their programs and to choose algorithms and data structures that give optimal performance.

Process control
This integrated treatment of the theoretic hardware, software, and control theoretic problems of process control systems would include hardware characteristics, operating systems for real-time applications, the process concept, synchronization, and scheduling theory. Students would learn how to prove that their systems will meet deadlines and how to design for fail-safe behavior. A course in control theory should be prerequisite.

Computing systems architecture and networks
This fairly standard course, now taught in both electrical engineering and CS departments, would cover the structure of a computer and multicomputer networks, communications bus design, network performance analysis, etc. A knowledge of assembly language should be assumed. Students should be taught to avoid buzzwords and discuss the quantitative characteristics of the systems they study.

Numerical analysis
This course, which could be taught as either computing science or mathematics, would cover the study of calculations using finite approximations to real numbers and would teach round-off, error propagation, conditioning of matrices, etc.

Digital system principles/logic design
This standard one-semester course for electrical engineers should cover the basics of combinational circuit design, memory design, error correction, error detection, and reliability analysis. The emphasis should be on systematic procedures. The course could be offered as either computing science or electrical engineering.

As in any academic program, the above program includes compromises. Many topics, such as databases, compilers, and operating systems, were considered and omitted because of time limitations. It is not that these areas are uninteresting, but rather that I have chosen the oldest, most mature, most fundamental topics over those that are relatively recent and likely to be invalidated by changes in technology. Some may find the program old-fashioned. I prefer to call it long-lasting.

One obvious exception to the "older is better" rule is the course on computer system documentation. I would like to think that its inclusion reflects its importance, but it may simply reflect my own research interests.

The program is rather full and far more closely resembles a heavily packed engineering program than the liberal arts program to which CS educators have become accustomed. The educational philosophy issues behind this traditional split are clearly outside the scope of this article. Personally, I would welcome a five-year undergraduate engineering degree to allow a broader education, but would find it irresponsible to make substantial reductions in the technical content of four-year programs.

3.8 Projects versus cooperative education

CS students are burdened by many courses that require hours of struggle with computing systems. Programming assignments include small programs in introductory courses, larger programs in advanced courses, and still-larger projects that comprise the main content of entire courses. This "practical content" is both excessive and inadequate. Much effort is spent learning the language and fighting the system. A great deal of time is wasted correcting picayune errors while fundamental problems are ignored. "Practical details" consume time better spent on the theoretical or intellectual content of the course.

Also, the programs that students write are seldom used by others and rarely tested extensively. Students do not get the feedback that comes from having a product used, abused, rejected, and modified. This lack of feedback is very bad education. Students and faculty often believe that they have done a very good job when they have not. Inadequate analyses and unsystematic work are often rewarded and reinforced by high grades.

There is no doubt that students cannot learn programming without writing programs, but we should not be teaching programming. Small assignments should have the same role as problems in a mathematics class and often should be graded the same way. The computer and the person grading the program both provide feedback, but the computer is often quite demanding about arbitrary details while ignoring substantial weaknesses in the program. The person who grades the program should be tolerant on matters of arbitrary conventions but should pay attention to the fundamental issues.

Properly run cooperative education programs provide the desired transition between academia and employment. Students produce a real product and get feedback from interested users. Review and guidance from faculty advisors is essential to integrate the work experience with the educational program. Project courses can and should be replaced by such a program. The use of the computer in academic courses can be greatly reduced.

3.9 Student needs versus faculty interests

I do not expect these remarks and proposals to be popular with the faculty of CS departments. We all have considerable emotional investment in the things that we learned and intellectual investment in the things we teach. Many faculty want to teach courses in their research areas in the hope of finding students to work on their projects. Moreover, my criticism of the education we now provide is unavoidably a criticism of the preparation of my younger colleagues.

A university's primary responsibilities are to its students and society at large. It is unfortunate that they are often run for the comfort and happiness of the teachers and administrators. In this matter, the interests of the students and society coincide. It is not in the students' interest to make them perform engineering without being prepared for that responsibility. Nor is it in their interest to give them an education that prepares them only to be technicians. Too many graduates end up "maintaining" commercial software products, which is analogous to electrical engineers climbing poles to replace cables on microwave towers.

3.10 Conclusions

My industrial colleagues often complain that CS students are not prepared for the jobs they have to do. I must emphasize that my proposals will not produce graduates who can immediately take over the responsibilities of an employee who has left or been promoted. That is not the role of a university. Universities should not be concerned with teaching the latest network protocol, programming language, or operating system feature. Graduates need the fundamentals that will allow a lifetime of learning new developments; the program I have proposed provides those fundamentals better than most current CS programs.

CS departments should reconsider the trade-off in their courses between mature material and new developments. It is time for them to reconsider their role, to ask whether education of computing professionals should not be the responsibility of engineering schools.

Acknowledgements

I have developed these views through a great many conversations with engineers, mathematicians, and computer professionals around the world. The contributors are too numerous to mention. Selim Akl, David Lamb, and John van Schouwen made helpful suggestions about earlier drafts. The referees made several helpful comments.

Teaching programming as engineering

4.1 Introduction

In spite of unheralded advances in computer hardware and software, most of today's introductory programming courses are much like courses taught 30 years ago. Although the programming languages have changed, we continue to equate teaching programming with teaching the syntax and semantics of programming languages. This paper describes a different approach being taken in the Faculty of Engineering at McMaster University. Our course emphasizes program design rather than language syntax, insisting that the program design is something distinct from the detailed code. It allows students a choice of programming languages for use in their laboratory work. Students learn a mathematical model of programming and are taught to use that model to understand program design, analysis, and documentation. Considerable effort is spent on teaching the students how to apply what they see as "theory" in practice.

4.2 Programming courses and engineering

Professional engineers are expected to use discipline, science, and mathematics to assure that their products are reliable and robust. We should expect no less of anyone who produces programs professionally.

In most jurisdictions, engineers are expected either to be graduates of carefully accredited University programs or to have passed exams that demonstrate that they have the knowledge that they would have obtained in such a program. It is unfortunate that there is no corresponding registration process for those who design programs.

This paper treats programming as an engineering discipline and describes a course that is intended to teach the fundamental knowledge that should be expected of any professional programmer. Because we believe in teaching good programming design habits from the start, this is our student's first course in programming. Unfortunately, many students come to University having learned to use a computer in High School or elsewhere. With rare exceptions those students

TEACHING AND LEARNING FORMAL METHODS   ISBN 0-12-349040-5

have learned to program intuitively and resist learning a new, more disciplined, approach.

4.3   The important characteristics of programming courses

For many years, the first question asked about any introductory programming course for engineers was "What programming language do you teach?" If one examines the many textbooks available for such courses, one finds that at least half of the book, and usually more, is simply a description of the syntax and interpretation of a particular language. The situation is exactly as if courses on circuit design were dominated by a description of one model of oscilloscope. We seem to have forgotten that our task is to teach students how to design programs, not the characteristics of one or two human artifacts.

Engineering educators have long known that their students must be prepared to work in rapidly changing fields. We have recognized that the educational programme must stress fundamentals — science, mathematics, and design discipline — so that graduates will find their education still valid and useful late in their careers. Most of the books that I used in my own engineering education are still correct and relevant, several decades later. In contrast, many introductory programming books are considered out of date before the students who use them have graduated.

The approach taken by those who teach programming differs greatly from the approach taken by those who teach engineering. All aspects of computing have developed very rapidly and will continue to do so. Instead of reacting to rapid change by focusing on fundamentals, programming books and courses try to keep up with the latest developments. Each new language, each new operating system, each new database package, each new windowing system, and each new programming fad, gives rise to another wave of books. The few books that claim to focus on fundamentals are highly theoretical. Instead of learning the latest tools, students are given theories that, while they don't get out of date, do not seem relevant to the task of programming.

The subject matter of most introductory programming courses is material that many engineers of previous generations learned on their own. Just as we did not have courses devoted to the use of slide-rules, we did not need an academic course to learn FORTRAN. In fact, many students of my generation found that a one-week evening course, offered by the computer centre (without credit), was sufficient as an introduction to the tools that were available.

If we are to include a course on programming as part of a university education, we must focus on programming fundamentals and their application, not on tools.

4.4   The role of mathematics in engineering

One of the clear differences between typical programming courses and most engineering courses is that the programming courses neither teach, nor make much use of, mathematics.

Those who do not have an engineering education often do not realise how much mathematics is taught to engineers. At my university, approximately 30% of an engineer's education is devoted to things that are explicitly titled mathematics. There is also a great deal of mathematics taught in specialized engineering courses. The ability to use mathematics is one of the things that differentiate professional engineers from technicians.

In engineering education we emphasise the concept of professional responsibility. Engineers are taught from their first day at University, that their products must be "fit for use". They learn that they cannot rely on intuition alone. Much of their education is devoted to learning how to perform both mathematical analysis and carefully planned testing of their products. My own engineering education included approximately as much mathematics as would have been taken by a mathematics major and, at my alma mater, many of the courses were the same ones taken by the mathematics majors. However, we did not learn math as an "end" but as a "means". We learned how to use mathematics in developing and analyzing product designs.

In spite of the fact that, in every other area of engineering, students are expected to learn the relevant mathematics, most programming courses treat the mathematics of programming as if it were (a) too difficult and (b) not relevant to programming. Moreover, many of those who advocate the use of mathematical methods in analyzing programs disparage the use of testing. They treat complementary methods of assuring quality as if they were alternatives. Students should be taught how to use mathematics, together with testing, to increase the reliability of their programs.

In fact, the mathematics needed to understand modern programming techniques is elementary and entirely within the capability of anyone who can learn differential and integral calculus. That includes all engineers and scientists.

4.5   The role of programming in engineering, business, and science

There is no longer any question about whether or not engineering, business, and science students should take courses in programming. Computers and software are now ubiquitous in those fields. Many engineering products include computers and software; most others are designed and analysed using computers. Hardly a week passes in which we do not hear some anecdote about the failure of an engineering product caused by an error either in the software contained in the product or in the software used to design it. Since people rarely talk loudly about their failures, we can assume that these anecdotes are just the "tip of the iceberg". The question is no longer "Do we teach our students about programming?", but "What do we teach our students about programming?" Educators should insist that courses on programming be more substantive than is currently the case.

4.6   The content of most "standard" programming courses

It is time to question the intellectual content of many courses in computing. We need to ask whether these courses are comparable to other engineering, mathematics or science courses. The typical programming course simply teaches about a programming language, an artifact designed by a few fallible human beings. Most of the time is spent on things that are neither mathematical truths nor facts about the world; they are just human design decisions. Such courses are analogous to teaching about a particular calculator, including the location of its buttons, how to turn it on, how to change the display, etc. I often hear complaints that many of these courses teach almost the same artifacts that were taught 30 years ago; computer scientists think that we should teach more modern languages than FORTRAN. I believe that the teaching of "old" languages is not the real problem; the real problem is that the subject of the course is an artifact, any artifact.

At my University, we were teaching two distinct courses under a single number (to preserve the illusion that we had a common first year for all engineering students). One "section" was a FORTRAN course; the other a course in Pascal. Because these two languages are quite different, the material taught to one section differed greatly from material taught to the other. For example, Pascal users learn about records; FORTRAN users do not. In fact, the concept of a record is an important one that can be used in FORTRAN even though the language has no explicit facilities for it; if one group of students should learn about records, so should the other.

4.7   Programming courses are not science courses

We must recognize another difference between engineering education and the education of scientists and mathematicians. In Engineering schools there is great emphasis on design, i.e. on how to invent useful things. Science courses can focus on science, i.e. on facts about the world. Like engineering courses, programming courses should emphasize how to apply those facts. This has very practical implications. Every course is limited in the amount of contact and student time; when we choose to stress the application of science, we are choosing not to teach certain facts or theories that might be interesting and elegant for all involved.

As part of a course in programming, students must learn problem solving skills. They must learn how to formulate problems, how to decompose a problem into smaller problems, how to integrate solutions, etc. The emphasis in many courses taught in Computer Science departments is quite different. Computer Scientists are interested in programming languages, (and the science of programming), for their own sake. There is more emphasis on the syntax and semantics of a language, than on how to use the language or how to decide when to use them. Computer Scientists are also interested in models of programming and often teach automata theory, language theory, etc. in introductory courses. The material is elegant and has great intellectual value; there is rarely emphasis on how to use it. In Engineering courses we teach theory and models, but the emphasis is always on the application of what we teach to design problems. Design and analysis may be viewed as complementary skills. Design is inherently creative and most of the things we can teach about design are heuristics, things that don't always work. Because a heuristic, intuitive, design process often yields designs that are "almost right" (i.e. wrong), solid, disciplined analysis of the results of the design process is essential. In engineering, mathematics is most often used as a means of design analysis. In contrast, many Computer Scientists talk about systematically deriving programs from specifications. Program derivation is analogous to deriving a bridge from a description of the river and the expected traffic. Refining a formal specification to a program would be like refining a blueprint until it turned into a house. Neither is realistic; the creative steps in design are absolutely essential. This is as true in programming as it is in any other area of Engineering. Engineers have learned to make a clear distinction between the product itself and a description of it. This distinction seems to have been lost in the Computer Science literature on programming. Mathematical tradition, in which formulae are the products, has led computer scientists to view programs and their mathematical descriptions as if they were the same things.

Those who chose engineering as a career path are often people with a fairly pragmatic view of life. They appreciate mathematics that is simple and elegant, but they want frequent assurance that the mathematics is useful. It is important to show them how to use a mathematical concept, not simply to teach them the definitions and theorems. In engineering mathematics, the emphasis has always been more on application of theorems than on proofs. Computer Science has followed the approach taken by mathematicians. When most Computer Scientists design a course, they will discuss proof of correctness more they discuss design.

4.8 A New Approach to Teaching Programming

We are currently teaching a novel programming course for all first year Engineering Students. It differs from conventional programming courses in two ways:

- ♦ The early part of the course teaches the basic mathematics of programming with emphasis on the use of mathematics to describe what a program does, or must do. Programming assignments are expressed as mathematical specifications. Students learn to compare programs with mathematical descriptions.

- ♦ We stress that the programming language is not the subject of the course. Students are given a choice of programming languages that can be used in the laboratories. Two of the three lectures per week were taught in an algorithmic notation based on Dijkstra's guarded commands (Parnas, 1983, 1986). The third, "laboratory", lecture uses a "real" language. Currently we offer FORTRAN and C. Lectures are scheduled so that students who wish to do so can attend both C and FORTRAN lectures. A system of bonus-points rewards students who learn both languages. The lectures present the same algorithms. Students see every algorithm at least twice, once in pseudocode, once in FORTRAN or C.

Our course emphasizes both the creative steps in programming and the analytical steps needed to confirm the correctness of a design. Students are taught a "divide and conquer" approach to programming in which problems are systematically reduced to simpler problems and programs can be inspected in a disciplined, systematic way.

4.9   The mathematics needed for professional programming

This section describes the mathematical content of this first course on programming. Although the material would be familiar to any Computer Scientist, it will be unfamiliar to most Engineers; most engineers have not kept up with developments in Computer Science or software design methods.

4.9.1   Finite state machines

The first step in getting students to take a professional approach to programming is to get rid of the "giant brain" and "obedient servant" views of a computer. It is essential that students see computers as purely mechanical devices, capable of mathematical description. Students learn that "remembering" or "storing" data is just a state-change, and are then taught to analyse simple finite state machines to verify that they accomplish specified tasks. The Moore–Mealy model is used. Students are also taught how to design finite state machines to perform simple tasks. We do not present the usual "automata theory". The emphasis is on understanding how the machines function and on designing them. A simulator is provided so that students can test their designs. The use of the state machine concept allows students to take a disciplined approach to designing systems that process sequences of data.

4.9.2   Sets, functions, relations, composition

We present a naive set theory in which all sets consist of a finite number of elements selected from previously defined finite universes. It is important to present the students with examples of the use of these concepts and exercises in their use. We want the students to know far more than the definitions and the algebraic laws; we ask them to use the concepts to provide precise models of real-world situations. We show how state machines can be described by a pair of mathematical relations and how to use the operations of union, intersection, negation and relational composition. This is the first step towards describing programs using functions and relations.

4.9.3   Mathematical logic based on finite sets

In the first two sections, finite state machines, and sets have been kept not just finite, but small, so that they could all be described by enumeration. The next step is to point out that these are unrealistically small sets, that it is not practical to describe most sets by enumeration, and that we must be able to make general statements about classes of states. We then introduce an interpretation of classical predicate logic in which expression denotations are finite sets and show how to use predicate calculus to characterise sets, including functions and relations. By restricting the definitions to finite sets, we eliminate all the problems that Mathematicians and Computer Scientists find interesting, and can focus on the use of these concepts in program design.

We define the logic formally, but unlike most Computer Science and Mathematics courses, we do not give proof rules. Instead we give the evaluation rules, which are much simpler. We use logic to describe program behaviour, not to prove theorems.

The logic allows use of partial functions (defining all primitive predicates on undefined values to be *false*). It is important to provide numerous examples in which the students use predicate logic to characterise the states of something real. Arrays (viewed as partial functions) provide a rich source of examples such as, "Write a predicate that is *true* if array A contains a palindrome of length 3." We repeatedly use the mathematics to say things about programs, and teach students to use, as contrasted to prove theorems about, logic (Parnas, 1993).

4.9.4   Programs as "initial states"

We briefly present an unconventional view of programming as picking the initial state of a finite state machine. This helps to explain such concepts as table driven programs, interpreters, etc. It allows us to explain von Neumann's insight about the interchangeability of program and data and the practical implications of his contributions. We show practical examples of "trade-offs" made by moving decision logic between program and data, e.g. introducing table driven programs.

4.9.5   Programs as descriptions of state sequences

Next, we present a more conventional view of programs as descriptions of a sequence of state changes. This concept is presented abstractly; we do not give any programming language notation for describing the sequences.

4.9.6   Programs described by functions from starting-state to stopping-state

After pointing out that programs can be characterised as either terminating or non-terminating we indicate that our course focuses on programs that are intended to terminate after computing some useful values. We explain how the most important characteristics of programs can be described by a mathematical relation between its starting-states and stopping states. The exact model used is LD- relations (Parnas, 1983, 1986). We provide examples in which the students use relations to describe distinct sets of sequences that are equivalent in the sense of having the same set of (start-state, final-state) pairs. We show how these relations can be used to describe a class of programs that are equivalent (in the sense of getting the same answers) but may differ in the algorithms that they use. We show that this allows a mathematical description of a program that is simpler, and easier to understand than the program itself because it omits information about the intermediate states in the state sequences.

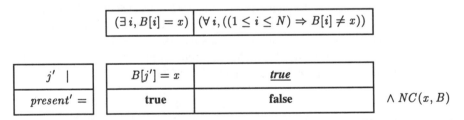

Figure 4.1: Specification of a programming assignment

4.9.7   Tabular descriptions of functions and relations

We extend the notation of predicate calculus by introducing 2-dimensional tableaux, which we call simply tables, whose entries are predicate expressions or terms. We show that these are equivalent to more conventional notation, but much easier to read. Students are given many examples in which we describe mathematical functions using these tables (Parnas, 1992). Figure 4.1 is an example of a complete specification of a program.

4.10   Teaching programming with this mathematical background

Although we teach a lot of mathematics, the purpose of the course is teaching students to program well. We must teach them to use the mathematics. We stress four points: (1) postponing program design until one has a precise statement of the requirements, (2) producing a precise program design before starting detailed coding, (3) constructing programs from components rather than simply "writing" the lines down in execution order, detailed checking of algorithms using a "divide and conquer" philosophy.

4.10.1   Programming professionally

Students are taught that they should never begin coding until they have a precise description of the program that they are trying to produce. All programs are introduced, not just with a natural language description, but with a mathematical description of the required behavior.

4.10.2   Program construction

A main theme of the course is that engineers should *not* program by "thinking like a computer"; they should not plan the steps to be followed by the computer in the order that the computer will follow them. Instead, they are told that their job is to assemble new programs from previously constructed "building-blocks", simpler programs. They are reminded that, if they are successful, their products will later be used as components of still larger programs. They are also taught that they may have to deal with programs that are thousands, even millions, of lines long. They cannot expect to understand all lines of the program. They must have precise "blackbox" descriptions of the program building-blocks. They are shown how to use mathematical descriptions instead of examining the code for the programs they will use as building-blocks.

4.10.3   A simple language of program constructors

To keep the main lectures "language neutral" we introduce a stripped-down nota-tion for describing programs. The syntax is shown in Figure 4.2. The language is introduced in a way consistent with the idea that we are constructing programs from building-blocks. The language provides four "constructors" or "constructs" that are used to construct programs from components. The simplest, ";", provides sequential execution. The others provide conditional execution, alternatives, and iteration. The programming notation is defined using the mathematical concepts taught earlier (Parnas and Wadge, 1986). We begin with very simple programs and continue, always using the "divide and conquer" discipline, to construct programs that solve more complex engineering problems. The students see every program twice, first developed systematically in the program planning notation, then translated into the programming language of their choice. A discipline of program design is stressed in every example. We systematically decompose a problem into simpler problems, then construct the complete solution from the components. We show how this program design notation, together with the mathematics, provides a method of analysis that can be used to validate a design.

<simple program>::= <primitive program> | (<program>)
          | it <program> ti

<guard>::= <boolean expression>

<guarded program>::= <guard> <simple program>

<guarded program list>::= <guarded program>
          | <guarded program list> | <guarded program>

<composed program>::=
          <simple program>;<simple program>
            | <composed program>; <simple program>

<program>::= <simple program> | <composed program>
          | <guarded program list>

<primitive program>::= <expression> | <assignment> | ●
          | ☞ | **skip** | **abort** | **init**

Figure 4.2: Syntax of the program design notation

Students are shown how to systematically determine whether or not a design covers all cases and does the right thing in each case. Although, we never talk of "correctness proofs", we do use correctness concepts to explain programs. For example, we usually identify an "invariant" when explaining a loop, and demonstrate that the invariant is maintained by an execution of the body of the loop. We demonstrate how thinking in terms of "invariants" makes it unnecessary to try to enumerate all the execution sequences that might arise. Students learn these concepts in a language-independent way and come to understand that they can be applied in any imperative programming language.

4.10.4 Turning designs into programs

The course stresses a separation between algorithm design and detailed implementation. The Program Design Notation is used to develop and analyse the algorithm. Students are then required to translate the design into correct code in FORTRAN or C and to test those programs thoroughly. Both the language lectures and the tutorials stress that there must be a correspondence between the running program and the pseudocode so that the latter serves as a documentation for the former. We tell the students about studies that show that this "design and then code" process greatly reduces errors in program design. Points are deducted if they have not kept the two versions of their program in correspondence. Homework assignments are specified using the tabular notation. Each problem must be done twice. The student must first do it using the program design notation and have that solution checked by the syntax checker that we provide. He/She then translates the program into the language that they are using in their laboratory work. This must be tested thoroughly. Both versions are graded. We have learned that the tutorials and the grading must stress that the pseudocode is used for a preliminary design before the coding. If we don't enforce this, students fall back to their high-school habits, write the running code using intuitive methods, and then write the "design" as an afterthought.

4.10.5 Tests

The first test deals entirely with mathematical concepts and state machines. The second tests the student's ability to match pseudocode programs with mathematical specifications. In the third, the student deals with more complex programs and specifications. In the second and third test, and the final exam, students are also asked to match pseudocode programs to programs in their chosen "real" language.

Because it is impossible to grade 400 student programs accurately, we actually ask students to complete programs, using a multiple choice format, so that there is only one correct answer and the tests can be graded mechanically.

4.11 Experience

The course has been taught three times, each time to about 400 first year engineering students. In the first year there was strong student resistance to the change. Students who turned to upper year students for help found that they were being asked to learn more than the students in previous years. "Why do we have to learn this when they did not?" was a frequent remark. Some of the strongest resistance came from students with previous computer experience; they thought that they already "knew" how to program (often in Basic) and did not need to be taught theory, design methods, or mathematics. However, at the end of the term many confessed that they now understood the material and could not explain their original resistance.

In the second year, there was much less resistance, but students learned the "theory" without applying it to practice. Many students observed that they could learn the program design aspects without actually running C or FORTRAN programs. We discovered a great deal of copying of those by the end of the term. By the third year, we felt we had the basic material correct and focused on changing the delivery so that students would see the connection between the design lectures and producing working programs. We made several changes:

- ◆ We changed our illustrative examples to illustrate the practical relevance of the methods. For example, instead of using recognizers to explain state tables, we had a series of problems on the mode control in a bicycle-computer.

- ◆ We provided consultants in the Computer Labs to help people who got stuck because of "mysterious" details about the compiler languages. We did this to remove any excuse for copying another student's work. In previous years students justified copying by claiming that they had no other source of help.

- ◆ We introduced a "laboratory exam" in which students were required to debug a simple program under supervision of Teaching Assistants (TAs). Students were given a correct pseudocode design for the program a week before the exam, but had to find the errors in the C or FORTRAN in "real time".

- ◆ We changed our grading procedure to increase the likelihood of detecting copying and treated all copying as academic dishonesty.

- ◆ We introduced carefully worked out tutorial sessions in which problems similar to the assignments were solved using exactly the methods called for in the design lectures. The TAs who presented these tutorials were carefully selected for their familiarity with the design method and mathematics.

Some instructors from other courses complained after the second year saying that we were teaching theory not programming. In part, this was justified. The students who had cheated on their homework did not learn how to get a program to run. However, an instructor whose classes included both students from the old, language-oriented, course, and students from the new course, found that the students from the old course were equally weak on the practical aspects. Computer assignments are far too easy to copy. Busy students will cheat to buy time.

Instructors in other subjects, e.g. Chemical Engineering, Civil Engineering, were also resistant because the material was new to *them*. One Department accused us of teaching "recent research" claiming that "finite state machines" were an example of recent theoretical advances; discussion revealed that they had never seen that half-century old concept. We often forget how little people in other areas understand about the advances made in Computer Science and Programming Methods in the last 30 years. They still program in the same way that people programmed 30 years ago. To be successful in such an environment, those who hope to upgrade programming courses must devote more effort than we did to the education of their colleagues.

Our goal is to improve student's ability to program in any language throughout their careers. It will be years before we can know how well we have succeeded.

4.12 Conclusions

Programming should be taught as if it were engineering because it is engineering. We should not be satisfied with teaching the detailed characteristics of one of today's tools. To prepare students for the rapidly changing world of computing, we must focus on fundamentals and design discipline. First year engineering students can be taught the mathematics and discipline necessary for professional programming

It is difficult to teach students with programming experience and novices in one class. We must choose between boring the experienced and confusing the novices.

Acknowledgements

These thoughts have been strongly influenced by H.D. Mills and N.G. de Bruijn. I am also deeply grateful to Professor E.M. Williams, former Head of the Department of Electrical Engineering at Carnegie Institute of Technology (now deceased) for having taught me his philosophy of engineering education. Referees have contributed to clarification of an earlier version of this chapter. Brian Bauer, Dennis Peters, Ruth Abraham, and Preeti Rastogi, made wonderful contributions in the third year.

References

Parnas, D. L. (1983) A Generalized Control Structure and Its Formal Definition. *Communications of the ACM*, **26**(8):572–581, August.

Parnas, D. L. (1992) *Tabular Representation of Relations*, CRL Report 260, Communications Research Laboratory, McMaster University, October.

Parnas, D. L. (1993) Predicate Logic for Software Engineering. *IEEE Transactions on Software Engineering*, **19**(9):856–862, September.

Parnas, D. L. and Wadge, W.W. (1986) *Less Restrictive Constructs for Structured Programs*, Technical Report 86-186, Computer and Information Science Department, Queen's University, Kingston, Ontario, Canada, October (available from the author).

Hints to specifiers

5.1   Motivation

Over the years I have been accumulating hints that I give students in response to common problems and recurrent questions that arise as they try their hand at writing specifications. I often remind myself of these hints when I write specifications too. I've broadly categorized them along the following dimensions:

- Figuring out *why* you are going through this specification effort (Section 5.2). What do you hope to get out of using formalism?

- Figuring out *what* of the system you want *to specify* (Section 5.3).

- Figuring out *how* to specify (Section 5.4). The most important hurdle to overcome is learning to abstract. I also give specific suggestions on how to make incremental progress when writing a specification.

- Figuring out *what to write down* (Section 5.5). Learn and abide by a formal method's set of conventions but do not feel unduly constrained by them. Also, we all make logical errors sometimes; I point out some common troublespots in getting the details of a specification right.

My hints are targeted for the novice specifier, but experts, such as teachers of formal methods, may also find them useful.

I will illustrate my points with examples, usually in Z or Larch. Many actually make more than one point.

5.2   Why specify?

You should first ask yourself this question, "Why specify?" You might choose to specify because you want additional documentation of your system's interfaces, you want a more abstract description of your system design, or you want to perform some formal analysis of your system. What you write should be determined by what it is you want to do with your specification.

Copyright © 1996 Academic Press Ltd
TEACHING AND LEARNING FORMAL METHODS
All rights or reproduction in any form reserved
ISBN 0-12-349040-5

You should then ask yourself "Why *formally* specify?" Your answer determines what is to be formalized, what formal method to use, and what benefits you expect from a formal specification not attainable from an informal one. When I have asked this question of system builders, here are the kinds of responses I have heard:

♦ Showing that a property holds globally of the entire system.

    ◊ I want to characterize the "correctness condition" I can promise the user of my system.

    ◊ I want to show this property is really a system invariant.

    ◊ I want to show my system meets some high-level design criteria.

♦ Error handling

    ◊ I want to specify what happens if an error occurs.

    ◊ I want to specify the right thing happens if an error occurs.

    ◊ I want to make sure this error never occurs.

♦ Completeness

    ◊ I want to make sure that I've covered all the cases, including error cases, for this protocol.

    ◊ I'd like to know that this language I've designed is computationally complete.

♦ Specifying interfaces.

    ◊ I'd like to define a hierarchy of C++ classes.

    ◊ I'd like a more formal description of this system's user interface.

♦ Getting a handle on complexity.

    ◊ The design is getting too complicated. I can't fit it all in my head. I need a way to think about it in smaller pieces.

♦ Change control.

    ◊ Every time I change one piece of code I need to know what other pieces are affected. I'd like to know where else to look without looking at all modules, without looking at all the source code.

Judicious use of formalism can help address all these problems to varying levels of detail and rigor.

5.3 What to specify?

Formal methods are not to the point where an entire large, software system can be completely specified. You may be able to specify one aspect of it, e.g., its functionality or its real-time behavior; you may be able to specify many aspects of a part of it, e.g., specifying both functionality and real-time behavior of its safety-critical part. In practice, you may only care to specify one aspect of a part of a system anyway.

In writing a specification, you should decide whether it is describing *required* or *permitted* behavior. Must or may? Since a specification can be viewed as an abstraction of many possible, legitimate implementations, you might most naturally associate a specification with describing permitted behavior. An implementation may have any of the behaviors permitted by the specification, but the implementor is not required to realize all. For example, a nondeterministic *choose* operation specified for sets will have a deterministic implementation. However, the expression "software system requirements" suggests that a customer may in fact *require* certain behavior. For example, in specifying an abstract data type's interface, the assumption is that all, not some proper subset, of the operations listed must be implemented.

Once it is clear what you want from the specification process, you can turn to determining exactly what should be formalized.

In increasing order of level of detail, you might want to formalize a global *correctness condition* for the system, one or more system *invariants*, the *observable behavior* of a system, or *properties* of entities in a system.

Correctness conditions
You usually have some informal notion of a global *correctness condition* that you expect your system to maintain. It might be something as standard as serializability, cache coherence, or deadlock freedom. Or, it might be very specific to the protocol or system at hand. If it is standard, then very likely someone else has developed a formal model for characterizing a system and a logic within which the correctness condition can be formally stated and proved. For example, serializability has been thoroughly studied by the database community from all angles, theoretical to practical. If your correctness condition can be cast in terms of a well-known theory, it pays to reuse that work and not invent from scratch.

If it is not standard then an informal statement of the correctness condition should drive the formalization of the system model and expression of the correctness condition. For example, in work by Mummert *et al.* (1994), the authors started with this informal statement of cache coherence for a distributed file system:

> If a client believes that a cached file is valid then the server that is the authority on that file had better believe that the file is valid.

They developed a system model (a state machine model) and logic (based on the logic of authentication (Burrows *et al.*, 1990)) that enabled them to turn the informal statement into the following formal statement:

> For all clients C, servers S, and objects d for which S is the repository,
> if C *believes valid*(d_C) then S believes *valid*(d_C).

where clients, servers, objects, repository, **believes** and *valid* are formally defined concepts. The point is that the formal statement does not read too differently from the informal one.

Keep in mind this rule-of-thumb when formalizing from an informal statement: Let the things you want to describe formally drive the description of the formal model. There is a tendency to let the formal method drive the description of the formal model; you end up specifying what you can easily specify using that method. That is fine as far as it goes, but if there are things you cannot say or that are awkward to express using that method, you should not feel bound by the method. Invent your own syntax (to be defined later), add auxiliary definitions, or search for a complementary method.

The process of constructing a formal model of a system and formally characterizing the intended correctness condition can lead to surprises. More than once I have seen Ph.D. students start formalizing the systems that they were building and then have to back off from their expected and desired correctness condition. They end up realizing that it was too strong, not always guaranteed (e.g., not guaranteed for some failure case or for a "fast-path" case), or only locally true (holds for a system component but not the entire system). Correctness conditions for distributed systems are likely to be weaker than expected or desired because of the presence of failures (nodes or links crashing) and transmission delays; the time to recover from failures and the time to transmit messages introduce "windows of vulnerability" during which the correctness condition cannot be guaranteed.

Invariants

The most common way to characterize certain kinds of correctness conditions is as a *state invariant*. An invariant is a property that does not change as the system goes from state to state. Remember also:

♦ An invariant is just a predicate. Given an appropriate assertion language, it is usually not a big deal to express an invariant formally.

♦ "True" is an invariant of any system. It's the weakest invariant and hence not a very useful one; you probably want to say something more interesting about your system. If "true" ends up being your strongest invariant, revisit your system design.

♦ An invariant can serve multiple purposes. It is usually used to pare down a state space to the states of interest. For example, it can be used to characterize the set of *reachable* states or the set of *acceptable/legal* ("good") states. (These two sets are not always the same. For example, you might want the set of acceptable states to be a subset of the set of reachable ones.) *Representation invariants* are used to define the domain of an abstraction function, used when showing that one system "implements" another (Liskov and Guttag, 1986).

♦ Different formal methods treat invariants differently. (See *Implicit versus Explicit* in Section 5.5.1 for an elaboration of this point.) Make sure you understand invariants in the context of the formal method you are using.

♦ Hard questioning of system invariants can lead to radically new designs.

To illustrate the last point, consider this example from the garbage collection community. One class of copying garbage collection algorithms relies on dividing the heap into two semi-spaces, *to-space* and *from-space*; in one phase of these algorithms, objects are copied from from-space to to-space (Baker, 1978). Traditional copying garbage collection algorithms obey a "to-space invariant": The user accesses objects only in to-space. Nettles and O'Toole (1993) observed that breaking this invariant and maintaining an alternative "from-space invariant" (the user accesses objects only in from-space) leads to simpler designs that are much easier to implement, analyze, and measure. This observation led to a brand new class of garbage collection algorithms.

Observable Behavior
State invariants are a good way to characterize desired system properties. Formalizing state transitions will allow you to prove that they are maintained. When you specify state transitions, what you are specifying is the behavior of the system as it interacts with its environment, i.e., the system's observable behavior.

It might seem obvious that what you want to specify is the observable behavior of a system, but sometimes when you are buried in the details of the task of specifying, you forget the bigger picture. Suppose you take a state machine approach to modeling your system. Here is a general approach to specifying observable behavior:

1. Identify the level of abstraction (see Section 5.4.1) at which you are specifying the system. This level determines the interface boundary that you are specifying; it determines what is or is not observable. For example, a bus error at the hardware level is not expected to be an observable event in the execution of an text formatter like Word, but `core dumped` is certainly an observable event when using a text editor like `emacs`.

2. Characterize the observable entities in a state at that given level of abstraction. These entities are sometimes called a system's *state variables* or *objects*. This step forces you to identify the relevant abstract *types* of your system. (See the section on *Properties of State Entities* below.)

3. Characterize a set of initial states, and if appropriate, a set of final states.

4. Identify the operations that can access or modify the observable entities. These define your state transitions.

5. For each operation, characterize its observable effect on the observable state entities. For example, use Z schemas, Larch interfaces, or VDM pre-/postconditions.

Observable behavior should include any change in state that is observable to the user. If you are specifying an operation, then the kinds of observable state changes include changes in value to state entities, observable changes in the store (new entities that appear and old entities that disappear), results returned by the operation, and signaled exceptions or errors.

Another way to think about observable behavior is to think about *observable equivalence* (Milner, 1980; Jones, 1986). Ask "Can I distinguish between these two things?" where "things" might be states, individual entities in a state, traces of a process, or behavior sets of a process, depending on what you are specifying. If the answer is "yes", then there must be way to tell them apart (perhaps by using unique names or perhaps by defining an *equal* operation); if "no", then there must not be any way for the observer to tell them apart.

Properties of state entities

The most important property to express of any entity in a system is its *type*. This statement is true regardless of the fine distinctions between the different type systems that different formal methods and specification (and programming) languages have. Since for a specification we are not concerned about compile-time or run-time costs of checking types, there is never a cost incurred in documenting in a specification an entity's type.

Since a type can be viewed as an abbreviation for a little theory, declaring an entity's type is a succinct way of associating a possibly infinite set of properties with the entity in one or two words. A truly powerful abstraction device!

For entities that are "structured" objects (e.g., an object that is a collection of other objects), when determining its type, the kinds of distinguishing properties include:

♦ Ordering. Are elements ordered or unordered? If ordering matters, is the order partial or total? Are elements removed FIFO, LIFO, or by priority?

♦ Duplicates. Are duplicates allowed?

♦ Boundedness. Is the object bounded in size or unbounded? Can the bound change or it is fixed at creation time?

♦ Associative access. Are elements retrieved by an index or key? Is the type of the index built-in (e.g., as for sequences and arrays) or user-definable (e.g., as for symbol tables and hash tables)?

♦ Shape. Is the structure of the object linear, hierarchical, acyclic, *n*-dimensional, or arbitrarily complex (e.g., graphs, forests)?

For entities that are relations, the kinds of distinguishing properties include whether the relation is a function (many-to-one), partial, finite, defined for only a finite domain, surjective, injective, bijective, and any (meaningful) combination of these.

Finally, algebraic properties help characterize any relational entity or any function or relation defined on a structured entity. The standard algebraic properties include: idempotency, reflexivity, symmetry, transitivity, commutativity, associativity, distributivity, existence of an identity element, and existence of an inverse relation or function. Algebras are well-known mathematical models for abstract data types and for processes (Hoare, 1985; Milner, 1980; ISO, 1987). For example, this algebraic equation characterizes the idempotency of inserting the same element into a set multiple times:

$$insert(insert(s, e), e) = insert(s, e)$$

and this characterizes *insert*'s commutativity property:

$$insert(insert(s, e_1), e_2) = insert(insert(s, e_2), e_1)$$

It also makes sense to ask about whether algebraic properties hold for operations on processes. For example, for CSP processes, parallel composition is both commutative and associative:

$$P \parallel Q = Q \parallel P$$
$$P \parallel (Q \parallel R) = (P \parallel Q) \parallel R$$

5.4 How to specify?

Given that you understand why you are specifying and what it is you want to specify, in what ways should you try to think about the system so that you can begin to specify and then make progress in writing your specification? The fundamental techniques are *abstraction* and *decomposition*. In specifying large, complex systems, abstraction is useful for focusing your attention to one level of detail at a time; decomposition, for one small piece of the system (at a given abstraction level) at a time. Both enable local reasoning.

5.4.1 Learn to abstract: try not to think like a programmer

The skill that people find the most difficult to acquire is the ability to abstract. One aspect of learning to abstract is being able to think at a level higher than programmers are used to.

Try to think definitionally not operationally
A student said the following to me when trying to explain his system design:

> If you do this and then that and then this and then that, you end up in a good state. But if you do this and then that and then this, you end up in a bad state.

When specifying concurrent systems, rather than thinking of what characterizes all good states, people often think about whether a particular sequence of operations leads to a good or bad state. Taking this operational approach means ending up trying to enumerate all possible interleavings; this enumeration process quickly gets out of control, which is typically when a student will come knocking at my door for help. This problem is related to understanding invariants (see *Invariants* in Section 5.3). Invariably, the very first thing I need to teach students when I work with them one-on-one is what an invariant is.

Try not to think computationally[1]

When writing specifications, abstraction is intellectually liberating because you are not bound to think in terms of computers and their computations.

The following predicate

$$s = s' \frown \langle e \rangle$$

might appear in the postcondition of the specification of a *remove* operation on sequences. Here, s stands for the sequence's initial value; s', its final value; e, the element removed and returned. You most naturally might read = as assignment (especially if you are a C programmer) and not as a predicate symbol used here to relate values of objects in two different states. You may need to stare at such predicates for a while before realizing the assertional nature (and power) of logic.

Try constructing theories, not just models

Building models is an abstraction process; but defining a theory takes a different kind of abstraction skill. When you construct a model of a system in terms of mathematical structures like sets, sequences, and relations, you get all properties of sets and relations "for free". This has the advantage that you do not have to spell them out every time you specify a system, but the disadvantage that some of those properties are irrelevant to your system. Thus, in a model-based constructive approach, you also need to provide a way to say which properties about the standard mathematical structures may be irrelevant. (You might strip away some of the properties by using invariants.) For example, you might specify a stack in terms of a sequence, where the top of the stack corresponds to one end of the sequence. Then, you need not only to state which end of the sequence serves as the top of the stack, but also to eliminate some sequence properties, e.g., being able to index into a sequence or concatenate two sequences, because they have no relevance for stacks.

By contrast, in a theory-based approach you state explicitly exactly what properties you want your system to have. Any model that satisfies that theory is deemed to be acceptable. For example, the essence of stacks is captured by the well-known equations:

$$pop(push(s,e)) = s$$
$$top(push(s,e)) = e$$

Sequences, or any other data structure, do not enter the picture at all.

Like many, you may find methods like Z and VDM appealing because they encourage a model-based rather than theory-based approach to specification. You can build up good intuition about your system if you have a model in hand.

However, to practice learning how to abstract, try writing algebraic or axiomatic assertions about the model.

5.4.2 How to proceed: incrementally

In the procedure below, at any given level of abstraction, we ignore some detail about the system. You might feel anxious to specify everything for fear of being "incomplete". Learning to abstract means learning when it is okay to leave something unspecified. This aspect of the abstraction process also allows incremental specification. In general, it is better to specify something partially than not at all.

Here are four common and important examples of incremental abstraction techniques: (1) first assume something is true of the input argument and capture this assumption in a precondition, then weaken the precondition; (2) first handle the normal case, then the failure case; (3) first ignore the fact that ordering (or no duplicates, etc.) matters, then strengthen the postcondition; (4) first assume the operation is atomic, then break it into smaller atomic steps. Let's look in turn at each of these examples in their generality and in more detail.

Use preconditions

Putting your "programmer's" cap on, think of preconditions in the context of procedure call. A precondition serves two purposes: an obligation on the caller to establish before calling the procedure and an assumption the implementor can make when coding the procedure.

More generally, preconditions are a way of specifying assumptions about the environment of a system component. Such assumptions can and should be spelled out and written down explicitly. By doing so, you can specify and reason about a piece of the system without having to think about the entire system all at once. Thus preconditions assist in partial specification, incremental design, and local reasoning — all attractive means of dealing with the complexity of large software systems.

One technical difficulty that trips some people is what a specification means if a precondition is not met. In many specification techniques (like Z and Larch), when an operation's precondition is not met, the interpretation is "all bets are off". The interpretation is that the precondition is a *disclaimer*.[2] In other words, the operation is free to do anything, including not terminate, if the precondition does not hold. The technical justification is that when an operation is specified using pre- and postconditions, the logical interpretation of the specification is an implication:

$$pre \Rightarrow post$$

When the precondition is "false" then the implication is vacuously true, so any behavior should be allowed.

Some formal methods (like InaJo (Scheid and Holtsberg, 1992) and I/O automata (Lynch and Tuttle, 1987) use the term "precondition" but mean something entirely different. The precondition is interpreted as a *guard*; no state transition should occur if the guard is not met. Here the interpretation is conjunction:

$$pre \land post$$

The difference is that under the disclaimer interpretation, for any state s in which the precondition does not hold, the state pair, $\langle s, s' \rangle$, for any state s', would be in the state transition relation; under the guard interpretation, no such state pair would be in the relation.[3]

There are other possible interpretations: For example, if the precondition is not met, it could mean that the state transition always goes to a special "error" state and termination is guaranteed, or it could mean the state transition leads to either an "error" state or nontermination. The point is that you must understand in the notation you are using what it means when a precondition is met or not met.

Finally, in the presence of concurrency, you need to specify both kinds of conditions for an operation: a precondition (as a disclaimer) and a guard. The precondition is evaluated in the state in which the operation is called; the guard, in the state in which the operation begins executing. Because of concurrency, a scheduler may delay the start of the execution of an operation to some time after the call of the operation; since there is time between the state in which the operation is called and the state in which it starts executing, an intervening operation (executed by some other process) may change the system's state. Thus, a predicate that holds in the state when the operation is called may no longer hold in the state when the operation begins to execute. The point is to realize that in the presence of concurrency, there is a new kind of condition to specify.[4]

Specify errors/exceptions/failures

It is as important to specify erroneous or exceptional behavior as it is to specify normal behavior. If an operation can lead to an undesired state, you should specify the conditions under which this state is reachable. If you are lucky, the specification language has some notational convenience (e.g., Larch's **signals** clause) or prescribed technique (e.g., Z's schema calculus) to remind you to describe error conditions; otherwise, handling errors may have to be disguised in terms of input or output arguments that serve as error flags.

There is a close correlation between preconditions and handling errors. Z specifiers draw this connection by abiding by this convention using schema disjunction:

$$TotalOp = NormalOp \lor ErrorOp$$

where *NormalOp* is the specification (schema) of the *Op* operation under normal conditions, and *ErrorOp* is the specification of *Op* under the condition in which the precondition (which must be *calculated* (Spivey, 1988) from *NormalOp*) does not hold. Thus, *TotalOp* gives the specification of *Op* under all possible conditions.

Larch specifiers, on the other hand, draw the connection by weakening the precondition, e.g., defining it to be equivalent to "true", and correspondingly strengthening the postcondition. Thus,

Op = **op**()
    requires P
    ensures Q

turns into:

Op = **op**() **signals** (error)
    requires true
    ensures if P then Q else **signal** error

For interfaces to distributed systems, you cannot ignore the possibility of failure due to network partitions or crashed nodes. You could abstract from the different kinds of failures by introducing a generic "failure" exception that stands for errors arising from the distributed nature of your system.

The two main points to remember are (1) in support of incremental specification, specify the normal case and then handle the error cases, but (2) do not forget to handle the error cases!

Use nondeterminism
Introducing nondeterminism is an effective abstraction technique. Nondeterminism permits design freedom and avoids implementation bias.

Nondeterminism may show up in many ways. It may be inherent to the behavior of an operation or object. Consider the *choose* operation on sets:

choose = **op** (s: set) **returns** (e: elem)
    requires $s \neq \varnothing$
    ensures $e \in s$

The postcondition says that the element returned is a member of the set argument; it does not specify exactly which element is returned.

You can express nondeterminism by explicit use of disjunction in a postcondition:

traffic_light = **op**() **returns** (c: color)
    ensures $c = red \lor c = amber \lor c = green$

If the type color ranges over *red, amber, green*, and *blue*, the use of negation allows you to express the same property more succinctly:

traffic_light = **op**() **returns** (c: color)
    ensures $c \neq blue$

You can express nondeterminism by explicit use of an existential quantifier, which is the more general case of disjunction:

positively_random = **op** () **returns** (i: int)
    ensures $\exists x : int . i > | x |$

From a state machine model viewpoint (for instance when discussing deterministic and nondeterministic finite state automata), nondeterminism should not be confused with choice. Suppose δ is a state transition relation,

$\delta : State, Action \rightarrow 2^{State}$

Then an example of choice is:

$$\delta(s, a_1) = \{t\}$$
$$\delta(s, a_2) = \{u\}$$

which says from state s you can either do the action a_1 (and go to the next state t), or do the action a_2 (and go to the next state u). However, an example of nondeterminism is:

$$\delta(s, a_1) = \{t, u\}$$

which says from state s you can do action a_1 and go to either state t or u.

Some formal methods for concurrent systems introduce their own notions of nondeterminism/choice; for example, CSP has two operators, one for internal choice ($\sqcap$) made by the machine and the other for external choice ($\square$) made by the environment.[5] CCS has yet a different way to model nondeterminism.

The two main points are that (1) nondeterminism is a useful and important way to abstract, but (2) be careful to understand any given method's way of modeling nondeterminism/choice to use it properly.

Use Atomic Operations

For any system it is important to identify what the *atomic* operations are. An atomic operation is one whose execution is indivisible; only the states before and after its execution are observable. At any level of abstraction an atomic operation may be implemented in terms of sequences of lower-level atomic operations (e.g., a *write* operation to a file on disk might be implemented in terms of a sequence of *write* operations to individual disk blocks). Even assignment can be broken down into sequences of loads and stores to/from memory and registers.

It is usually assumed that each procedure of a sequential program is executed atomically; this assumption is rarely stated explicitly.

For a concurrent system, it is critical to state explicitly what operations are atomic. The atomicity of an operation, Op, guarantees that no other operation can interfere with Op's execution and that you can abstract away from any intermediate (lower-level) state that it might actually pass through.

5.5 What to write?

With your pen poised over a blank sheet of paper or fingers over your keyboard, you now face the problem of what to write down. If you are using a specific formal method like Z, VDM, or Larch, you must know the syntax and semantics of its specification language. It is not enough to know what the syntactic features are; you need to understand what each means.

It is important to understand the difference between syntax and semantics. For example, a typical algebraic specification language has grammatical rules for formulating syntactically legal terms out of function and variable symbols. Each syntactically legal term denotes a value in some underlying algebraic model. For example, the term $insert(insert(\varnothing, e_1), e_2)$ is a syntactic entity that denotes the set value $\{e_1, e_2\}$, which is a semantic entity. For a standard model of sets, the syntactically different term $insert(insert(\varnothing, e_2), e_1)$ denotes the same semantic set value.

Associated with any formal method is its *assertion language*, usually based on some variation of first-order predicate logic. With assertions you nail down precisely your system's behavior. It is in your assertions where the smallest change in syntax can have a dramatic change in semantics. Getting the details of your assertions right is typically when you discover most of the conceptual misunderstandings of your system's design.

5.5.1 General rules-of-thumb

What distinguishes a formal method from mathematics is its methodological aspects. A specification written in the style of a given formal method is usually not just an unstructured set of formulae. Syntactic features make it easier to read the specification (e.g., the lines in a Z schema), remind the specifier what to write (e.g., the **modifies** clause in Larch), and aid in structuring a large specification into smaller, more modular pieces (e.g., Z schemas, Larch traits).

Implicit vs. explicit
Most formal methods have well-defined specification languages so the choice of what you explicitly write down is guided by the grammar and constructs of the language.

However, there is a danger of forgetting the power of the unsaid. What is *not* explicitly stated in a specification often has a meaning. A naive specifier is likely to be unaware of these implicit consequences, thereby be in danger of writing nonsense. Here are three examples.

The first example is the *frame* issue. If you are specifying the behavior of one piece of the system in one specification module, you should say what effects that piece has *on the rest* of the system. In some formal methods (e.g., InaJo), you are forced to say explicitly what other pieces of the system do not change (NC''):

$$NC''(x_1, \ldots, x_n)$$

This is sometimes impractical if n is large, or worse, if you do not or cannot know what the $x_1, \ldots, x_n$ are in advance.

In some methods (e.g., Larch), you say only what may (but is not required to) change; anything not listed explicitly is required *not* to change:

$$\textbf{modifies } y_1, \ldots, y_m$$

This says $y_1 \ldots y_m$ may change but the rest of the system stays the same.

A subtler point about the Larch **modifies** clause is that there is significance to the omission of the clause. The absence of a **modifies** clause says that no objects may change. Thus, if you write a postcondition that asserts some change in value to an input argument or global, the assertion would be inconsistent with an omitted **modifies** clause.

Z's Δ and Ξ operators on schemas are similar to InaJo's *NC* construct; they allow you to make statements local to individual operations about whether they change certain state variables or not. Use of these schema operators on say the schemas, S_i, leaves implicit the invariant properties of the system captured in S_i. These properties can be made explicit by "unrolling" the schemas S_i.

This feature of Z is related to my second example of implicit vs. explicit specification, which has to do with invariants. In some formal methods like Z, state invariants are stated explicitly. They are a critical part of the specification, i.e., the "property" component of a Z schema, and used to help calculate operation preconditions. In others like Larch, they are implicit and must be proved, usually using some kind of inductive proof rule. Finally, in others like the 1980 version of VDM (Jones, 1980), they are redundant. They are stated explicitly and contribute to the checklist of proof obligations generated for each operation.

Finally, the third example has to do with implicit quantification. In many algebraic specification languages the *i* equations in this list

$$e_1$$
$$\vdots$$
$$e_i$$

are implicitly conjoined and quantified as follows:

$$\exists f_1 \ldots \exists f_n . \forall x_1 \ldots \forall x_m . e_1 \wedge \ldots \wedge e_i$$

where $f_1, \ldots, f_n$ are the function symbols and $x_1, \ldots, x_m$ are the variables that appear in $e_1, \ldots, e_i$.

This kind of implicit quantification has subtle consequences. Consider the following (incorrect) equational specification of an operation that determines whether one set is a subset of another:

$$s_1 \subseteq s_2 = (e \in s_1 \Rightarrow e \in s_2)$$

What you really mean is:

$$s_1 \subseteq s_2 = \forall e.(e \in s_1 \Rightarrow e \in s_2)$$

but in most algebraic specification languages, writing a quantifier in the equation is syntactically illegal; the tipoff to the error is the occurrence of the free variable e on the right-hand side of the first equation.

Auxiliary definitions
Do not be afraid to use auxiliary definitions:

◆ To shorten individual specification statements. For example, when argument lists to functions get too long (say, greater than four), then it probably means the function being defined is "doing too much".

♦ To "chunkify" and enable reuse of concepts. When a long expression (say, involving more than two logical operators and three function symbols) appears multiple (say, more than two) times, then it probably means that chunk of information can be given a name and the name reused accordingly.

♦ To postpone specifying certain details. When you find yourself going into too much depth while specifying one component of the system in neglect of specifying the rest of the system, then introduce a placeholder term to be defined later.

Notation

If your primary purpose in specifying is the tangible end-product, i.e., the specification, and you have chosen a particular formal method to use, stick to its notation. Presumably you chose this formal method for its brand of expressiveness or for its known applicability to your problem domain. A carefully designed specification language should have just the right number and kinds of syntactic constructs to let you express all of what you want to say. The constructs provided by the language let you highlight those aspects of the system that are important to record, e.g., side effects in a Larch **modifies** clause. At the same time, they also force you to express yourself in a stylized way using a restricted vocabulary. So, once in a while the notation may force you to express something more awkwardly or more verbosely than you wish; however, either situation may actually be a sign to rethink your abstractions and decompositions.

If you are primarily interested in gaining a deeper understanding of your system through the use of formalism and the formal specification you write is a means toward your end, then do not feel overly constrained by notation. You might happen, not necessarily out of choice, to be using a formal method not specifically designed for your problem domain. If there is a concept you want to express and you cannot express it easily in the given notation, invent some convenient syntax, say what you want, and defer giving it a formal meaning till later. Don't let notation get in the way of your making progress in writing your specification. On the other hand, don't forget to define your inventions. It may be at odds with the rest of the semantics. (If you're lucky, however, you will have thought of a new specification language idiom that is more generally useful than for just your problem at hand.)

Since no one method is suitable for specifying all aspects of a system or all kinds of systems, you might choose to resort to the only practical strategy known today: to mix methods, and hence, to use a mix of notations. For example, you might use Z to specify the static properties of your system (state space); and CSP, its dynamic behavior (sequences of state transitions). Mixing methods, however, is dangerous: If you use different notations from different methods, then because they are based on different semantics (e.g., state machines and process algebras), you are less likely to detect that you have specified something that is actually semantically inconsistent. Combining different formal methods is a subject of current research (e.g., see ISO, 1987; Nielsen *et al.*, 1989; Zave and Jackson, 1993).

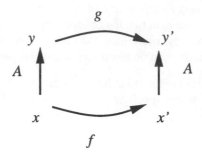

Figure 5.1: A commuting diagram

Proofs

Most likely you will not be proving theorems about your system from your specifications, but if you are, the first difficult aspect about doing proofs is knowing how formal to be. For realistic systems or large examples, it's impractical to do a completely formal proof, in the strictest sense of "formal" as used in mathematical logic. What you should strive for when writing out an informal proof is to justify each proof step that in principle could be formalized.

Given that you are doing only informal proofs, the second difficult aspect is knowing when you can skip steps. Some steps are "obvious" but others are not. Also, what may seem "obvious" often reflects a hole in your argument.

It is possible to do large formal proofs using machine aids like proof checkers and theorem provers. There is of course a tradeoff between the effort needed to learn to use one of these tools and its input language and underlying logic and the benefit gained by doing the more formal proof. If what you are trying to prove is critical, it may pay to invest the time and energy; moreover, this cost need be paid only once, the first time. If you plan to do more than one (critical) proof, it may be worth your while. Finally, using machine aids keeps you honest because they do not let you skip steps.

Choosing the degree of formality and how much proof detail to give takes experience and practice, gained by both reading other people's proofs and constructing your own. A background in mathematics usually helps.

There are common proof techniques that you should have in your arsenal: proof by induction, case analysis, proof by contradiction, and equational reasoning (substituting equals for equals). You should be familiar with natural deduction though you probably would use it for only small, local proofs.

Finally, the familiar commuting diagram from mathematics plays a central role in proofs of correctness for software systems. For example, an interpretation for Figure 5.1 in the context of state machines is to suppose that f is an action of a concrete machine on the concrete state x. If $\langle x, f, x' \rangle$ is a state transition of the concrete machine, then there exists an abstract action g such that $\langle A(x), g, A(x') \rangle$ is a state transition of the abstract machine.

In the context of abstract data types, the interpretation is that given that x is a concrete representation for y, the concrete function f *implements* the abstract function g under the abstraction function A. That is,

$$A(f(x)) = g(A(x))$$

More elaborate diagrams, for example, that allow sequences of actions rather than single actions generalize this basic idea. The "CLInc Stack" case study (Bevier *et al.*, 1989) of proving the correctness of the implementation of a small programming language down to the hardware level relies fundamentally on a stack of commuting diagrams.

5.5.2   The details

I now turn to the nitty gritty of specification: getting the technical details right.

Logical errors
Common logical errors that I have seen specifiers (including myself) make involve implication and quantification.

Implication. Remember that *false* implies anything so that

$$false \Rightarrow \ldots$$

is vacuously true, and that anything implies *true* so that

$$\ldots \Rightarrow true$$

reduces to true.

Quantifiers
Problem spots include nested quantifiers, ordering of quantifiers (especially modal operators for a temporal logic), and combining quantifiers and implication (e.g., what happens to a formula when bringing a quantifier outside an implication). Another confusion arises when qualifying a quantified variable with set membership, $\in$. That is,

$$\forall x \in T . P(x)$$

translates to

$$\forall x . x \in T \Rightarrow P(x)$$

but

$$\exists x \in T . P(x)$$

translates to

$$\exists x . x \in T \land P(x)$$

If you have a complicated predicate with a lot of embedded quantifiers, you may find it helpful to break the predicate into pieces, where each piece is in prenex normal form and has only one or two quantifiers.

Properties of sets, functions, and relations
When specifying objects such as sets, bags, and sequences that are collections of objects you may be prone to making the following common errors.

Saying

$$x \in s'$$

in the postcondition of an *insert* operation on sets is not enough. It does not say that elements in the set that were originally in s are still there.

Suppose you are specifying the behavior of a *remove* operation, which extracts and returns an element, x, from a set, s: Saying

$$s' = s - \{x\}$$

in the postcondition is too weak. You need to say

$$s' = s - \{x\} \wedge x \in s$$

since in the first case x may not be a member of s and the postcondition could hold by returning an arbitrary value; in that case, the set would also not change in value, probably not the intended behavior for a *remove* operation.

Saying

$$s - s' = \{x\}$$

is also not strong enough. Here you need to add that s' is a proper subset of s:

$$s - s' = \{x\} \wedge s' \subset s$$

since the first case allows s' to have extra elements.

Some specification languages allow functional notation to be used for relations that are not functions. If you try to do ordinary mathematical (and specifically algebraic) reasoning with formulae written using that notation, you are headed for trouble. For example, suppose *choose* is a relation that is not a function; it returns some element from a set. Saying something like

$$f(choose(s)) \wedge g(choose(s))$$

in the postcondition of an operation is weaker than saying

$$\exists x . x = choose(s) \wedge f(x) \wedge g(x)$$

since in the first case the different occurrences of *choose* could return different values. Of course if *choose* is a function, then it is guaranteed to return the same value.

Recursive definitions, commonly found in algebraic specifications, may at first look puzzling. For example, in specifying the *delete* operation for sets

$$delete(insert(s, e_1), e_2) = \text{if } e_1 = e_2 \text{ then } delete(s, e_2)$$
$$\text{else } insert(delete(s, e_2), e_1)$$

a common error is to forget to reapply *delete* recursively if e_1 and e_2 are equal or to forget to "reinsert" e_1 if they are not. Without reapplying the *delete* you get a bag, not a set, and without reinserting the e_1 you lose an element from the set.

5.6 Summary

The process of writing specifications borrows from and is similar to the processes of writing prose, writing programs, and writing mathematics. You need to worry about the big picture (e.g., the overall structure, organization, and meaning of concepts) as well as the fine details (e.g., punctuation, spelling, and special symbols). There are rules that you must always obey and rules that you may break once in a while. There are stylistic conventions to learn and follow. As with writing prose, programs, and mathematics, writing specifications well takes practice and patience.

There are many books on how to write good prose (e.g., Strunk and White, 1972) and even some on how to write good programs (e.g., Bentley, 1986). This chapter is my attempt, and perhaps the first such attempt in the formal methods community, to cull out some common rules-of-thumb for writing specifications. Maybe these hints can serve eventually as a basis for a set of organized guidelines for specifiers.

Acknowledgements

This chapter is based on research sponsored by the Wright Laboratory, Aeronautical Systems Center, Air Force Materiel Command, USAF, and the Advanced Research Projects Agency (ARPA) under grant number F33615-93-1-1330. Views and conclusions contained in this chapter are those of the authors and should not be interpreted as necessarily representing official policies or endorsements, either expressed or implied, of Wright Laboratory or the United States Government.

My views on writing specifications have been greatly influenced by John Guttag and Jim Horning, originating from our joint paper written in 1982 (Guttag *et al.*, 1982). More recently, David Garlan and Daniel Jackson have helped identify common specification stumbling blocks that we see our students frequently face in our teaching of the Models, Methods, and Analysis courses for the Carnegie Mellon MSE program. I thank David and Daniel also for their useful feedback on an earlier draft of this paper.

I thank Jim Horning, Leslie Lamport, David Parnas, and Leo Marcus for their critical remarks on the AMAST'95 version of this paper. Jim, as usual, helped polish my writing. They all helped clarify my comments on nondeterminism and the Larch **modifies** clause. They also convinced me that the AMAST'95 paper's original title was terribly misleading.

Finally, I thank all the students with whom I have worked over the years for their interest and patience in trying their hand at formal specification.

Notes

1. Another way of saying the same thing as in the previous section.
2. Thanks to Daniel Jackson for this term.
3. There is further confusion in understanding preconditions in Z because even though you might write explicitly in your schema the conjunction, $xpre \land post$, where $xpre$ is the "explicit" precondition, the meaning is the implication, $pre \Rightarrow post$, where pre is the calculated precondition and usually not identical to $xpre$ (Garlan, 1991).
4. Larch calls the guard a *when-condition* to distinguish it from the standard precondition written in a **requires** clause.
5. Hoare calls the former "nondeterministic or" and the latter "general choice".

References

Baker, H.G. (1978) List Processing in Real Time n a Serial Computer. *Communications of the ACM*, **21**(4):280–294, April.

Bentley, J. (1986) *Programming Pearls*, Addison-Wesley, Reading, MA.

Bevier, W.R., Hunt, W.A., Jr., Moore, J.S. and Young, W.D. (1989) An approach to systems verification. *Journal of Automated Reasoning*, **5**:411–428.

Burrows, M., Abadi, A. and Needham, R.M. (1990) A logic of authentication. *ACM Transactions on Computer Systems*, **8**(1):18–36, February.

Garlan, D. (1991) Preconditions for understanding. In *Proceedings of the Sixth International Conference on Software Specification and Design*, pp 242–245, October.

Guttag, J.V., Horning, J.J. and Wing, J.M. (1982) Some remarks on putting formal specifications to productive use. *Science of Computer Programming*, **2**(1):53–68, October.

Hoare, C.A.R. (1985) *Communicating Sequential Processes*, Prentice Hall International Series in Computer Science, Hemel Hempstead.

ISO (1987) *Information Systems Processing — Open Systems Interconnection — LOTOS*, Technical Report DIS 8807, International Standards Organization.

Jones, C.B. (1980) *Software Development: A Rigorous Approach*, Prentice Hall International Series in Computer Science, Hemel Hempstead.

Jones, C.B. (1986) *Systematic Software Development Using VDM*, Chapter 15, Prentice Hall International Series in Computer Science, Hemel Hempstead.

Liskov, B. and Guttag, J.V. (1986) *Abstraction and Specification in Program Development*, McGraw-Hill/MIT Press, Cambridge, MA.

Lynch, N. and Tuttle, M. (1987) *Hierarchical Correctness Proofs for Distributed Algorithms*, Technical Report, MIT Laboratory for Computer Science, Cambridge, MA, April.

Milner, A.J.R.G. (1980) *A Calculus of Communicating Systems*, Lecture Notes in Computer Science **92**, Springer Verlag, Berlin.

Mummert, L., Wing, J.M. and Satyanarayanan, M. (1994) Using belief to reason about cache coherence. In *Proceedings of the Symposium on Principles of Distributed Computing*, pp 71–80, August; also available as Technical Report CMU-CS-94-151, School of Computer Science, Carnegie Mellon University.

Nettles, S.M. and O'Toole, J. (1993) Real-time replication garbage collection. In *SIG-PLAN Symposium on Programming Language Design and Implementation*, ACM Press, June.

Nielsen, M., Havelund, K., Wagner, K.R. and George, C. (1989) The RAISE language, method and tools. *Formal Aspects of Computing*, 1:85–114.

Scheid, J. and Holtsberg, S. (1992) *InaJo specification Language Reference Manual*, Technical Report TM-6021/001/06, Paramax Systems Corporation, June.

Spivey, J.M. (1988) *Introducing Z: a Specification Language and its Formal Semantics*, Cambridge University Press, Cambridge.

Strunk, W. and White, E.B. (1972) *The Elements of Style*, second edition, The Macmillan Company, London.

Zave, P. and Jackson, M.A. (1993) Conjunction as composition. *ACM Transactions on Software Engineering and Methodology*, 2(4):379–411, October.

Moore formal methods in the classroom: A how-to manual

6.1 Introduction

Doing something once qualifies one as a researcher in an area; doing it twice means one is an expert. Using the Moore method (Albers *et al.*, 1990; pp 287–294), we have twice taught a course on program derivation, a sub-topic of formal methods (Cohen, 1990; Dijkstra, 1976). The course, taught in the semesters Fall 1993–94 and Spring 1994–95, uses Cohen's text, *Programming in the 1990s* (Cohen, 1990). This text teaches a programming methodology based on the predicate calculus in the process of program development. An earlier paper (Foster *et al.*, 1995) reviews our first attempt from the perspective of the teachers, students, and observers. Building on that experience and from our second semester, we now present a *how-to* manual directed primarily at teachers. We hope that after reading this you will be encouraged to use the Moore method to teach formal methods.

We believe very strongly in the application of formal methods to programming. Formal methods, a very important component of a computer science curriculum, are often, if not always, under-represented in the curriculum. Sadly, in our department (as in many), if students see any formal methods at all, it is late in their careers. Yet, the only real prerequisite to a practical introduction to program derivation is some familiarity with the predicate calculus, found in any typical discrete mathematics course.

For programming "in the small", program derivation allows students to write imperative programs with a high degree of confidence in the correctness of their efforts. It is a top-down, stepwise refinement calculus: a mixture of heuristic and (semi)-mechanical steps that are performed in a calculational way. The resulting programs are *provably correct* in that they can be verified to meet their *specifications*. A specification is a formal, logical, statement of the desired program behavior.

However, gaining facility with program derivation (and formal methods in general) requires a large investment of time. (In this it shares much with other forms of calculus.) Traditional lecture-based pedagogies do not provide enough practice for the students to feel comfortable applying the techniques. Because of this, we had been disappointed with our experiences teaching formal methods courses that rely on traditional pedagogics.

The Moore method is a non-lecture oriented pedagogy that places a premium on student participation. We turned to the Moore method for several reasons. First, formal methods are not significant if they are of only theoretical interest and we wanted our students to have hands-on experience. Second, we are convinced that most students retain information better if they discover it for themselves, than if they hear it second-hand in lectures. Third, we desire the collaborative research atmosphere the Moore method permits in the classroom.

In addition, we team-taught this course in order to support the extra classroom requirements of the students, and to allow one instructor to be free during class to be an observer while the other functioned as a discussion prompter.

The body of the chapter is organized as follows. Section 6.2 presents a brief introduction to formal methods: Section 6.2.1 explains what a specification is, Section 6.2.2 discusses derivational programming, and Section 6.2.3 provides a small example of a program derivation. Readers familiar with program derivation and formal methods may wish to skip this section. In Section 6.3 we present a full discussion of the Moore method. Section 6.4 details the syllabus. Section 6.5 discusses our experiences with the method and presents some analysis of the results. Finally, in Section 6.6, we distill our experience into a list of caveats for prospective teachers that wish to use the method and present some conclusions.

6.2   Formal methods

The area of formal methods is not, in itself, a subject matter, but an approach to any subject matter within computer science. A good source for current information is the World-Wide Web Virtual Library on Formal Methods located at:

http://www.comlab.ox.ac.uk/archive/formal-methods.html

There is not a single, agreed-upon definition, but in the broadest terms formal methods are the application of appropriate mathematical tools for solving problems (in computer systems).

Of course, such a broad definition can hardly be argued with: but in terms of programming, it refers to an attempt to find the right mathematical tool(s) with which to treat programs as mathematical objects. In a fundamental sense, this is unavoidable — programs *are* formal mathematical objects, since a computer is just a machine that performs formal symbol manipulation. Formal methods are most often identified with the area of *program correctness*: using mathematical analysis to predict program properties. The common starting point for all formal methods is a formal specification, i.e., a formula in the predicate calculus that expresses the input–output relationship the program is intended to produce. Formal methods provide for a rigorous, mathematical correspondence between the formal specification of what a program is intended to do and the program itself, which specifies what the computer actually will do. It is in this sense that the resulting programs can be said to be "provably correct".

6.2.1 Specifications

A *specification* is a statement of *what* a program is to do, as opposed to *how* it is to do it. That is, it is a non-operational description of the program's behavior. A specification can be expressed in many different ways. We are primarily interested in *formal specifications*: ones written as mathematical statements, usually in first-order predicate calculus. Formal specifications have the advantage of precision and can provide guidance for the development of a program.

We concentrate on programs that can be specified as a black box: we are interested solely in the input they must be provided and in the logical relationship of this input to the desired output. While this does not cover all types of programs (most notably, it leaves out reactive programs such as operating systems), it does treat most programs that computer science students encounter.

As an example of the difference between a specification and an implementation, consider the difference between the two functions *square* and *square-root*. A specification for setting y to be the square of x would state that the program should make the equation $y = x^2$ true upon termination. This is so simple that it is hard to see the difference between *what* and the *how*; its implementation corresponds directly to the specification. However, a specification for *square-root* stating that the program should set y to be the square root of x would use the equation $y^2 = x$, which does not lend itself to direct implementation.

A specification is the starting point for derivational programming. In the course, we spend some time on the crucial and important task of developing formal specifications, but it is far too vast an area to treat without an entire course devoted to it.

6.2.2 Derivational programming

In this space, it is not possible to do more than give a brief overview of this topic: complete treatments can be found in Cohen (1990), Dijkstra (1976), Dijkstra and Scholten (1990) and Kaldewaij (1990).

Derivational programming is a particular methodology within formal methods that uses the tools of the predicate calculus to *create* programs hand-in-hand with their proofs — indeed, the search for a proof is what guides the writing of the program. This contrasts with attempting to prove that a program corresponds to its specification in a *post-hoc* manner, which is how formal methods are usually introduced to computer science undergraduates (unfortunately).

Using a set of heuristics as a guide, a programmer decomposes the specification into sub-problems, letting the *shape* of the formulas drive the search for program structure. For example, a universally quantified formula indicates that a predicate must hold over an entire domain. A loop is the most common program structure causing iteration over a domain (recursion being the other). The derivational methodology provides a checklist which, if met, guarantees a loop will satisfy its specification.

Each step in a program derivation is a calculation in the predicate calculus; just as students cannot solve physics problems without practice in the integral calculus, students cannot hope to derive programs without being well versed in the predicate calculus.

6.2.3   An example

We use an example adapted from Cohen (1990) to illustrate the basic techniques of derivational programming. A familiarity with the predicate calculus is assumed. In the interests of brevity, and because of the simplicity of the example, we do not present a formal specification.

The table of squares of the natural numbers is the sequence

$$0, 1, 4, 9, 16, \ldots$$

The problem is: Given integer $N \geq 0$, write a program that prints the first N entries in the tables of squares. We refer to this as the *postcondition* of the program; the result desired from the execution of the program. Further, no exponentiation or multiplication is allowed in the solution. (Without this restriction, the program is trivial. The reader is invited to solve the problem — with the restriction — before continuing.)

Obviously, a program containing a loop is required, with one iteration for printing each entry in the table; we use an alternative notation for a while loop with B as the condition (guard) and S the body:

```
do B --> S od
```

We also use the multiple assignment statement, where all of the expressions on the right-hand side are evaluated, then assigned, simultaneously, to the variables on the left-hand side.

When faced with a postcondition that cannot be immediately met, a heuristic suggests replacing the constant N by a fresh variable n to obtain a new, but equivalent, assertion:

the first n entries in the table of squares have been printed $\wedge \ n = N$

This decomposes the problem into two smaller ones: how to print the first n entries of the table, and then how to reach a state where $n = N$. When this conjunction holds, then it is equivalent to the postcondition. When it fails to hold because of the second conjunct, the program is not finished: we have not printed all of the entries in the table. The negation of the second conjunct can function as the guard of the loop. The first conjunct becomes the *invariant*: a condition that encodes the relationships maintained during the execution of the program. After each iteration of the loop, the first n entries will have been printed, but execution should increase n and print more entries. An invariant does not mean that there are no values being changed, else the program would be useless!

In this case, two invariants are created:

> *P0* : the first *n* entries in the table of squares have been printed
>
> *P1* : $n \geq 0$

The invariant *P1* guarantees that *P0* is defined. This immediately yields the program:

```
var n : int;
n := 0; { P0 ∧ P1 }
do n ≠ N -->
   print(n^2);  // requires an exponentiation operator
   n := n + 1
od
{ P0 ∧ P1 ⇒ postcondition }
```

Of course, this is not much better a solution, because it contains an exponentiation, which is disallowed. Again, we follow the heuristic by introducing another fresh variable, *x*, with the invariant:

> *P2* : $x = n^2$

P2 can be initialized before the loop by an assignment; the "trick" is to see if it can be maintained during the execution of the loop. Since incrementing *n* violates *P2*, a new value for *x* must be derived that re-establishes the invariant:

```
var n, x : int;
n, x := 0, 0; { P0 ∧ P1 ∧ P2 }
do n ≠ N -->
   print(x);
   n, x := n + 1, E
od
{ P0 ∧ P1 ∧ P2 ⇒ postcondition }
```

The unknown value *E* is calculated by using the weakest precondition calculus, which has the axiom:

$$wp.x := E.P \;=\; P^x_E \tag{6.1}$$

The left-hand side can be read as "the weakest precondition of the assignment of *E* to *x* in order to achieve the postcondition *P*". The expression P^x_E represents the expression obtained by replacing all (free) occurrences of *x* in *P* by the expression *E*. One way to understand this axiom is that *after* the assignment statement the predicate $x = E$ is certain to hold, so for *P* to hold afterwards, whatever conditions it imposes on *x* must hold for *E* *before* the assignment statement. We assume that the evaluation of the expression *E* has no side effects.

The calculation proceeds as:

$$wp.n, x := n + 1, E.P2$$
$$=\quad \langle \text{ Axiom (6.1) } \rangle$$
$$P2^{n,x}_{n+1,E}$$
$$=\quad \langle \text{ Substitution } \rangle$$
$$E = (n + 1)^2$$
$$=\quad \langle \text{ Arithmetic } \rangle$$
$$E = n^2 + 2n + 1$$
$$=\quad \langle \text{ Invariant } P2 \rangle$$
$$E = x + 2n + 1$$
$$=\quad \langle \text{ Introduce a new variable } y \rangle$$
$$E = x + y$$

Of course, in order to introduce a new variable y, we must have an invariant that goes with it:

$$P3 \quad : \quad y = 2n + 1$$

It is easy enough to initialize $P3$ by assigning 1 to y before the loop. Once again, incrementing n violates the invariant $P3$, so a new value must be assigned to y that re-establishes it:

```
var n, x, y : int;
n, x, y := 0, 0, 1; { P0 ∧ P1 ∧ P2 ∧ P3 }
do n ≠ N -->
   print(x);
   n, x, y := n + 1, x + y, E
od
{ P0 ∧ P1 ∧ P2 ∧ P3  ⇒  postcondition }
```

And again, we have to calculate the value for the new expression E:

$$wp.n, x, y := n + 1, x + y, E.P3$$
$$=\quad \langle \text{ Axiom (6.1) } \rangle$$
$$P3^{n,x,y}_{n+1,x+y,E}$$
$$=\quad \langle \text{ Substitution } \rangle$$
$$E = 2(n + 1) + 1$$
$$=\quad \langle \text{ Arithmetic } \rangle$$
$$E = 2n + 3$$
$$=\quad \langle \text{ Invariant } P3 \rangle$$
$$E = y + 2$$

The expression $y + 2$ can be implemented directly, so no new variables are required; the program is complete:

```
var n, x, y : int;
n, x, y := 0, 0, 1; { P0 ∧ P1 ∧ P2 ∧ P3 }
do n ≠ N -->
   print(x);
```

```
    n, x, y := n + 1, x + y, y + 2
od
{ P0 ∧ P1 ∧ P2 ∧ P3 ⇒ postcondition }
```

The soundness of the axioms with which we justified the steps of the calculations guarantees that if the loop ever terminates, all of the invariants will still hold, and together they imply that the desired postcondition will hold.

The only uncertainty is whether the loop will terminate or not. For that, we need a *metric*: this is a function, t, which acts as a yardstick to measure how much longer the program will execute. We do not explicitly indicate t's parameters; they may be any of the program variables. The metric and the program must meet all of the following conditions:

1. t is an integer-valued function.

2. Execution of the body will definitely decrease the value of t.

3. Decreasing the metric is guaranteed to falsify the loop condition: $P \wedge t \leq 0 \Rightarrow \neg B$ where P is the conjunction of all of the invariants.

Given those properties, we are guaranteed that the loop **will** terminate. If the loop condition holds, then by the last item, t has some positive value. When the body is executed, by the second item, t will decrease. At some point in time, it must drop to zero or below, at which time the last item guarantees that the condition will become false, and the loop will stop. For this problem, the obvious metric is $N - n$.

An important point to notice is that the introduction of each new variable did not require us to go back and re-prove all of the previous invariants were maintained. We assume that assigning a value to a new variable cannot change any of the values of other variables.

6.3   Moore method

R.L. Moore, a professor of mathematics at the University of Texas at Austin in the 1940s, created the Moore method (Albers *et al.*,1990; pp 287–294). It is still in use in some courses within that department. One of us (Barnett) took courses taught using the method in the departments both of mathematics and of computer sciences while in Austin in the 1980s. We describe the method as it was experienced at that time.

The method forces students to learn a subject by rediscovering it from first principles. It is related to the Socratic method in its reliance on eliciting the answer from the students. However, in the Socratic method the teacher's role is very active, while in the Moore method, the teacher remains more passive. Students, upon entering the course, are given a packet of basic theorems in the field, and are required to prove the theorems at the board during class. (Originally, to assist the students — and to prevent their becoming tainted by having the material explained to them — Moore would remove all relevant texts from the library. Clearly, this was before the current age of computer networks and interlibrary loans.) The professor's role is that of passive observer: to sit at the back of the class and merely mark down the names of the students who go to the board. A mark is made regardless of the success or failure of the student, and encouragement, criticism, and help are all allowed from the other students. The entire grade for the course depends solely on a student's number of board appearances.

Obviously, such a course is extremely sensitive to the dynamics between the students and the professor, as well as those between the students themselves. When it works well, the classroom is a bubbling laboratory of exploration as students present their work, receive criticism and help from other students, explore alternative solutions, and chase down blind alleys. When students are uninterested in the material and come to class unprepared, then long hours can drag by as little or no work is presented on the board.

Based on our experiences in the first semester, we modified the Moore method by reducing the percentage of the semester grade dependent on board work to 60%. We required the students to turn in journal entries each week. Worth 10% of the final grade, the journals consisted of a report on how many hours were spent each day on the material. The other 30% was split evenly among three exams: two written exams during the semester, and one oral final. Journals and exams were added to the second semester in order to get some insight into the students' reactions to the course, and to satisfy our colleagues' need for some "objective" measure of performance. (Our contention is that even with a traditional pedagogy, a subjective component of grading remains.)

6.4 Course description

The first time we taught the course was in a 15 week semester; the second was in a 16 week semester. Both times we offered the course as a three-credit upper-division elective. It also counted for graduate credit the first year. For such a course there are about 150 minutes of class time per week. We elected to split this into two meetings a week, each of 75 minutes. We split the material into two main parts: learning propositional calculus and predicate calculus (about 6 weeks); applying the calculii to the problem of program derivation (about 9 weeks). Figure 6.1 shows how much time was spent on each chapter of Cohen's text (1990).

The first part of the course was oriented to teaching not only the two calculii, but also enforcing a uniform proof format. The format, shown in Figure 6.2, serves as a concise vehicle for performing proofs, and is a useful pedagogical tool (Dijkstra and Scholten, 1990; Gries and Schneider, 1993). Requiring a hint in between each step, and allowing at least an entire line for it, encourages giving a full justification for each step. At the same time, using a standard layout made it easier for the students to follow each other's proofs.

Chapters 2 and 3 in the text introduce the predicate calculus; Chapter 4 introduces specifications and a notation for their use; Chapter 5 introduces the

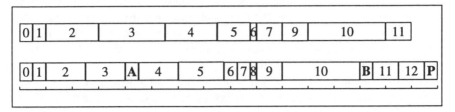

Figure 6.1: Amount of time spent on each chapter in the text. The numbers within the boxes are chapter numbers. Each tick mark on the scale represents one week. The top bar is for the first year, the bottom bar is for the second year. In the second year, there were two written exams, which were given in class and are marked as **A** and **B**; a party was held on the last class (**P**) (the last problem was, literally, a piece of cake)

Theorem: $X \vee \text{true} \equiv \text{true}$

$\quad X\vee \text{true}$
$\equiv \quad \langle P \equiv P \equiv \text{true}, \text{with } P := Y \rangle$
$\quad X \vee (Y \equiv Y)$
$\equiv \quad \langle \vee \text{ distributes over } \equiv \rangle$
$\quad X \vee Y \equiv X \vee Y$
$\equiv \quad \langle P \equiv P, \text{with } P := X \vee Y \rangle$
$\quad \text{true}$

Figure 6.2: A proof in the standard format. In this case, it is a sequence of equivalence-preserving transformations, with the justification for each step in angle brackets following the equivalence symbol that connects adjacent lines. Each hint lists the theorem applied, along with the substitution employed. := is the substitution operator. Other connectives than equivalence are also allowed, such as implication

programming notation. Chapter 6 is an intermediate discussion of the connection between proof formats and theorems. Chapters 7–10 present program derivation using all of the previously introduced tools for imperative programs with assignment statements, conditionals, and loops. In Chapter 11, recursion is presented from the standpoint of deriving tail-recursive functions from general recursive ones; a standard program for implementing tail-recursion with iteration is then used to implement the programs. Chapter 12 discusses the problem of developing formal specifications from a problem description.

The opening class was the only instance of our standing and lecturing to the students. At this class, we stressed that both the method and the content of the class would place demands on them unlike any other class that they had taken. We outlined the responsibilities they would have to take on. We then presented the first problem in the book, which introduces them to the calculational style of the book. The calculational style is like a foreign language: one's first sentences are awkward and even simple phrases take time to master. An entire class period is never too long to spend on this first problem.

For the rest of the semester, we provided lists of all of the problems in the book, both within the chapters and in the exercises at the end of each chapter. Class would begin by students proceeding to the board and putting up their solutions. As a chapter would progress, we would remind them of problems still left "open". Each student at the board would then present their solution to the class. At the beginning, they tended to speak only to us, and not to the other students. During this time, it was important to ask questions that demonstrated the type of constructive criticism we hoped the students would use with each other.

We realized that this approach would require a great many office hours, perhaps even an "open door" policy (which was customary with us in any case). This expectation did in fact prove true. Students often came to the professors' offices to work through proofs, more for confirmation than because the students were completely stumped. The painfully shy students tended to show us work in our offices before showing it to the class.

6.5 Results

It is difficult, if not impossible, to determine the true effects of an experiment like ours. But rather than just presenting an anecdotal account, we tried to assemble some quantification of our experience. Section 6.5.1 presents a picture of the students as they entered into the course. A snapshot of their behaviour during the course is shown by their attendance (Section 6.5.2) and their performance (Section 6.5.3). Finally, in Section 6.5.4, we try to measure any lasting effects from the course.

6.5.1 The students

The first time we offered this course, we had no prerequisites, and students from all academic standings enrolled: from freshmen to graduate. Our professorial colleagues were concerned lest a student could get graduate or upper division credit for the same work as a lower division student. Also the course had to have a course number, and the course number indicates the level at which the course should be taught. So, the second time we offered the course as an upper-division undergraduate course with a prerequisite of Junior standing; the class was much more homogeneous relative to class standing than the first time around. We believe that the only real prerequisite for the material is a first course in discrete mathematics covering the propositional calculus and the predicate calculus, simple set theory, and types such as sequences and trees. Unfortunately, such courses sometimes emphasize mathematical results and facts over the *act* of proving theorems.

Interestingly, though, the academic preparation of the students, as measured by GPA, was considerably different the second time. The first time, the distribution of GPAs across math and computer science courses was nearly normal, with lower math GPAs overall. So, students in the first section were, overall, *poorly* prepared for the course. In the second section, the mean GPA was considerably higher, with much superior math scores at the upper end of the distribution. See Figure 6.3 for these data. This difference in formal preparation may have been reflected in the relative ease with which we covered the propositional and predicate logics in the second section (see Figure 6.1 for the distribution of topics in the semester).

These observations may be somewhat skewed, however. The first section had several "misfits" from our department. These were the hackers: students who avoid tedious distractions from banging on keyboards, distractions such as tests and lectures. These are the "promising" students whose classroom efforts, and consequently GPAs, are abysmal. They may have been attracted to our course precisely because it was designed to avoid the usual "academic" trappings. The second time around, the students were a more traditional bunch.

Results from the first section are described in (Foster *et al.*, 1995). Students in the second section seemed less willing to take personal responsibility for the course. They did do so, with 178 student presentations in the semester, but they seemed hesitant, and often presented their results to the professors rather than to their peers. Few students in the second section were willing to go out on a limb and lead a discussion on a problem which no one, themselves included, had already solved. In the first class, this happened often toward the end of the semester. We missed this spontaneity in the second class.

6.5.2 Attendance

Attendance in this course was in general high, as Figure 6.4 illustrates. There was the usual slight drop in attendance early in the semester, as those who were tentatively enrolled made up their minds which courses to take. Interestingly, both

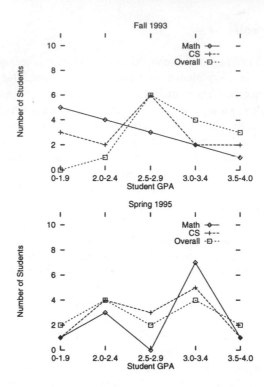

Figure 6.3: Math, computer science, and overall GPAs for students

sections had a marked decrease in attendance when we covered Chapter 3 of the text. This chapter introduced quantification, using a syntax which was unfamiliar to all the students.

Initially, students expressed much discomfort with this material. Some of the problems became more challenging and unfamiliar at this point, too. Students who continued to attend class did master this material, to the point that it was second nature by the end of the semester.

There are also clearly noticeable drops in enrollment around weeks 16 and 27 which are not correlated to the chapters in the text. It is not a coincidence that these are the usual times for midterms and finals. Many students told us that they tended to spend less time on our class when the coursework in their other classes was particularly high.

The instructor should be on guard for these trying periods, and should warn the students against relaxing their efforts. One weakness of the Moore method is that students without very strong organizational skills (which is usually a majority) tend to concentrate their resources on what they perceive to be the most immediately pressing needs. However, formal methods build steadily on previous material, so that students who fail to master one part will have difficult for the remainder of the course.

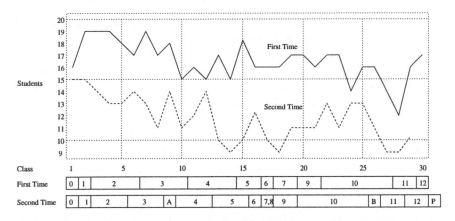

Figure 6.4: Attendance. The number of students in class is displayed by week for each semester. The chapter of the text being covered is also listed by week

Exam	Points	Min	Max	Avg.	Std. Dev.
1	50	37	50	41.53	3.42
2	50	13	46	34.21	9.23

Figure 6.5: Exam results for the second section. The second exam was open book and slightly more difficult than the first

6.5.3   Examinations and journals

As we mentioned in Section 6.3, in the second semester, we required the students to keep a weekly journal, and had two written examinations, and one oral final.

The students were asked to record in their journals: time spent on this course each day of the week; the hardest and easiest problems they faced that week; why they selected these problems; and some problems which we assigned to exercise skills with which they were having particular difficulty.

Students actually provided very little feedback in their journals, which was a great disappointment to us. Their time records were spotty, but overall seemed to confirm our suspicions that they would stop working on our course when the workload in their other courses increased. They rarely thought about *why* a problem was hard or easy for them, often saying only "I was able to solve it, so it was easy" or "I couldn't solve it, so it was hard".

The written examinations were rigorous tests of both conceptual knowledge and ability to apply techniques. They were examinations of the sort which one would find with more traditional presentations of the material. Matching the level of difficulty of the material, students did much better on the first exam than they did on the second, as shown in Figure 6.5.

Scores on these examinations almost exactly mirrored the number of times students went to the board, with two interesting exceptions. Two of our students scored poorly on written examinations, but were often going to the board and scored very highly on their oral examinations. These were students with low GPAs who were clearly uncomfortable taking written examinations. They knew the material very well, but would not have done well in a traditional "lecture and test" setting. We feel that traditional pedagogy may discard and discourage more of these students than we care to admit, and alternatives such as the Moore method ought to be tried more often.

Interestingly, students commented that they appreciated having the examinations. It comforted them to have a familiar measure of success or failure. Clearly, being kept assured of their progress is important to students, even if this means taking tests —an activity with which they are rarely comfortable.

The oral examinations were very revealing. We gave each student an individual oral examination, lasting one hour, in which we required them to demonstrate technique *and* to explain why the technique worked (or didn't). The examinations were designed to determine the extent to which they had mastered basic skills from derivational programming and formal proofs, and to probe the depth to which students had assimilated the theoretical material. That is, we tested *what*, *how*, and *why*. The *why* of formal methods was not covered explicitly in the text, though it did surface in some in-class discussions — so this was truly a test of their mastery of the subject matter.

Although it was time-consuming, it clearly showed what the students knew, and what they didn't. Students with very deep understanding were sometimes those who scored poorly under the time pressure of a written examination. Conversely, some students had mastered technique, and so would score well on written examinations, but hadn't considered the justification for these techniques. This, too, came out in the orals.

But, the oral examinations did more than merely test the students' grasp of the material: it was a genuine capstone experience bringing the course together for them, raising questions of relevance and justification which had not occurred to them before. Many students commented that the oral examinations were a revelation to them.

Orals are, of course, time consuming for the professor (requiring one hour per student, two or three hours preparation, and ten to fifteen minutes per student to evaluate their performance). But when one considers time to write, grade, and take written tests the time commitment isn't that much greater. And the payoff is great for both the instructor and the student.

6.5.4 Effectiveness

We designed this class to educate the students in two ways: to teach them about program derivation, and to give them facility with formal manipulations. Anecdotal evidence from professors (including peer reviews) and from students supported our belief that we succeeded at both in the first class (Foster *et al.*, 1995). Examinations (see Subsection 6.5.3) provided further evidence of our success in the second class.

To get another possible measure of the courses' effectiveness, we have tracked the GPAs of students who have taken this course in both math and computer science courses. We have one semester's worth of data on the students from the most recent section of our course, and two year's worth from students in the first section. We feel that the patterns we have observed will be accentuated as more of the course alumni progress toward their degrees.

Students have shown a significant improvement in their academic performance in computer science courses, and their performance in mathematics courses has remained virtually unchanged. This is interesting in that computer science courses are rarely taught with any attention to formalism, whereas math courses almost always are. See Figure 6.6 for the data. This confirms our belief that the type of mathematics required by computer science students is not that traditionally taught in mathematics programs.

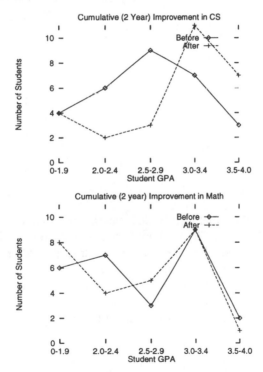

Figure 6.6: Improvement in computer science and math GPAs before and after the course

There are two possible alternative explanations for these data. One might think that students did well in our course, due to "easy" grading policies (the first section of the course did have a reputation among students for an "easy A"), and that this raised their GPA. In fact, there were more A grades awarded than one would expect from a normal distribution. See Figure 6.7 for the distribution of grades in the two sections. However, over two years of grades for students in the first section would dilute this effect.

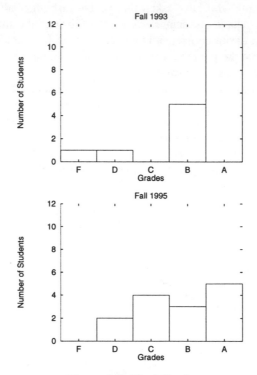

Figure 6.7: Final Grades

Another possibility is that students do better in their upper division courses. We cannot discount this possibility without determining the distribution of GPAs by year for all computer science majors. However, our suspicion is that students who do not perform well in lower-division computer science courses will not remain computer science majors. Moreover, the courses with reputations for being "hard" are usually the upper division courses, with the exception of the few lower division courses which "weed out" students who are not really competent to be computer science majors.

6.6   Warnings and conclusions

In order to succeed in this type of course, there are three things that are vital for the students to possess: maturity, maturity, and maturity. Not only are they confronted with new material that depends on familiarity with an uncomfortable tool (predicate calculus), but they are being asked to take charge of their education in a way that they have probably never experienced before.

Now, if our students are at all representative of other students, it is likely that your students lack at least one of the three qualities. In such a case, we have several recommendations.

Set them up properly: make sure to begin the course by discussing how the class will differ from a traditional pedagogy. Make sure to stress the increased responsibility that devolves upon them. They will need to pace themselves over the semester. There are two traps associated with the kind of work demanded in such a course. The first is that students will spend all of their time on it to the detriment of their other courses. The second is that since there are no assignments with due dates, students can allow the work to slide while they meet their deadlines in their other classes. Having exams during the semester helps a bit with this, but it also allows the students to think that the same ignore-then-cram methods they are used to will work for this course. They will not. Repeat these warnings as necessary during the semester. We did so, with increasing severity, at least three times.

Provide several avenues of interaction during the course: we required written journals as well as personal office hours. Encourage students to work together outside of class. Although we were disappointed with the use of the journals, we believe that it is important to provide that channel of communication for students that might take advantage of it.

Similarly, provide several avenues for testing their comprehension: we used standard-style written exams, oral exams, and essay feedback. We believe the oral exams are the best way to measure their comprehension.

For the teacher, there are also three vital qualities: patience, patience, and patience. The hardest thing to do is to sit quietly when students direct their presentations and questions to you instead of their peers, or when they arrive unprepared. This is a common problem with students in any class, but this method is more susceptible to it.

If you are at all like us, you also probably lack at least one of these qualities. Perhaps the easiest response is to take an absolutist position and never say one word in class. We found ourselves unable to do that; instead we tried to gauge when the class was floundering and engaged them in a Socratic dialogue. It is a variant of the halting problem — one never knows what the students will come up with on their own if you had just waited that extra minute. We were surprised on many occasions when a silent stare in response to a question like "what does question 4.5 want us to do?" would lead to a deep, significant discussion from the students — after a long, embarrassing silence. This actually happened, more than once.

We believe that one of the most positive aspects of the Moore method is that it is able to use the peer pressure that exists in any classroom and turn it to the teacher's benefit. Usually, students huddle together in a protective shield of cooperation aimed at circumventing the teacher and the work. No one wants to stick their neck out and answer a question unless they are sure of the answer, or unless they are one of the few students in each class that monopolizes the classroom. But the Moore method, by its nature, forces *all* of them to go to the board and present their work.

No one wants to look bad in front of their peers, so the students struggle to come up with excellent work to present at the board. The more they do, the more their classmates have to work to be able to present their own material. Once started, this dynamic maintains its own momentum for the entire semester.

Many of our colleagues have remained skeptical about the grading methods for this class. The first semester we gave credit for each visit to the board, even if a student was going to the board as part of a group. This led to abuse (Foster *et al.*, 1995), so we introduced more classical testing methodologies (see Section 6.5.3). Even with these, however, the grade distribution (see Figure 6.7) was not normal. We felt that there were a few students in the first semester whose grades were higher than their knowledge of the material would warrant—but that this was not the case the second time. Indeed, there were students whose knowledge was deeper the second time than would have been recognized by written examinations.

We feel that our testing methods the second time were very good at identifying students who had mastered the material. Even though grading was primarily based on the objective criteria of number of trips to the board (see Section 6.3) the final letter grades reflected mastery of the material. We believe that those students who received an A had a deep understanding of both technique and theory, those with a B were skilled with the techniques, those with a C had minimal comprehension of both, and a D was better than nothing.

These were not criteria which we set up beforehand, but they happened to correspond to the grades actually received. However, we were not happy having to resort to written examinations, when we had specific cases where we knew the results were misleading.

We are completely confident that our grading methods were at least as objective as standard ones, which are often less accurate and objective than many professors are willing to admit. We hope that other professors will explore other grading schemes and let us know how they work out.

Our experiences have confirmed us in our belief that it is important to teach formal methods and, moreover, that it is important to use an effective pedagogy. For material that requires a large investment of time in order to master the "tools of the trade", the Moore method is particularly effective.

Recently, a course similar to ours was offered at the University of Luton in England (Allum, 1995). The Moore method can also be used for other computer science material. For example, we are aware of it being used in a compiler class in Spain (Forcada, 1995). Reports from these locations have been very positive. We look forward to hearing from others experimenting with this or similar techniques.

Acknowledgements

Abby Howell helped significantly in the editing of this account. We would like to thank Dr. Karen Van Houten, who participated in the first section and whose comments were invaluable. Luke Sheneman, a student from the first section, also provided valuable comments. We would like to thank John Dickinson, the chair of the Department of Computer Science at the University of Idaho and the College of Engineering for providing the time necessary to teach this course (twice). We also gratefully acknowledge the help and support of Dr. James Alves-Foss and Dr. Deborah Frincke and the Laboratory for Applied Logic, where formal methods are appreciated daily. And, most importantly, we thank the students who took our course—without whom the experiment would surely have failed.

References

Albers, D.J., Alexanderson, G.L. and Reid, C. (1990) *More Mathematical People*, Harcourt Brace Jovanovich, London.

Allum, D. (1995) Personal Communication.

Cohen, E. (1990) *Programming in the 1990s: An introduction to the calculation of programs*, Springer-Verlag, New York.

Dijkstra, E.W. (1976) *A Discipline of Programming*, Prentice Hall, Englewood Cliffs, NJ.

Dijkstra, E.W. and Scholten, C.S. (1990) *Predicate Calculus and Program Semantics*, Springer Verlag, New York.

Forcada, M. (1995) Personal Communication.

Foster, J., Barnett, M., van Houten, K. and Sheneman, L. (1995) In *Formal methods: Teaching program derivation via the Moore method*, Technical Report, University of Idaho, Department of Computer Science, also to appear in *Compuer Science Education*.

Gries, D. and Schneider, F.B. (1993) *A Logical Approach to Discrete Math*, Springer Verlag, New York.

Kaldewaij, A. (1990) *Programming: The Derivation of Algorithms*, Prentice Hall International Series in Computer Science, Englewood Cliffs, NJ.

Formal methods and modeling in context

7.1 Introduction

Formal methods are widely cited as a way to achieve high–integrity software, and indeed are mandated in certain circumstances. They are now also recognized as having benefits at the level of industrial application (Hinchey and Bowen, 1995; Naftalin *et al.*, 1994), yet they remain one of the most controversial areas of contemporary software engineering practice. Part of the reason for this controversy lies in the unfortunate choice of term *formal methods*, a term taken from formal logic but now used in computing to cover a wide range of mathematically based activities. It would seem pedantic, however, to argue in favour of a more suitable phrase. Furthermore, formal methods are subject both to the hyperbole of self–styled "experts", who fail to understand the nature of formal methods, and to the criticism of others who see formal methods as merely an opportunity for academics to exercise their intellects. After a quarter of a century, one would have hoped that the half–truths and unwarranted prejudices that abound in the software engineering industry would have died out. Unfortunately this is not the case (Bowen and Hinchey, 1995; Hall, 1990).

At least part of the blame for such ignorance and prejudice falls on formal methods educators. Students are led to believe that formal methods are difficult to use and involve complex mathematics. The examples used are based upon trivial systems for which programs may be written in a fraction of the time it takes to write a formal specification. It is no wonder then that students fail to see the benefits of using formal methods in the development of complex systems, and to recognize the invaluable contributions that formal methods can make at *all* stages in the development lifecycle. Clearly there is a need to educate students in a way which places formal methods in a realistic perspective.

Unquestionably, formal logic has an important role to play in the development of high–reliability software; a complete education in software engineering should reflect this. Nevertheless it is important to develop skills in building mathematical models, to which formal reasoning may then be applied. Furthermore, it is important to develop attitudes which value the various skills of formal methods, including formal reasoning and modeling, and which place these skills in a realistic context of software engineering taken as a whole.

The author has been developing such an approach to teaching formal methods involving the use of role–play. By acting as a client, the instructor in a formal methods course can interact with students to develop the general attitudes and skills referred to. The students learn to appreciate that formal methods comprise a range of tools and ideas which can greatly enhance software development at all stages, especially in requirements capture. The approach is centred around a realistic case study; unlike many introductory textbooks on formal methods, this case study does not depend on an over–simplified file–processing system. Furthermore the case study is presented as a problem through which the students are guided rather than as a *fait accompli* which is then analyzed; this is important for developing applicable skills rather than just understanding. The use of rôle play is important in helping develop attitudes. In order to develop modeling skills, we have found the Z notation particularly useful.

The instructor acts as a system procurer, while the class is divided into development teams each of which must elicit the requirements from the instructor, specify the system, and work towards a design that implements the specification. The students are in the second year of an undergraduate course in computing science or software engineering at Anglia Polytechnic University; they thus represent a typical mix of abilities rather than the "high–flyers" that might be encountered at, say, University of Cambridge. They already have experience of more traditional approaches to software development, but have little or no experience of system development in a real–life industrial setting. Each student is expected to commit about 100 hours to the exercise.

The role–play approach can thus be used to give students a greater appreciation of the relevance of formal methods to *all* phases of system development, including requirements capture, and to enhance their understanding of the nature of system evolution (in particular why simple "waterfall" models of development are unrealistic).

7.2   Teaching Aims and Objectives

The course details as given to the students are summarized in Table 7.2.

From the instructor's viewpoint, a rather more extended statement of aims is given in what may be regarded as teaching aims. These are as follows.

1. *Give students experience in tackling problems ab initio.* We are dubious of the benefits of giving students artificial, unambiguous, trivial statements of requirements; such statements are only a small step from specifications in any case. Instead, we want students to learn how to *start* the process of formal specification, how to begin to formulate their understandings, and how to deal with abstraction.

2. *Develop confidence in building and manipulating models, rather than just reading models developed by others.* We believe that understanding abstraction and the ability to write good formal specifications only comes with

practice. Yes, it is important to read specifications written by others, but there is no substitute for experience and hard work.

3. *Develop a better understanding of the system development process.* In particular we want the students to realize that requirements capture is much more than simply getting the procurer to write a natural language description of the requirements; it depends upon an interactive process between procurer and requirements analyst, a process which can be made more effective through the use of formal notations. Natural language is ambiguous; furthermore procurers often have only a half–formed idea of what is really needed. We also want students to get some understanding of the nature of refinement, and of how it is possible to demonstrate that a design is indeed an implementation of the specification. The students should learn something about proof; not necessarily formal proof, but rather informal and rigourous proof. Finally the importance of testing at all stages of the development process, and its relationship to formal methods, needs to be considered.

4. *Demonstrate that formal methods are not a panacea.* Formal methods should be seen as complementary to and not incompatible with structured development methods and notations.

5. *Provide some realistic examples that demonstrate the usefulness of formal methods.* If we use trivial examples that can be easily handled using more conventional development methods, the advantages of formal methods are not highlighted.

6. *Develop confidence and competence in the application of one particular formal notation.* For reasons we will explain later, we chose to focus on the Z notation.

7.3 The teaching approach

To achieve these aims we felt that a novel approach was required. Traditional approaches fail to highlight the need to use formal methods at early stages in the development. In general, they tend to concentrate on simple information systems for which the task is to write operations to read, add and delete records from a file, and produce status reports. While such information systems make nicely sized and relatively simple case studies, they tend to be dull and uninteresting, and do little to develop modeling skills. Case studies are needed which explore the possibilities of formal methods more fully; for example, reactive systems. Furthermore, while most textbooks expound a particular notation and give some simple examples, they fail to demonstrate how to *apply* formal methods; the skill of building models is not developed. The latest textbooks such as that by Bottaci and Jones (1995) go some way towards resolving our objections, but the development of any skill requires a more active involvement than simply reading a book, no matter how good that book may be.

We have therefore sought an approach which is based on the active involvement of the students in modeling, and which requires personal interaction both between students and between students and instructor.

7.4   Notation

An important aspect of the approach adopted is the stress placed upon modeling rather than writing using a particular formal notation and upon the idea that the resulting model should specify the goal of *what* the system should do rather than *how* it should achieve that goal. Nevertheless, it is necessary eventually to express the model using some notation. The notation chosen should therefore be able to reflect closely the model which is being developed. We feel that the best notation satisfying these requirements is Z.

7.4.1   What is Z?

The Z notation is based upon the concepts of set theory and logic. It is not possible in this brief paper to present a comprehensive exposition of the Z notation; a small example must suffice. For a description of the underlying mathematical concepts the reader is referred to (Dean, 1996); for an introduction to the Z notation itself the reader is referred to Hinchey and Dean (1997) or Wordsworth (1992). The approach to Z used is perhaps slightly different to that used in the standard and indeed in many textbooks: these books tend to emphasize the nature of Z as a formal language with a deductive system (that is as a formal logic), whereas in the case study the emphasis is more towards the use of Z in building a model. One particular aspect of the approach we adopt is to introduce various aspects of Z in a way which can help the modeler. In order to illustrate this, and also to introduce the novice to the Z notation, a brief summary of some of the key aspects of Z will now be considered. An example is given based around the case study itself although it is not taken directly from the models discussed in that case study.

Suppose we have a rail system serving a network of stations, and that we wish to model a passenger inquiry system whereby a passenger can specify a journey (in terms of a start and destination) and obtain a suggested route for that journey.

We begin by introducing a set of *PLACES* as a "given type". A finite subset of *PLACES* will have stations, so we declare *Stations* : $\mathbb{F}\,PLACES$. The railroad company will operate over a finite set of *Routes* linking these *Stations*, where each route can be modeled as a partial, injective function between stations.

$$Routes : \mathbb{F}(Stations \rightarrowtail Stations)$$

$$\mathrm{dom}(\bigcup Routes) = Stations \qquad\qquad (1)$$
$$\mathrm{ran}(\bigcup Routes) = Stations \qquad\qquad (2)$$
$$\forall\, r : Routes \bullet r^{+} = \mathrm{dom}\, r \times \mathrm{ran}\, r \qquad\qquad (3)$$

This is an example in Z of an axiomatic definition (sometimes called an axiomatic declaration). Axiomatic definitions are used to introduce sets which are constant for the system under consideration. In this case we are modeling an inquiry system in which we do not want the passenger to be able to alter the set of *Routes* in the network! The axiomatic definition consists of two parts. Above the horizontal dividing line is the "declaration" which declares the nature of the set *Routes*; in this case *Routes* is a finite set of (partial) injective functions from *Stations* to *Stations*. Below the horizontal dividing line is the "predicate" which sets out the properties that the declared set(s) must have. In this case we see that the whole network can be modeled by a relation, $\bigcup$ *Routes*, which includes all pairs of stations which are adjacent along at least one route. Clearly we must be able to leave any station for another (1), and to arrive at any station from another (2). Furthermore, every route *r* must be continuous (3). Notice how in the last sentence the word "continuous" may be somewhat ambiguous, but expression (3) is not and clarifies what *we* mean by "continuous". Note that the predicate in this axiomatic definition consists of three components (1), (2) and (3) which are conjoined; by convention the conjunctive symbol $\wedge$ is understood at the end of each component. The predicate part is important in capturing the required properties of the set.

The set of *Stations* is also a constant set and is properly introduced by an axiomatic definition before that for *Routes*.

$$\mid \quad Stations : \mathbb{F}\, PLACES$$

Note that in this case, the only property being captured for *Stations* is that it is finite. This is done in the declaration part itself rather than as a separate predicate, hence we do not need the horizontal dividing line. This "trick" of implying a predicate within the declaration part is common in Z. Really the axiomatic definition as just given is no more than an abbreviated form for

$$\mid \frac{Stations : \mathbb{P}\, PLACES}{\#Stations \in \mathbb{N}}$$

The set of integers $\mathbb{N}$ is understood in Z and does not need a special introduction. Of course we may feel that another essential property of *Stations* is that it contains at least one member. The full definition would then be

$$\mid \frac{Stations : \mathbb{P}\, PLACES}{\begin{array}{l}\#Stations \in \mathbb{Z} \\ \#Stations > 0\end{array}}$$

(Notice that $\mathbb{Z}$, the set of integers, has been used rather than $\mathbb{N}$.) Again this can be abbreviated to

$$\mid \quad Stations : \mathbb{F}_1\, PLACES$$

The set *PLACES* is also a constant, but is not introduced by an axiomatic definition since an axiomatic definition can only define sets in terms of existing sets. We therefore need to build our models from one or more "given sets". This is done by writing the set(s) between square brackets.

[*PLACES*]

A useful convention is to write all constant sets with an initial capital letter (for example *Routes*) and to write a given type entirely as capitals (for example *PLACES*).

Many books refer to *PLACES* as a "given type" and may even distinguish between the type and the "carrier set" associated with it. This is correct, but is not necessarily that helpful to the modeling process. Furthermore a given type such as *PLACES* (or strictly the carrier set associated with this type) is often described loosely as a set of all possible values. Since the set of *Stations* is a subset of *PLACES*, the implication is that a passenger may be able to input a place which is not a station. If a keyboard is being used for data entry, this is indeed the case; however, we may well insist that the interface itself will only permit the input of known stations. (For example by displaying station names on a touch–sensitive screen.) In that case it might be more appropriate to use *STATIONS* as the given set, although in that case we lose the required properties of *STATIONS*. (There is a way round this difficulty using what is known as a "free type"; a good discussion of that is given in Wordsworth (1992).

In the course of a particular journey a train will travel along a specified *route*, and will either be at rest at a *station* or travelling towards the next *station*. The state of a train can thus be defined by a "schema":

$$
\begin{array}{l}
\underline{\quad TrainInTransit\quad} \\
route : Routes \\
station : Stations \\
\hline
station \in \mathrm{ran}\ route \cup \mathrm{dom}\ route \qquad\qquad (4)
\end{array}
$$

As a general rule, schemas have names; in the example given the name is *TrainInTransit*.

In many ways a schema is like an axiomatic definition in that entities are declared (in this case *station* and *route*) and properties captured in the predicate part below the horizontal dividing line. In this case we need to capture the property that a *station* must lie on the *route* (4).

The main difference between an axiomatic definition and a schema is that the entities in a schema (such as *station* and *route*) are variables; as the system state changes so do the values of *station* and *route*. Thus we can imagine a constant set associated with the schema such that every element in the set represents one possible state of the system. For example each element could be an ordered pair with the first coordinate being a *route* and the second element a *station*; in this case the schema can be regarded as defining a relation between *Routes* and *Stations*.

Schemas can also be used to model changes in state. For example, the schema $\Delta TrainInTransit$ refers to any possible change.

```
┌─ ΔTrainInTransit ──────────────────────────────────────────
│ route : Routes
│ station : Stations
│ route' : Routes
│ station' : Stations
├────────────────────────────────────────────────────────────
│ station ∈ ran route ∪ dom routestation' ∈ ran route' ∪ dom route'
└────────────────────────────────────────────────────────────
```

where *route* and *station* refer to the state of the system before a change, and *route'* and *station'* refer to the state of the system after the change. Associated with this schema is a set of ordered 4–tuples; the first two coordinates refer to the state before the change, and the last two refer to the state after the change.

In fact we can regard this new schema, $\Delta TrainInTransit$, as made up of two parts: *TrainInTransit*, as defined above, and *TrainInTransit'* which is equal to:

```
┌─ TrainInTransit' ──────────────────────────────────────────
│ route' : Routes
│ station' : Stations
├────────────────────────────────────────────────────────────
│ station' ∈ ran route' ∪ dom route'
└────────────────────────────────────────────────────────────
```

Thus a shorter way of defining $\Delta TrainInTransit$ is to write:

```
┌─ ΔTrainInTransit ──────────────────────────────────────────
│ TrainInTransitTrainInTransit'
└────────────────────────────────────────────────────────────
```

This way of defining $\Delta TrainInTransit$ also suggests an alternative set to be associated with the schema; the set of ordered pairs in which the first element is an ordered pair representing state before and the second element is an ordered pair representing state after.

Of course this schema covers *any* possible change; often we want to be more restrictive. For example, suppose we want to model a change in which a train stays on the same *route* but departs from *station* for *station'*, the next destination on *route*. We can model this by the schema:

```
┌─ TrainDepartsForNextStation ───────────────────────────────
│ ΔTrainInTransit
├────────────────────────────────────────────────────────────
│ route' = route                                          (5)
│ station ↦ station' ∈ route                              (6)
└────────────────────────────────────────────────────────────
```

Essentially this is the same as $\Delta TrainInTransit$ except that extra conditions (5) and (6) have been added to the predicate part to restrict the changes to those in which the *route* stays the same and the *station'* after the change is next along the *route* from the *station* before the change. The new set associated with *TrainDepartsForNextStation* is in fact a subset of that associated with Δ*TrainInTransit*. If we associate the new schema with the set of ordered pairs of states before and after the train departs for the next station, we in fact have a function on the set of states associated with *TrainInTransit*. This function is not total; once the train has reached the end of the *route* then there is no further *station'* to which it can proceed along that *route*. The domain of the function is in fact a subset of the set of states given by *TrainInTransit*. A schema which defines this domain is known as the "precondition". In this case the precondition is equal to

```
┌─ pre TrainDepartsForNextStation ──────────────────────
│ route : Routes
│ station : Stations
├───────────────────────────────────────────────────────
│ station ∈ dom route
└───────────────────────────────────────────────────────
```

7.4.2 Why Z?

There are several reasons why we chose to use Z:

1. Z is the most common formal method in use in Europe, both in academia and in industry. We believe that its use is rapidly becoming more common in the US also.

2. The Z notation is simple; it is based on Zermelo set theory and simple logic. Students will already have taken courses in discrete mathematics, and therefore should be familiar with most of the mathematical concepts used. Schemas and the schema calculus are the only major novelty, and we avoid introducing these until somewhat later in the course.

3. Z is a wide–spectrum formal specification notation; it has a broad application base, and is suitable for use at all levels of abstraction.

4. There is a wide range of support materials for Z. There are many good textbooks (although as we have already pointed out, we have problems with using these alone), a number of very cheap or free support tools such as type–checkers, LATEX stylefiles, type–setters, and theorem provers, most of which will run in an MS–DOS environment.

5. We have found that Z helps to enforce abstraction, something which students find very difficult and which they will avoid if possible. When using VDM, say, they try to write programs, introducing the equivalent of for–loops and while–loops. This is not a criticism of VDM as such, but rather an observation of the 'hacking' mentality that is instilled in undergraduates in programming courses.

With these factors in mind, we decided to use Z. Although it has its limitations, for example in specifying real–time systems, these actually serve to highlight to students that no single specification language is definitive.

7.4.3   Prerequisite knowledge

It is important that students are well prepared mathematically in order to tackle the case study. Before beginning the case study, students are expected to be familiar with the basics of discrete mathematics. This does not mean that they should be taught a wide range of topics such as graph theory, formal proof and combinatorics, but rather that they grasp the *essence* of discrete mathematics: this not only refers to a knowledge of the basic concepts of sets, logic, functions and relations, but also to an understanding of the idea of modeling, to confidence and competence in handling mathematical notations, and, above all, to an attitude of believing that mathematical modeling has a very important role to play in computing. This approach to teaching the basics of discrete mathematics which gives an appropriate basis for developing modeling with sets and logic is described more fully in Dean (1995).

It is also our experience that there is no suitable text which prepares students in the way that they need. We do not seem to be alone in this; in Garlan (1994) it is stated that there is a lack of texts which "concentrate primarily on the broader underlying principles" [of formal methods]. It has therefore been necessary to write a new book (Dean, 1996). Students have to work through this book and pass a multiple choice test before they can begin the case study. A feature of this material is the inclusion of activities which foster an understanding of the role of modeling and of the close relationship between the mathematics and computing; it also encourages an approach to learning based upon activity and analysis rather than just reading and memorizing. This active attitude is essential for attempting the case study.

7.4.4   Corequisite learning

Students taking the course should already have *some* background in discrete mathematics. Nevertheless there are certain aspects of Z which they will not have encountered previously; furthermore, it is likely that the students will be familiar with a notation which differs from Z.

We generally find that students require some revision of set theory and simple logic, during which the Z notation can be introduced as the standard. They are also introduced to the idea of "types" in Z.

At a later point the notion of Z schemas, schema types and the schema calculus are introduced. We are not in favour of introducing these concepts too early, as it results in many students thinking that for some reason schemas are essential to Z, almost something magical.

Longer courses, or courses with more advanced students, may continue with the more sophisticated aspects of Z, and with refinement in Z.

Some reasoning should be covered in any formal methods course. We do not hold that this *has* to be formal reasoning; indeed, full formal proof is rarely employed in practice. At this stage, informal, intuitive reasoning suffices, with obvious equivalences and deficiencies highlighted. More rigourous reasoning should clearly be integrated at a later point.

7.5 An overview of the case study

We build the entire course around a single large (and extensible) case study — that of a metropolitan rail system. We believe this to be a very useful case study; it is a realistic application in a domain that should be reasonably familiar to all. Furthermore it is possible to tackle real–time and safety–critical aspects if desired. Rail systems are one of those domains that have proven themselves to be very amenable to formal specification, and much success has been reported in the use of formal methods in the railway industry (Dehbonei and Mejia, 1995; Dürr *et al.*, 1995; King, 1994; Hansen, 1994; Simpson, 1994).

Rail systems have also become a recognized comparison testbed for real–time development methods (Young, 1995), and CENELEC, the European body governing safety in railroad system software, is advocating the use of formal methods in the development of such systems.

Perhaps more importantly, the case study is easily extended, and can be tailored to the ability of the students and the length of the course.

In addition to a student guide, each student receives a case study booklet through which they are expected to work. This booklet comprises several chapters.

1. **Introduction** which gives a brief overview of the nature of formal methods, modeling and their interrelationship. It also outlines what the student should learn from the working through the case study, and the role of the instructor in helping to bring about this learning (see Table 7.2). Essentially the introductory chapter is a summary of this book chapter.

2. **Guide to the case study** which explains the stresses modeling as a process, and provides instructions on how to work through the case study. It also includes a brief statement of the problem itself.

3. **An electronic map** which states more fully the systems to be modeled, and takes the student through a number of stages towards a mathematical model of the map of the rail network. Before beginning each stage in the work, the students are given a brief explanation of what is needed, some guidance on completing that stage and perhaps some further information (Table 7.5). This is followed by specific tasks to attempt in the form of an "Activity". Possible "Answers" to that activity are mostly given in an appendix at the end of the booklet, while the main body of the text builds on and evaluates

the models arising from the activity (Table 7.5). At the end of each chapter, further activities are given to which no possible answers are given and which form the basis of student assessment.

4. **The Passenger Inquiry System** which builds on the model of the rail network to build a model of the inquiry system itself. The student is introduced to Z schemas, schema types and their use in modeling input and output. An important aspect of the modeling process stressed in this chapter is refinement. Often refinement is treated as a mathematical process which is only used when attempting to produce a final program design from a specification. We prefer to stress the usefulness and practicality of refinement at all stages in the software development process, and which provides an integrated view of this development.

5. **A system to update the electronic map** which now builds a new model for a different system, namely one to update the information held in the electronic map. This new model will use many of the ideas already developed in the earlier model; this is considered important in helping maintain confidence. This chapter also concentrates on the use of schemas to model operations, that is changes to the state of the electronic map.

6. **A control system** which presents the student with yet another system to model. Experience with the earlier modeling exercises is helpful in giving the student ideas of the sort of approach which can be adopted, yet the ideas from the earlier models cannot be used directly; attempts to do that tend to result in great difficulties. Thus the student is gradually moved towards being able to build models for novel systems.

We begin by considering models of the network itself; this introduces the students to the idea of abstraction and axiomatic definition. The natural progression is then to introduce the state of the system — station positions and attributes, trains, status of signals, and operations that change the state (at which point schemas are introduced). Later we can begin to deal with entire sections of line, rather than operations at specific points (promotion).

As time (and student ability) permits, it may prove possible to extend the case study to considering realistic scheduling policies and train timetabling.

Another aspect of the case study is an inquiry system that keeps a record of timetables, routes, etc.

7.6 An evaluation

We have found the course outlined in this paper to be very effective. We find that our students gain a better understanding of the process of system development, and that "hands–on" experience with formal specification and modeling helps to encourage the required "mind–set". These benefits are still important even if the students never have to use formal methods.

The students' natural reaction is to take the initial statement of requirements and to rewrite this in Z. They then generally submit what they claim is an appropriate formal specification; usually this specification is incomplete, or wrong, or a mixture of Z and programming language constructs; often it is unnecessarily full of sophisticated features of the Z notation. The instructor interacts with the students to make them realize that they need first to analyze the problem more deeply using *simple* mathematical concepts; this can be very demanding for both the instructor and the students. At this stage the students start to see the ambiguities in the original statement of requirements, and may even berate the instructor for giving them a vaguely worded assignment — the role play aspect of the case study needs to emphasized at this juncture! (If the initial statement of requirements is sufficiently ambiguous, much frustration can ensue.)

The students then begin to structure their questions more carefully, so that they can attempt to remove much of the ambiguity. This process usually continues for a few sessions, with the more able students asking the more appropriate questions early. Gradually the procurer allows them to start formalizing small portions of the system. The instructor must act the part of the customer, dismissing formalized specifications as unintelligible, until the students annotate them liberally with natural language.

By the end of the course, most (teams of) students will have produced an intelligible specification which they claim adequately describes the system required by the procurer. They will also have done some informal proofs. The more able students will have derived a simple design for the system.

We do not claim that as a result of role–playing the students produce perfect specifications. Some still find the task of realizing a specification difficult and daunting; however, we feel that although they may not necessarily have succeeded in their stated task, they have learned a lot about how to begin producing a formal specification and how to apply formal methods. Furthermore they almost invariably comment that they have found the challenge rewarding, are convinced of the usefulness of mathematical methods, and have a better comprehension of the depth of analysis that is required at the start of any project, whether or not formal methods are to be used.

The approach also has the advantage that more advanced students can be allowed to continue at a faster pace, and are not constrained by the weaker members of the class.

A major difficulty arises with students who have already "done" Z (or VDM or some other specification "language") on another course, and who seem to have a deeply embedded idea that the purpose of the exercise is to write a "program" to include as many of the more esoteric aspects of the notation that they can squeeze in. We are rather alarmed at the thought that many students from other courses are entering industry with such a distorted view that can only do a great disservice to formal methods, and which can only lead to a deeper entrenchment of practitioners opposed to these methods, which have so much to offer.

7.7   Conclusions

We have developed an approach to learning formal methods which concentrates on developing skills and attitudes rather than facts and methodologies. Educational theory suggests that such an approach is best developed through role play. We have found that a simple role play situation in which students constitute software teams, and the instructor a client, is effective in achieving our aims.

Like all role play exercises, there needs to be a well–thought–through body of preparatory and support material for both the students and the instructor. Students seem to enjoy and are motivated by the challenges of the active approach.

As a result of the approach, students appreciate that there are many aspects to formal methods, and that *some* of these aspects should be present in most, if not all, software projects. In particular the students see formal methods as a range of ideas and tools which complement existing methodologies, not replace them.

7.8   Future developments

So far the role play has been based upon the instructor taking the part of the client. Ideally, it would be good if the students themselves could play the client. This would not only have the advantage of relieving some of the burden from the instructor, but would also give the students the valuable experience of seeing the software development process from the other side. Furthermore, it would also necessitate the students' reading the master model, and thus give them extra practice at reading formal specifications and answering simple questions about them. Unfortunately the skills required for the student to play the client probably mean that such role play could only be used at a late stage in the case study, or even in a second case study.

Acknowledgements

This chapter is an extended and revised version of a short paper (Dean and Hinchey, 1995) presented at the 26th SIGCSE Technical Symposium on Computer Science Education, Nashville, 1995 and published by the Association for Computing Machinery.

References

Bottaci, L. and Jones, J. (1995) *Formal Specification Using Z — A Modelling Approach*, International Thomson Publishing, London.

Bowen, J.P. and Hinchey, M.G. (1995) Seven More Myths of Formal Methods, *IEEE Software*, **12**(4):34–41, July; also appears in a shortened form in (Naftalin *et al.*, 1994), pp 105–117.

Dean, C.N. (1995) Mental Models of Z: I — Sets and Logic. In J.P. Bowen and M.G. Hinchey, editors, *ZUM'95: 9th International Conference of Z Users*, pp 498–507, Lecture Notes in Computer Science **967**, Springer Verlag, Berlin.

Dean, C.N. (1996) *The Essence of Discrete Mathematics*, Prentice Hall Essence of Computing Series, Hemel Hempstead.

Dean, C.N. and Hinchey, M.G. (1995) Introducing Formal Methods Through Rôle–Playing. *SIGCSE Bulletin*, **27**(1):302–306, March.

Dehbonei, B. and Mejia, F. (1995) Formal Development of Safety–Critical Software Systems in Railway Signalling. In (Hinchey and Bowen, 1995), pp 227–252.

Dürr, E.H., Plat, N. and de Boer, M. (1995) CombiCom: Tracking and Tracing Rail Traffic using VDM^{++}. In (Hinchey and Bowen, 1995), pp 203–225.

Garlan, D. (1994) Integrating Formal Methods into a Professional Master of Software Engineering Course. In J.P. Bowen and J.A. Hall, editors, *Z User Workshop, Cambridge, 1994*, pp 71–85, Workshops in Computing, Springer Verlag, London.

Hall, J.A. (1990) Seven Myths of Formal Methods. *IEEE Software*, **7**(5):11–19, September.

Hansen, K.M. (1994) Validation of a Railway Interlocking Model. In (Naftalin *et al.*, 1994), pp 582–601.

Hinchey, M.G. and Bowen, J.P., editors (1995) *Applications of Formal Methods*, Prentice Hall International Series in Computer Science, Hemel Hempstead.

Hinchey, M.G. and Dean, C.N., editors (1997) *A Handbook of Z*, Academic Press, London, to appear.

King, T. (1994) Formalising British Rail's Signalling Rules. In (Naftalin *et al.*, 1994), pp 45–54.

Naftalin, M., Denvir, T. and Bertran, M., editors (1994) *Industrial Benefits of Formal Methods, Proceedings of FME'94*, Lecture Notes in Computer Science **873**, Springer–Verlag, Berlin.

Simpson, A. (1994) A Formal Specification of an Automatic Train Protection System. In (Naftalin *et al.*, 1994), pp 602–617.

Wordsworth, J.B. (1992) *Software Development with Z*, Addison–Wesley, Reading, MA.

Young, W.D. (1995) Modeling and Verification of a Simple Real–Time Railroad Gate Controller, In (Hinchey and Bowen, 1995), pp 181–201.

Table 7.1: A brief description of the content, learning aims and objectives from the student guide.

Contents

1. Introduction to formal methods and modeling.

2. Modeling with discrete mathematics. Abstraction. Animation.

3. Introduction to the Z notation. Types. Constants and axiomatic definitions; abbreviation definitions.

4. Variables and schemas. Schema types. Refinement.

5. Abstract state machines.

6. Generic definitions. Use of the mathematical toolkit.

7. Preconditions. Schema calculus.

Course Details

Aims

1. Develop ability to read formal specifications.

2. Develop ability to produce formal specifications.

3. Develop understanding of the role of mathematical models.

Objectives

1. Understand simple formal specifications.

2. Modify simple formal specifications.

3. Develop set–theoretic models of simple systems.

4. Express simple set–theoretic models in formal notation.

5. Write good specifications, based around formal notation, of simple systems.

6. Understand the role of formal methods.

Table 7.2: Extracts from Chapter 1 of the *Case Study Booklet*

Several essential aspects of modeling will be brought out in this case study including

♦ Abstraction using sets

♦ Strategies for building the model

♦ Extending and developing the model

♦ Informal reasoning about properties of the specification

♦ Testing that requirements have been captured

♦ A simple introduction to animation

♦ Refining the model

In order to bring out these particular aspects most effectively, the tutor will act as a system procurer for the system; using this system as the basis of a case study, you will need to determine the system requirements, deriving a system specification.

⋮

It is unlikely that you will become proficient modelers; what you should gain, however, is an understanding of the skills and knowledge which you will need, and you should lay the foundations of these.

Table 7.3: Information Extract from Chapter 3 of the *Case Study Booklet*

What we need now is some form of test which will enable us to decide whether any given 'map' is acceptable or not; this is what *abstraction* is about. We express this test as a predicate

$\vdots$

The following are all acceptable:

Accept

$\{x \mapsto \{A, B\}\}$

$\{v \mapsto \{A, B\}, w \mapsto \{A, D\}, x \mapsto \{B, C\}, y \mapsto \{D, C\}\}$

$\{v \mapsto \{A, B\}, w \mapsto \{A, D\}, x \mapsto \{B, C\}, y \mapsto \{D, C\}, z \mapsto \{C, E\}\}$

$\{u \mapsto \{A, B\}, v \mapsto \{A, B\}, w \mapsto \{A, D\}, x \mapsto \{B, C\}, y \mapsto \{D, C\}, z \mapsto \{C, E\}\}$

Five examples of unacceptable maps were given in the text. The values of *EndSet* for the first three of these are:

Reject

$\{x \mapsto \{\}\}$

$\{x \mapsto \{A\}\}$

$\{x \mapsto \{A, B\}, y \mapsto \{B\}\}$

Table 7.4: Activity Extract from Chapter 3 of the *Case Study Booklet*

━━━━━━━━━━━━━ **Activity** ━━━━━━━━━━━━━

What do the **Accept** values of *EndSet* have in common which the first three **Reject** values do not? What is the significance of this difference?

━━━━━━━━━━━━━ **Activity** ━━━━━━━━━━━━━

Write down a predicate which is true for the **Accept** values but false for the **Reject** values.

━━━━━━━━━━━━━ **Answers** ━━━━━━━━━━━━━

$\forall\, set : \mathbb{P}\, STATIONS \bullet set \in \mathrm{ran}\, EndSet \Rightarrow \#set = 2$

At this stage it might be tempting to assume that is all that is required. But the next example shows that is not the case.

━━━━━━━━━━━━━ **Activity** ━━━━━━━━━━━━━

The value of *EndSet* for the fourth **Reject** map is

$$\{x \mapsto \{A, B\}\}$$

Is the predicate obtained above, true or false in this case? If the predicate is true, what modification needs to be made?

An empirical study of specification readability

8.1 Introduction

Experience in the teaching of mathematics at any level reveals the difficulty that a large proportion the population have with the use of abstracted symbolic notations (Hackney, 1991). Some, who have mastered arithmetic and can cope with geometry, reach an insurmountable barrier with algebra. A recent Assessment of Performance Unit (APU) report shows decreases in U.K. pupil's ability to cope with algebra and number, whilst reporting small increases in ability in geometry and data handling (Burghes, 1992). Reasons cited include: the sudden introduction of modern mathematics; a serious cutback in work involving natural numbers; a massive reduction in the basic algebraic content of the GCSE syllabus and indiscriminate use of calculators both in the classroom and in all examinations (Roy, 1992). The ability to read and interpret information condensed into equations and to be at ease with abstract notation seems to be increasingly rare among the student body. Similar problems occur in the teaching of programming languages when introducing concepts of variables and parameters.

In formal methods the aim is to express the essence of a specification in a mathematically precise form using a concise, well-founded notation, therefore some of these same difficulties will occur. There are many claims and counter claims about formal methods and the ease with which they can be used but very little published empirical work. This paper reports the results of an initial experiment to test some aspects of specifications that may be pertinent to these claims. The aim was to try to quantify the effect of various factors on the ability to read and understand formal specifications and is part of broader on-going work examining and identifying metrics for them. The initial results and some experimental observations are reported in this paper.

8.2 Experimental context

The main factors to consider when undertaking this work were: the formal method to be examined, the attributes to be measured and the subjects of the experiment.

One of the frustrations of the existing studies of formal methods is the tendency of researchers to invent new versions of existing notations or even entirely new notations and methodologies. It was decided to use the Z specification language (Spivey, 1992) as the basis for the study to give the results wide applicability. The Z notation is becoming a *de facto* lingua franca within the software engineering and computer science communities. This breadth of applicability in both academia and industry is evidenced by the rapid rise in the number of publications about Z or using Z as a notation and the number of quoted applications. The schema structure of Z also lent itself to the presentation of part of a larger specification whilst still being a meaningful fragment.

As an initial study the main attribute of concern was the readability of the specification. This becomes quite a complex attribute because aspects of comprehension, interpretation and inference can all be considered as part of the skill of reading. This is reflected in the learning process which involves two distinct phases: comprehension and articulation. The testing of reading literature also brings these issues into focus. When children learn to read they are initially tested by reading out loud to see that they have mastered the mechanics of putting the letters together and joining the words into sentences. At this stage no comprehension is tested although some interpretation could be implied by phrasing and inflexion. A more advanced stage of reading is tested by a comprehension test which requires the child to answer questions to see if the passage has been understood, it being assumed that they have already mastered the initial mechanistic stage (Harris and Sipay, 1975). The experiment included both aspects of reading.

The comprehension of a language may be understood in three phases or levels: lexical, syntactic and semantic. By analogy, the way in which the child's reading material is written can make a difference to their ability to understand it. Familiar names which they can easily recognize give them key words to work round. Anyone reading a long novel with complicated Russian names will be familiar with the difficulty of maintaining the sense of the narrative whilst recalling the different characters' names. The presentation of the material also has some bearing on the ease with which it is read. The use of paragraphs and short sentences in the structure of the page will aid the reading process. Finally, illustrations in a book give valuable extra information in a visual form about the meaning of the text and give the child confirmation that their interpretation is correct or cues the child into the correct interpretation.

Formal specifications can become more user-friendly if they are presented in a way which increases readability. In an analogy with a child's reading three aspects of a specification were examined: the use of variable names, the inclusion of explanatory comments and text, and the decomposition of the schemas. These are each factors which have been considered essential to the production of quality software where, as in English prose, the style of writing can illuminate or obscure the ideas which are expressed. It is intuitively appealing and has long been generally accepted that the use of meaningful variable names and appropriate explanatory comments enhance program readability (Rushby, 1980) and the partitioning of large or complex programmes into smaller modules is essential to their intellectual manageability (Wirth, 1974). This has to some extent been confirmed by experiment (Harold, 1986) and (Tenny, 1988).

8.3   The experiment

The subjects of the experiment were undergraduate and postgraduate students at the University of Greenwich. They all had some knowledge of Z and were willing to spend time taking part in an experiment. The uniformity of the background and experience of the students also helped in the control of some of the bias to the results.

The students came from four classes which were, for the purposes of the experiment, called A, B, C and D. The students in A, B, and C were part-time evening computer science undergraduates. Those in Class A were nearing the end of a one semester unit in formal specification using Z and were at level 2, that is, the equivalent of the second year of a full time degree. Nine students participated in the experiment. Five of these where direct entrants having successfully completed an HND with appropriate grades. The sixteen students of Class B were also level 2 but had completed the formal methods unit the previous semester and were now on a theory of computation unit. Class C was in a level 3 software engineering unit, that is equivalent to the final year of a full-time degree. Of these, eleven students participated in the experiment. Their experience of Z had been part of a formal methods course in the previous year covering much of the same ground as the new formal specification unit taught to the current level 2 students. Twenty six students of Class D took part in the experiment. These were a mix of day-release part-time and full-time MSc software engineering students who had had one three-hour lecture on Z with tutorial exercises three weeks prior to the experiment. Five mini-specifications were prepared varying only in the naming of

Table 8.1: Experimental specifications

Specification	Comments	Meaningful names	Single schema
1	Yes	Yes	No
2	Yes	No	No
3	No	No	No
4	Yes	Yes	Yes
5	No	Yes	No

variables, the use of comments and the decomposition into more than one schema. Each specification was randomly assigned a number from a set of random number tables (Murdoch, 1974). These are summed up in Table 8.1. An example of a specification used in the experiment with comments but without meaningful variable names is given in Figure 8.1 and the same specification but without the the comments but with meaningul names is presented in Figure 8.2. The students were each given an instruction sheet and a sheet to record their responses. The

The new user's name is taken in and an identity number is assigned from the pool of unused numbers. The unused number set is amended and the new pair of user and their number are added to the existing users;

```
┌─Add────────────────────────────────────────────
│ ΔSystem
│ x? : Ngrp
│ n! : N
│ m! : Res
├────────────────────────────────────────────────
│ n! ∈ Avids
│ x? ∉ dom Net
│ Avids' = Avids \ n!
│ Net' = Net ∪ {x? ↦ n!}
│ m! = OK
└────────────────────────────────────────────────
```

Here error messages are generated by the failure of either of the two preconditions in the Add schema:

```
┌─AddFail────────────────────────────────────────
│ ΞSystem
│ x? : Ngrp
│ n! : N
│ e_m! : Res
├────────────────────────────────────────────────
│ (x? ∈ dom Net ∧ e_m! = error_type1) ∨
│ (Avids = ∅ ∧ e_m! = error_type2)
└────────────────────────────────────────────────
```

Finally the behaviors are combined:

$$AddUser \cong Add \lor AddFail$$

Figure 8.1: Specification 2

Add _____

$\Delta System$
$name? : Person$
$n! : N$
$message! : Response$

$n! \in Unused\_Ids$
$name? \notin \mathrm{dom}\ Users$
$Unused\_Ids' = Unused\_Ids \setminus n!$
$Users' = Users \cup \{name? \mapsto n!\}$
$message! = OK$

$AddFail$ _____

$\Xi System$
$name? : Person$
$n! : N$
$e\_message! : Response$

$(name? \in \mathrm{dom}\ Users \wedge e\_message! = name\_in\_use) \vee$
$(Unused\_Ids = \varnothing \wedge e\_message! = no\_id\_available)$

$AddUser \mathrel{\widehat{=}} Add \vee AddFail$

Figure 8.2: Specification 5

instruction sheet is reproduced in Figure 8.3. The students were thanked by the experimenter and told the experiment was being conducted as part of research into styles and metrics in formal specification. It was explained that the results would be treated confidentially and not used as part of any assessment. The instruction sheet was read through and any arising questions answered. The experiment was then conducted in two phases. In the first phase the students were asked to answer three questions about a randomly allocated specification and record the time as they responded to each question. These times were later translated into elapsed time. The questions were:

♦ What conditions give rise to error messages?

♦ The size of which set would give you the number of current users on the network?

♦ Which set or sets give you information about the total number of users the network will support?

In the second phase, when this task was completed, each student was given copies of all five specifications and asked to rank them in order of comprehensibility and record the ranking.

8.4   Results

The first analysis of the results was a simple examination of the differences in scores and times between the classes. Class D, as might be expected having had only one brief lesson in Z, were on average slower in completing the first phase of answering three questions. They took an average of 577 seconds. These students were postgraduates and therefore with a higher educational level, but they had also received the shortest amount of teaching time which seems to have led to a longer reading time. Class B, who had completed the course and taken an examination in Z a few months previously performed the best, taking an average time of 363 seconds. One outlier distorts the figures and ignoring this reduces their mean time to just 317 seconds. Class C, surprisingly, did better than A with an average time of 391 seconds as opposed to 541. However class A's times were distorted by an outlying result which if ignored reduced the class average time to 480 seconds. A graph showing the total time taken to complete the reading of the specification by the individual students, and grouped by class, is given in Figure 8.4. Only 58 students are represented here as four failed to provided either a start time or a finish time on their answer sheet and therefore their results had to be ignored. The scores obtained in answer to the three questions are shown in a bar chart (Figure 8.5). This reveals a high proportion (19 out of 62) of the students that could not answer any of the questions correctly, demonstrating a poor understanding of the specification. The bar chart also shows that a similar proportion (20 out of 62) could correctly answer every question implying that with Z, as with a lot of mathematics, it is common that students divide into those who

Instruction Sheet

Do not turn over the question paper until you are asked to.

Thank you for agreeing to participate in this experiment. It is being conducted as part of research into styles and metrics in formal specification. The results will be treated confidentially and will not be used as part of any assessment of you or any other person.

As well as this instruction sheet, you will be given an answer sheet to record your answers on and a question sheet which you must not look at until you are asked to do so. The experiment will take part in two phases.

Phase I
On the other side of the question sheet is a simple Z specification and three questions for you to answer about the specification. We would like you to answer those questions and time your response at each step.

When you are asked to start, turn over the question sheet and record the start time on the answer sheet. There are five different specifications of which you have been allocated one on a random basis. Working as quickly as you can record the number of your specification on the answer sheet and then read through the specification.

When you have finished reading through the specification and you are ready to answer the questions record the time again. Answer each question in turn noting the time as you complete each answer. Raise your hand when you have finished. Do not attempt to modify your answers after you have recorded your finish time.

Phase II
After you have looked at one specification you will be given all five and asked to compare them for comprehensibility.

Taking as much time as you need put the five specifications into order on the basis of how comprehensible you feel they are. Carefully sort the specifications until you feel you have ranked them with the least comprehensible first, and the one which is most understandable last. Write down the numbers of the specifications in order on the answer sheet.

Once again, thank you for your time and effort.

Figure 8.3: Student Instruction Sheet

have finished a problem and those who cannot even start. In Figure 8.6 the scores for answering the questions are plotted against the time taken to answer them. The mean times have been marked showing an inverse relationship suggesting that if students could read and understand the specification then they did not need a long time to do so, whereas those who took a long time to answer the questions got more of them wrong. Regression analysis was performed on the scores against the three attributes: comments, names and structure. We would like to note that this was done as an exploratory rather than definitive analysis. Since the response variable is ordered and discrete, a polytomous logistic regression would be an appropriate form of analysis. However, for indicative purposes we restrict ourselves to linear regression fitting by the ordinary least squares method.

The regression equation became:

$$score = 0.974 + 0.259c + 0.676n - 0.059s$$

where:

  c is the variable showing the presence or absence of comments;

  n is the variable showing the presence or absence of helpful names;

  s is the variable showing the presence or absence of blocked schemas.

As a result of the analysis only the use of meaningful or helpful identifier names in the schemas seemed to have a significant effect on the score with a p value of 0.05.

Finally the cumulative rankings of the five specifications in terms of their comprehensibility is shown in Figure 8.7. This clearly shows the specification with comments and meaningful variable names is rated as most comprehensible and that with neither is the least. These match closely the predicted order 1, 4, 5, 2, 3, only differing in the order of specifications 4 and 5. This implies that in order of importance for the readability of a specification, helpful names are more important than comment levels and least important by comparison is the blocking of one or more schemas together. It is clear that different comments may produce different rankings, similarly decomposition of schemas may be more important on large or complex specifications and further investigation does need to be conducted. The data was analyzed using Minitab[1] and any incomplete data was not included. As only four students did not have either scores or total times this had little overall effect. The different classes taking part were used as a blocking factor in the model.

8.5   Conclusions

Large claims for statistical validity and inferences of a far-reaching nature about the readability of Z could not be justified by such a small-scale experiment. However,

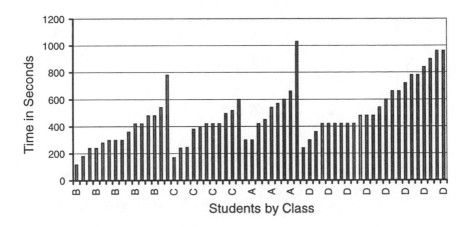

Figure 8.4: Individual student times

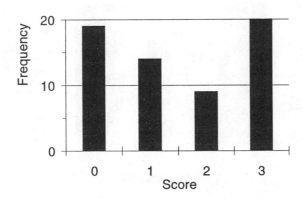

Figure 8.5: Student scores

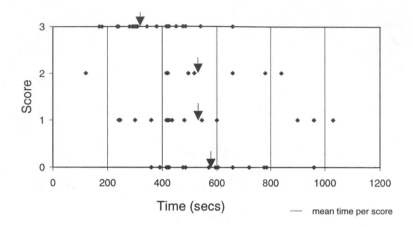

Figure 8.6: Scores and times

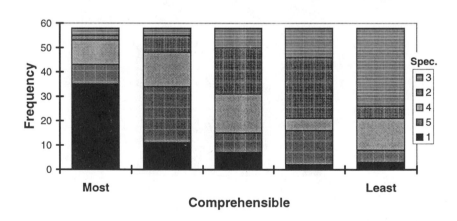

Figure 8.7: Specification rankings

there were sufficient subjects to make some limited observations and to give pointers for further work.

However, it can be concluded that a positive difference can be made to a specification in Z by the use helpful variable naming and the attachment of appropriate comments. Although there are compelling reasons to believe that large specifications are more readable when partitioned by judicious use of schemas, the scale of the specification used in this experiment was not large enough to show this effect.

From this experiment it seems valid to say that several lessons can be learnt for the teaching of formal methods. One should not underestimate the difficulty of reading a formal specification written in a mathematical notation. Specification must be recognized as a unique form of communication between human beings. Every opportunity should be taken to make the reading easier particularly by suitable naming of variables and data. Time to assimilate the techniques involved is important and reading does not always imply semantic comprehension or the higher skill level — the ability to articulate. As it was clear that 19 of the subjects did not understand the specification sufficiently to answer any of the questions correctly despite their background, then we should not expect clients and software engineers to master Z and other formal methods without training.

It is not only for the benefit of the client that the specifications should be read easily but also the author. It is well known in programming that a time lapse can create difficulties for the writers themselves with their own code. Indeed, the poor style of many programmers, use of C, for example, has given it the undeserved label of a write-only language.

Training practitioners from the start to have appropriate names for identifiers and to include suitable explanatory text will ensure good comprehension from clients, fellow software engineers and implementors.

8.6   Discussion

In the Educational Issues session of the 1994 Z User meeting Wordsworth (1994)[2] argued that almost everything that the software engineer does has a mathematical theory that can explain and illuminate it and therefore, that mathematics should be made the teaching medium and basis of an entire education program in software development. He acknowledges that software engineers may not be good at teaching mathematics and their students not good at understanding it. He concludes that universities have a critical part to play in changing this situation by finding ways to improve their teaching and enthuse their undergraduates, or improve selection of undergraduates.

There is no option of changing student selection criteria given the pressures political or otherwise. However, it is possible, as Wordsworth suggests, to look for new ways of improving our teaching and inspiring the students. We have, for example, found the use of Logica's Formalizer tool for writing and type checking Z specifications valuable in providing direct feedback to the student, in much the same way that a compiler provides feedback to a programming student.

This experiment suggests that in teaching formal methods it is crucial that appropriate time and effort is put into the early lexical and syntactic comprehension of the notation, supporting this through semantic cues in good choice of variable names and comments.

Whilst good software engineering does rest on mathematical rigor and formalism, teaching it in the abstracted way of many mathematicians with terse term identifiers will do nothing to enthuse the students, instead it will create feelings of confusion, demotivation and inevitably failure.

8.7   Future developments

The experiment has now been repeated with a further 71 students and although the analysis is not yet complete the preliminary results appear to confirm those presented here. To examine this further more research is needed, on a more in-depth and broader scale.

♦ A fully interactive approach could be used. This would entail writing further specifications so that all combinations of attributes are covered.

♦ More diverse subjects could be tested including representatives from industry who employ formal specifications.

♦ The experiments could be replicated in other institutions to see whether similar results occur.

Other attributes could be included or investigated separately in these further experiments.

The size of the Z specification needs to be increased to test further the effect of schema decomposition on readability and give a more realistic simulation of the type of specification normally encountered. Mitchell *et al.* (1994) suggest that different Z specification structurings can lead either to versions where it is easy to understand the component parts but harder to see how they fit together or to those where it is easier to get an overall view of the system's behavior but harder to understand the individual component parts. This implies that different styles of specification writing might be appropriate for different levels of abstraction and would need to be explored further.

Acknowledgements

The authors would like to thank K. Rennolls of the University of Greenwich for his invaluable help and encouragement with this work.

Notes

1. Minitab is a trademark of Minitab, Inc.
2. A revised version of that paper is to be found as Chapter 1 of this book.

References

Burghes, D. (1992) Recent changes in school curricula and their effect on university mathematics courses: a view from mathematics education, *Bulletin of the IMA*, **28**(1):17–20, January.

Hackney, J. (1991) The internalisation of symbolism, *Bulletin of the IMA*, **27**(10):214–216, October.

Harold, F.G. (1986) Experimental evaluation of program quality using external metrics. In E. Soloway and S. Iyengar, editors, *Empirical Studies of Programmers*, pp 153–167, Ablex Publishing Corp., New Jersey.

Harris, A.J. and Sipay, E.R. (1975) *How to Increase Reading Ability, A Guide to Developmental and Remedial Methods*, 6th Edition, McKay.

Mitchell, R., Loomes, M. and Howse, J. (1994) Structuring formal specifications — a lesson relearned, *Microprocessors and Microsystems*, **18**(10):593–599.

Murdoch, J. and Barnes, J.A. (1974) *Statistical Tables for Science, Engineering, Management and Business Studies*, 2nd Edition, Macmillan, London.

Roy, S. (1992) *No Maths Please, Bulletin of the IMA*, **28**(1):26–27, January.

Rushby, N. (1980) Other people's programs. In B. Meek and P. Heath, editors, *Guide to Good Programming Practice*, pp 152–159, Ellis Horwood, Chichester.

Spivey, J.M. (1992) *The Z notation: A Reference Manual*, 2nd Edition, Prentice Hall International Series in Computer Science, Hemel Hempstead.

Wirth, N. (1974) On the composition of well-structured programs, *Computing Surveys*, **6**(4):247–259.

Wordsworth, J.B. (1994) Educational issues relating to formal methods. In Proceedings of the Educational Issues of Formal Methods Session of the 1994 Z User Meeting, St. John's College, Cambridge, June, pp 29–36; included in revised form as Chapter 1 of this book.

Investigating student difficulties with mathematical logic

9.1 Introduction

In teaching the same course several times, one can begin to observe a core of misunderstandings that crop up with every new class of students. This phenomenon in an undergraduate computer science course covering topics in discrete mathematics and formal verification of computer programs led to the research reported here. Each semester, a large number of students demonstrated a predictable set of misconceptions about, and partial understandings of, logic concepts. Because logic is the foundation for formal verification, these misunderstandings tended to sabotage students' ability to grasp the more advanced concepts. This study investigated the question: *Do novice computer science students generally have more difficulty with the concepts of logic than they have with concepts in other areas of computer science?*

The concepts in the computer science subdomain of logic were described by means of a taxonomy, which served as the cornerstone of the rest of the research. The data for this research were based on the multiple-choice test questions and statistics from several publicly available versions of a standardized computer science examination. The questions were partitioned into three groups: those that were strongly related to logic, those that bore little or no relationship to logic, and those for which the relationship to logic was not sufficiently strong or weak. Questions in the last group were eliminated from further consideration.

In order to allocate questions to the appropriate group in a valid and reliable manner, the questions were classified using the research methodology of content analysis. Individuals with extensive experience in issues related to computer science education were invited to serve as judges in the content analysis procedure. The judges independently rated each question according to how strongly its content was related to logic, with the pooled results from all of the judges providing the basis for assigning questions to the groups. Finally, the patterns of responses by those who took the exams allowed comparative analysis of individual performance on the groups of questions strongly and weakly related to logic.

The remainder of this chapter is organized as follows. Two sections provide background for this study. The first discusses the role of mathematical logic in computer science, including curricular issues, programming languages, and formal methods. The second background section explores the relationship between logic and learning. Next, the research design is presented. This is followed by a section that describes the findings. The chapter ends with a discussion of the conclusions and ideas for future research.

9.2   Mathematical logic in computer science

Mathematical logic is pervasive in the field of computer science. Examples of the breadth and depth of the role of logic have been given by Galton (1992), Gries and Schneider (1993a), Myers (1990), and Sperschneider and Antoniou (1991), among others. This section focuses on three areas where mathematical logic is important in the context of this study: logic in the beginning computer science curriculum, programming languages, and formal methods for proving program correctness.

9.2.1   Logic in the computer science curriculum

In the evolution of undergraduate computer science curricula, attempts to recommend which mathematics courses should be required, the number of mathematics courses, and when the courses should be taken have been the source of much controversy (Berztiss, 1987; Dijkstra, 1989; Gries, 1990; Ralston and Shaw, 1980; Saiedian, 1992). A central theme in the controversy has been the course called *discrete mathematics*, which generally includes topics of formal logic.

The first widely accepted curriculum for academic programs in computer science was Curriculum '68 (Atchison, 1968), published by the Association for Computing Machinery (ACM). Curriculum '68 had a strong mathematical orientation, including a computer science course in discrete mathematics, Introduction to Discrete Mathematics, which included topics of logic. Some educators, however, found that Curriculum '68 was too strongly aligned with traditional mathematical studies, to the point of excluding some alternatives (Pollack, 1982). In the mid-1970s, the ACM initiated a new curriculum effort in response to the increased demand for practice-oriented computer science programs. This culminated in Curriculum '78 (Austing, 1979). Curriculum '78 included the course Discrete Structures as part of the general mathematical requirements but "did not define explicitly the details of topics to be covered in the course" (p. 208). The mathematics components of Curriculum '78 have been criticized as being essentially the same as those in Curriculum '68 except weaker (Ralston and Shaw, 1980). Ralston and Shaw predicted that, because the mathematics of central importance to computer science had changed drastically from 1968 to 1978, the impact of Curriculum '78 was less than it would have been had it had a stronger mathematics component.

In 1976 and 1983, the IEEE Computer Society published model programs in computer science and engineering (IEEE, 1976, 1983). The IEEE model programs, described as being strong mathematically (Shaw, 1985), cited mathematics as a subject area that is crucial to computer science and engineering. The discrete mathematics course, which was to be a pre- or corequisite for twelve of the thirteen core subject areas of the model program, included Introduction to Symbolic Logic as its first module (of eight).

An alternative model curriculum for a liberal arts degree in computer science was developed under the aegis of the ACM (Gibbs and Tucker, 1986). This report reaffirmed the view of computer science as a coherent body of scientific principles. It stressed the essential role of mathematics, "not only in the particular knowledge that is required to understand computer science, but also in the reasoning skills associated with mathematical maturity" (p. 207). The discrete mathematics course was recommended as either a pre- or corequisite for the second semester computer science course.

While the ACM and the IEEE curricula were widely used, the rapid rate of changes in the computing field soon rendered them outdated. In the late 1980s, a joint committee of the ACM and the IEEE Computer Society produced a document known as the Denning Report (Denning, 1989), which in its turn became the foundation for an effort to develop computer science curriculum guidelines suitable for use into the 1990s. The final report, Computing Curricula 1991 (Tucker, 1990), cited influences of the earlier ACM and IEEE guidelines as well as of other curricular recommendations produced during the previous 25 years. In recognition of the wide variety of institutions and types of programs it was addressing, Computing Curricula 1991 specifically avoided the definition of specific courses. Instead, a scheme was defined that allowed customized mappings between subject matter and courses, depending on the nature of the institution or program. In discussing the vital role of mathematics in the computing curriculum, the committee stated that "Mathematical maturity, as commonly attained through logically rigorous mathematics courses, is essential to successful mastery of several fundamental topics in computing" (p. 27). At least the equivalent of four or five semester-long courses were specified for all computer science students, including a discrete mathematics course. This course included many concepts of mathematical logic, with additional topics of logic to be covered in an optional logic or advanced discrete mathematics course.

Another viewpoint regarding logic and undergraduate computing education comes from educators specifically interested in mathematical logic. The Association for Symbolic Logic (ASL) is an international organization that has been devoted to the study of logic since 1936. In the summer of 1991, a committee was formed and charged with making specific recommendations about logic education for both pre-college and undergraduate programs. The committee's brief final report (ASL, 1995) recommended that all post-secondary students should be encouraged to take at least one introductory course that teaches the basic notions of logic, including informal strategies, propositional calculus, and predicate calculus. At the advanced post-secondary level (for example, at four-year institutions), the ASL Guidelines advocate an additional set of core topics in logic that are relevant to many areas of science and scholarship.

In the late 1980s, the Mathematical Association of America (MAA) sponsored a program to explore the issue of discrete mathematics at the undergraduate level (Ralston, 1989). An experimental program was run at six colleges and universities to foster "the development of a new curriculum for the first two years of undergraduate mathematics in which discrete mathematics [would] play a role of equal importance to that of the calculus" (p. 1). The committee recommended that discrete mathematics should be part of the standard mathematics curriculum for the first two years at all colleges and universities and that it should be taught at the intellectual level of calculus (that is, in such a manner that students are forced to think and to become skilled in proof techniques).

In an informal survey of approaches to teaching discrete mathematics, Franz-blau (1993) presented three "new" course models: (i) discrete mathematics courses with a focus on proof and (re-)writing, (ii) discrete mathematics as the first course for computer science majors, and (iii) discrete mathematics courses where logic is used as a tool. The third model has the strongest implications for this study. As an example of this model, Franzblau cited the "radically different and highly structured approach" of Gries and Schneider (1993a, 1993b, 1994). In a review of Gries and Schneider's textbook, *A Logical Approach to Discrete Math* (1993a), Warford (1994) described his experiences in using it as the text in a discrete mathematics course for computer science students. Warford found that the central role of the propositional and predicate calculus allowed a unified treatment of other discrete mathematics topics. He felt that the character of the course began to resemble that of the traditional calculus: in traditional calculus, students progress through a series of skill-based exercises such as differentiation, the chain rule, and integration; in the Gries and Schneider approach to discrete mathematics, the skill-based exercises include textual substitution, Leibniz's rule, boolean expressions, and quantification. In addition, the traditional calculus course and the logic-based discrete mathematics course have the same underlying theme: the development of students' skills with proofs and reasoning.

9.2.2 Mathematical logic in programming languages

There is an intricate relationship between the concepts of classic mathematics and the datatypes in programming languages. Fundamental building blocks of mathematics, such as integers and booleans, are included as simple data types in most programming languages. For many students, learning to write boolean expressions while learning to program is perhaps the first opportunity they have to perceive logic as a practical tool. In this section, we consider the role of logic in traditional imperative programming languages. Specifically, we focus on the data type boolean within imperative programming languages. Logic programming, for example using Prolog, is not considered.

In a majority of imperative programming languages, the use and understanding of mathematical logic is centered on data type boolean. For example, a program's control structure usually includes a series of decision points, with the choice at each decision point determined by the value of a boolean expression. In practice, however, data type boolean has often been treated as a "second-class" entity in programming languages. Programmers, whether professionals or students, have tended to use booleans differently from, for example, integers. For an entity to have "first-class" status in a given language, it must be usable without restriction in whatever ways are appropriate for the language. This encompasses three requirements: First, the data type should have as its basis a well-defined set of values. For example, datatype integer has as its basis the set $\{\ldots, -2, -1, 0, 1, 2, \ldots\}$ and data type boolean is based on the set $\{true, false\}$. Second, it must be possible both to evaluate expressions whose result is of that data type and to assign the result of expression evaluation to variables of that type. Third, it must be possible to pass arguments and return function values of the type.

Dijkstra and Feijen (1988) explained the contribution of Algol 60 in advancing the status of data type boolean. In the early days of programming, execution was viewed as the process of computing numbers and testing conditions. The act of computing numerical values generally resulted in a quantity that was stored for later use, while the act of testing a condition was used immediately in influencing further calculations. Algol 60 generalized the notion of computation to encompass the computation of truth values using variables of type boolean. Thus, the testing of a condition could be viewed as a computation in its own right. Dijkstra and Feijen observed that "This generalization of the idea of computation is a very important contribution: the proof of a theorem can now be regarded as the demonstration that the computation of a proposition yields the value *true*" (Dijkstra and Feijen, 1988, p. 43).

The understanding that a programmer, whether student or professional, has of fundamental computer science concepts is influenced by the features of the programming language(s) they use. As a result, many programmers fail to benefit from a full understanding of all of the characteristics of data type boolean. Algol 60 provided the mechanisms for using data type boolean as first-class entity. The programming language C, on the other hand, encourages the view of boolean as a special case of type integer. The confusion caused by such conventions may interfere with students' understanding of mathematical logic.

9.2.3 Logic as the basis for formal methods

Formal methods encompass a wide range of techniques and languages used in the development of software. Wing (1990) defined a method as formal "if it has a sound mathematical basis, typically given by a formal specification language" (p. 8). Cooke (1992) explained that the term "formal methods" is related to the facility of reasoning in a mathematically precise and logical way about software systems. He clarified that formal methods cover "not only programming languages and the common data types, their operators and their properties, but also logic, particularly the notion of deduction" (p. 420). Goldson *et al.* (1993) projected the "hope that the use of formal methods will make programs conform to specification and make them more reliable but [caution that] such 'methods' are really nothing more than a collection of techniques imported from discrete mathematics, logic and set theory" (p. 373).

Galton (1992) outlined a representative selection of the ways in which formal logic has been used in computer science. Applications of classical first-order predicate logic include program specification, program verification, program synthesis, and logic programming. Beyond classical logic, Galton sketched applications based on intuitionistic logic, temporal logic, modal logic, and logics for non-monotonic reasoning. He admitted that, even in his extensive survey, he neglected many areas of computing in which logic is important, a fact that underscores the breadth of the role of logic in computer science.

The remainder of this subsection focuses on a specialized area within the range of formal methods that evolved from work in the formal development of algorithms. In the 1960s, researchers who needed to manipulate formulae of the predicate calculus on a regular basis found that conventional logics, such as natural deduction, required a great deal of formal detail without providing much insight into the process of algorithm development (Gries and Schneider, 1994). The need for a better model gave rise to the development of a collection of formal methods referred to as *formal verification of program correctness* (where correctness of a program is established *a posteriori*) and *formal derivation of correct programs* (where the proof of correctness is developed as the program is developed).

Floyd (1967) was the first to suggest that the specification of proof techniques could provide an adequate formal definition of a programming language; he also analyzed the potential benefits of using an axiomatic approach for program proving and for formal language definition. In the seminal paper "An axiomatic basis for computer programming", Hoare (1969) implemented Floyd's suggestion. Whereas earlier language definitions had been primarily in terms of implementation, the use of axioms made it possible to define languages non-operationally (that is, independently of their implementations). Hoare presented an axiom system in which programs are expressed as formulae. Such formulae, called Hoare-triples, are predicates given in terms of triples $\{Q\}S\{R\}$. In this triple, S is a statement from the programming language while Q and R are predicates on the variables used in the statement. Referred to as the *precondition* and the *postcondition*, Q and R describe the initial and final program states of the statement S. By using axioms and rules of inference that specified the meaning of statements in a simple programming language, it was possible to verify the correctness of a given program written in that language. (This discussion ignores the steps that led from consideration of only "partial correctness" to "total correctness". Partial correctness does not address the issue of program termination. Minor notational changes that were a part of this evolution are ignored here in favor of the later notation.)

As an alternative to proving the correctness of given programs, Dijkstra (1968) proposed controlling the process of program generation. In the early 1970s, Dijkstra introduced the notion of *predicate transformers* as a systematic way to derive rather than verify programs. The process of program derivation with predicate transformers was described in Dijkstra's classic book *A Discipline of Program-*

ming (1976) and expanded by Gries in the textbook *The Science of Programming* (1981). Predicate transformers extended the Hoare axiom system and provided a means for defining programming language semantics in a way that would directly support the systematic derivation of programs from their formal specifications (Dijkstra and Scholten, 1990). A predicate transformer is a function of two arguments, a statement and a predicate, and returns a predicate as its result. In the Hoare-triple $\{Q\}S\{R\}$, the predicate transformer takes as arguments statement S and postcondition R. The output of the predicate transformer, Q, is a predicate called the *weakest precondition*. The weakest precondition is satisfied by all of the program states in which execution of statement S is guaranteed in a state satisfying predicate R (Gries, 1981). Predicate transformers provide a basis both for deriving correct programs and for verifying the correctness of existing programs.

Over time, the activities of program verification and program derivation have become more formal. As limitations in the use of predicate transformers were encountered, researchers undertook the task of defining the theory more formally. Dijkstra and Scholten (1990) explained the professional delight they experienced in adapting the predicate calculus to the task of expressing program semantics. By adopting a strict, carefully designed proof format using notational adaptations, they discovered they were "in possession of a tool that surpassed our wildest expectations". They observed that "we were forced to conclude that the formal techniques we were trying out had never been given a fair chance, the evidence being the repeated observations that most mathematicians lack the tools needed for the skillful manipulation of logical formulae" (p. vi).

Among other things, Dijkstra and Scholten's efforts contributed to the development of a calculational logic. The key difference between calculational logic and other forms of logic is the extensive use of value-preserving manipulations in the former rather than proofs composed exclusively of chains of implications. Calculational logic was used informally in the late 1970s and refined through the 1980s. In the early 1990s calculational logic has come into wider use, for example in discrete mathematics courses required of computer science students. This approach is represented by the presentation given in Gries and Schneider's text *A Logical Approach to Discrete Math* (1993a).

9.3   The relationship between logic and learning

Logic is often called the science of reasoning. Copi (1979) pointed out: "As thinking ... reasoning is not the special province of logic, but part of the psychologist's subject matter as well" (p. 1). For psychologists, reasoning is interesting from the point of view of process, as a model for human thought; for logicians, the correctness of the completed reasoning process is of the most interest. In the field of computing, the use of logic as a tool for expressing and proving theorems is a key focus. This section explores several aspects of the relationship between logic and learning. We begin by considering a study that explored the importance of analytical reasoning skills. Next, we look at the connection between logic and thought processes. Theories that consider ability in logic to be but one type of intelligence are discussed next. The section concludes with a discussion of several studies that have explored the relationship between ability to reason about logical propositions and success in science courses.

In 1986, Powers and Enright (1987) conducted a survey to determine the perceptions of a sample of college faculty members about the importance of analytical reasoning skills for graduate study. They noted, "Despite the perceived importance of reasoning, there seems to be no consensus regarding the impact of formal education on the development of reasoning abilities" (p. 659). The sample included 255 graduate faculty in six fields (chemistry, computer science, education, engineering, English, and psychology). The questionnaire asked about the importance of various reasoning skills as well as the extent to which each skill seemed to differentiate between marginal and successful students. It also addressed the importance and frequency of commonly observed errors in reasoning. The results showed that, regardless of discipline, the participants rated some reasoning skills as very important (for example, "detecting fallacies and logical contradictions in arguments", "making explicit all relevant components in a chain of logical reasoning", and "testing the validity of an argument by searching for counterexamples"). Other reasoning skills were rated as important within one discipline but not in others. For example, "knowing the rules of formal logic" was rated as one of the most important skills in computer science but was rated as quite unimportant in the other disciplines. The two reasoning skills rated most important by the computer science educators were "breaking down complex problems or situations into simpler ones" and "reasoning or problem solving in situations in which all facts underlying a situation are known".

While there appears to be an intimate relationship between the underlying reasoning processes and academic success, it is important to note that learning about logic is not synonymous with learning to reason. Specifically, logic is a *topic* in computer science, encompassing underlying skills as important for the student as the skills of arithmetic. This distinction is important when considering the role of logic in psychological studies: there has been a tendency to blend the two, despite the differences. Copi (1979) claims that "paradoxically enough, logic is not concerned with developing our powers of thought but with developing techniques that enable us to get along without thinking!" (p. 246).

Rothaug (1984) surveyed several views of the relationship between formal logic and the natural psychological logic of thought. The descriptive or rationalist view held that there is a close relationship between logic and reasoning. Another view held that the laws of logic are only normative and are not useful as a descriptive model for thinking and reasoning. Piaget and other researchers have postulated that higher-level psychological processes reflect logical principles, so that formal logic provides a useful way to characterize a significant component of thinking and reasoning. Anderson (1980), a cognitive psychologist, viewed the use of logic as a useful heuristic method for learning about a subject's behavior when the subject solves problems (rather than as a model for thinking). Anderson maintained that "Reasoning is fundamentally a matter of problem solving, not a logical activity

[and] deductive reasoning is a special case of problem solving rather than some special faculty of the mind" (p. 326).

Other views on the role of logic in psychology have been based on the assumption that human intelligence is not a single trait or process but is instead a collection of separate abilities. In these models, the ability to do logic is simply one of many abilities. For example, Guilford (1967) considered a three-dimensional model of intellect, organized around three main aspects of human functioning: operations, products, and content. In Guilford's theory, specific abilities involve a combination of each of these dimensions. Gardner (1985) argued for the existence of several human potentials, each of which is relatively autonomous. Gardner hypothesized seven intelligences: logical–mathematical, linguistic, musical, spatial, bodily–kinesthetic, interpersonal, and intrapersonal; hence, his theory has been called multiple intelligences theory. Gardner and Hatch (1989) explained that there is not necessarily a correlation between any two intelligences and that each may entail distinct forms of perception, memory, and other psychological processes. They characterized the key components of the logical–mathematical intelligence as "sensitivity to, and capacity to discern, logical or numerical patterns; ability to handle long chains of reasoning" (p. 6).

For science educators, the relationship between logic and science is of special interest because of important parallels between the two: both are systems that seek truth, and the systematic procedures employed by each resemble one another (Rothaug, 1984). Science educators have shown that, given their definitions of *reasoning* and *success*, an individual's ability to reason is strongly related to their success in science. Stofflett and Baker (1992) cited results that indicate that students who reason well score higher on content examinations, have stronger process skills, and have more interest in science. Various studies with students in college physics courses have shown correlations of 0.30 to 0.75 between a variety of measures of logic and achievement in the course (Lockwood *et al.*, 1980; Piburn and Baker, 1988; Seeber *et al.*, 1979). Similar results were obtained in studies of high school physics students (Lockwood *et al.*, 1982) and college chemistry students (Rothaug and Pallrand, 1982; Rothaug *et al.*, 1981).

One instrument that has been used to measure ability in logic in a number of studies is the propositional logic test (PLT). The PLT is a simple instrument used to assess a subject's ability to process propositional statements. In contrast to other measures of ability with propositional logic, error patterns on the PLT have revealed systematic relationships between age and ability that appear to reflect underlying reasoning processes (Piburn, 1989). A study with Australian high school science students considered whether achievement in science positively correlated with ability to reason about logical propositions (Piburn, 1990). It was shown that correlations between score on the PLT and achievement in science were significant and relatively high. The results revealed that advanced students received the highest scores and basic students the lowest, with the greatest difference showing up between advanced and intermediate students. The pattern of errors across ability groups in the Australian sample was the same as that across grade levels in cross-sectional studies of American students from grades 7 to the first year in college. In another study, Stager-Snow (1985) worked with students in an introductory computer science course for non-computer science majors. Her results indicated that for the females in the sample the PLT was a weak predictor of success in the course. For the males in this study, the PLT had no predictive power. Stager-Snow also found that knowledge of the `if-then` statement had predictive power for the females in her study.

9.4   Research design

This section presents the research design behind this exploratory and descriptive study. First, we describe preparatory activities, including development of the taxonomy used to describe logic concepts in the context of computer science and the process by which appropriate computer science material was identified. The next subsection elaborates the content analysis procedure that was used to classify the test questions according to the strength of their relationship to the concepts in the taxonomy and the data that were generated. Finally, we describe the analysis of the data.

9.4.1   Identifying concepts in the subdomain logic

In order to provide a concrete definition of concepts in the computer science subdomain of mathematical logic, a taxonomy of concepts was prepared for use in this study. The taxonomy, given in Figure 9.1, was an outline of logic concepts particularly relevant to this research.

The iterative development of the taxonomy was influenced by a wide variety of sources, including standard computing curriculum guidelines (Austing, 1979; Koffman *et al.*, 1984; Koffman *et al.*, 1985; Tucker, 1990), the way in which the concepts were presented in undergraduate textbooks (Dale and Walker, 1996) and more advanced texts (Gries, 1981; Sperschneider and Antoniou, 1991), and the draft of an international standard for datatypes (ISO, 1994). During its development, the taxonomy was reviewed by several computer science educators to ensure its content validity. The resulting taxonomy was a broad outline that provides a breakdown of advanced as well as basic concepts of logic.

9.4.2   Identifying a source of test items for analysis

This research required a source of data where novice computing students demonstrated their understanding of beginning computer science concepts. It was clear that this source would most likely be some sort of test. It was essential that a sufficiently large number of students should complete the test. In addition, the questions on the test had to lend themselves to being analyzed for strength of relationship to the concepts of logic. Finally, the students' answers to the ques-

1.0 Datatype boolean
   1.1 Set of values $\{true, false\}$
   1.2 Set of operations $\{equal, not, and, or, implies, nor, \ldots\}$
      1.2.1 Truth tables
      1.2.2 Precedence rules
   1.3 Properties
      1.3.1 Non-numeric
      1.3.2 Unordered
      1.3.3 Discrete
2.0 Related simple types
   2.1 Bit
   2.2 State, restricted to two values
   2.3 Two-valued subrange of integer
3.0 Boolean-based calculi
4.0 Boolean aspects of programming languages
   4.1 Realization of datatype boolean
   4.2 Boolean expressions
      4.2.1 constants / named constants
      4.2.2 boolean result / non-boolean arguments
      4.2.3 boolean result / boolean arguments (predicate calculus expressions)
      4.2.4 boolean-valued function calls
   4.3 Assignment
      4.3.1 right-hand side
      4.3.2 left-hand side
   4.4 Conditional control structures in imperative languages
      4.4.1 selection
         4.4.1.1 explicit boolean condition (`if`)
         4.4.1.2 implicit boolean condition (`case` in Pascal)
      4.4.2 iteration
         4.4.2.1 explicit boolean condition (`while` in Pascal, `for` in C)
         4.4.2.2 implicit boolean condition (`for` in Pascal)
   4.5 Boolean parameters
   4.6 Other uses
5.0 Assertions and formal verification
   5.1 Precondition / postcondition
   5.2 Loop invariant
   5.3 Calculation of weakest precondition
   5.4 Data transformations
6.0 Other topics / advanced topics

Figure 9.1: Taxonomy of concepts in the computer science subdomain of mathematical logic, as used in the content analysis procedure

tions needed to be available in order to allow analysis of their understanding of different concepts. After considering several alternatives, it was decided that using information from an existing body of data was preferable to designing and administering a custom-made test. Specifically, the Advanced Placement Examination in Computer Science (APCS exam) was found to meet all of the criteria.

The APCS exam is one component of the Advanced Placement Program, which allows pre-college students to demonstrate their knowledge of various college-level subjects and qualify for college credit. The AP program, which is oriented towards the American educational system, is run by the College Board and administered by Educational Testing Services (ETS). The AP program targets three groups: "students who wish to pursue college-level studies while still in secondary school, schools that desire to offer these opportunities, and colleges that wish to encourage and recognize such achievement" (College Board, 1990, p. i). Students who do well may be granted placement, appropriate credit, or both by colleges and universities that participate in the program.

The Advanced Placement Examination in Computer Science, offered annually since 1984, is designed to cover as closely as possible the topics recommended for the corresponding introductory college-level course(s), generally referred to as "CS1" and "CS2" (Austing, 1979; Koffman *et al.*, 1984; Koffman *et al.*, 1985). Because several thousand American students take the exam each year, statistics about the exam outcome provide a broad base of information about the performance of novice computer science students.

Each version of the APCS exam used in this study was made up of two parts, a multiple-choice section and a free- response section. Each multiple-choice section included from 35 to 50 questions while the free-response section included three or five items. A multiple-choice question comprised a problem statement and five alternative responses, one of which was correct. The multiple-choice questions were scored using a mechanical scanning and scoring system. Because the laws in several American states require that multiple-choice questions be disclosed every fourth year, the APCS exams for the years 1984, 1988, and 1992 could be used for this study. For each of these three years, Educational Testing Services (ETS) published a report that included the full text of all questions, the correct answers for the multiple-choice section, the grading guidelines for the free-response items, and selected statistical analyses (College Board, 1986, 1989, 1993). For this study, the multiple-choice questions were packaged into exam packets that were used in the content analysis procedure.

9.4.3   The content analysis procedure

Content analysis was used to classify each APCS multiple-choice question for the strength of its relationship to logic. The procedure was based on those in *Content Analysis: An Introduction to Its Methodology* (Krippendorff, 1980), which describes the philosophy, sampling techniques, and methods of validation and analysis to be used in designing and carrying out content analysis. The most

Table 9.1: Classification system for indicating strength of relationship between APCS multiple-choice questions and the computer science subdomain mathematical logic

CATEGORY	DESCRIPTION
"main concept"	The question deals directly with the concepts of mathematical logic.
"vital subconcept"	In this question, one or more concepts of mathematical logic are important subconcepts but not the primary focus.
"trivial subconcept"	In this question, one or more concepts of mathematical logic appear but have little bearing on the solution.
"not used"	In this question, the concepts bear no meaningful relationship to the subdomain of mathematical logic.

common use of content analysis has been to analyze written text or recorded conversation for the occurrence and meaning of certain words, phrases, and ideas. This study adapted the procedure to allow judges to rate each multiple-choice question according to how strongly it was related to the subdomain of logic.

Content analysis depends on having a set of criteria against which content can be measured. When carrying out the content analysis procedure, the content under consideration must be categorized based on these criteria. For this study, the criteria were derived from the taxonomy developed for this study (see Figure 9.1. Judges used the taxonomy and a four-category classification system to associate each multiple-choice question with one of four categories: "main concept", "vital subconcept", "trivial subconcept", or "not used". The categories were ordered, with "main concept" indicating the strongest relationship to logic and "not used" the weakest. The classification system is given in Table 9.1.

The judges for the content analysis procedure were selected for their expertise in computer science education. Each judge was in some way involved with the introductory computing curriculum.

In the content analysis procedure, each judge received a cover letter with instructions, the taxonomy of concepts, the four exam packets, a table with the correct answers to all of the multiple-choice questions, and four copies of the coding form. Judges were asked not to discuss their rating of the APCS exam questions with anyone until after the task was complete. This constraint avoided the situation where two judges, by collaborating, produced a single combined rating rather than two individual ratings. This constraint also reduced the likelihood of inconsistencies that could arise in a judge's ratings because of outside influences.

9.4.4   The data

The ETS data sets
Educational Testing Services (ETS) provided files that contained anonymous data for every person, referred to as a *respondent*, who had taken one of the five exams (1984, 1988A, 1988AB, 1992A, 1992AB). For this study, the only data that was relevant was the response on each multiple-choice question (or an indication that the question was not answered).

In analyzing the response data, several additional variables were calculated for every respondent. First, for each multiple-choice question, a variable indicated whether the respondent had answered the question at all. Second, also for each multiple-choice question, a variable indicated whether the respondent had answered the question correctly. Finally, a variable indicated the total number of multiple-choice questions that the respondent had answered correctly.

The content analysis data
Four distinct exam packets were considered in the content analysis procedure (1984, 1988, 1992A, 1992AB). The content analysis ratings identified the APCS questions most relevant to this research and were the basis for allocating the questions to groups. The 38 judges returned a total of 150 forms out of the 152 that were distributed: only 36 forms were returned for the 1988 exam packet. With few exceptions, the forms were complete and filled in correctly. In the instances where a judge had inadvertently omitted the rating for a question, the researcher contacted the judge directly for the missing rating.

The content analysis data included the number of judges as well as information about the classification system (the number of categories and a code for each). The ratings from the individual judges were accumulated into a ratings summary table, where the cells gave the frequency of occurrence of each category for each multiple-choice question. The ratings summary table provided the basis for the reliability calculations as well as for the grouping algorithm described in the next subsection.

Grouping of multiple-choice questions
A key goal of this study was to contrast performance on questions judged to have a strong relationship to logic with performance on questions that were judged to have little or no relationship to logic. A rating of "main concept" or "vital subconcept" for a question indicated that the judge perceived logic to be an important aspect of that question; a high occurrence of these two categories caused the question to be assigned to the *strongly related* group. Similarly, ratings of "trivial subconcept" or "not used" indicated that the judge perceived the concepts of logic to be unimportant in the context of the question; a high occurrence of these two categories caused the question to be assigned to the *not strongly related* group. All other questions were eliminated from consideration. Eliminating the mid-range questions compensated for chance choices by judges. This handled the problem of

"borderline" questions, the situation where a question could shift between groups based on a change in rating by only one or two judges. After the groups were established, two additional variables were developed for each respondent: the number of questions the respondent answered correctly in the *strongly related* and *not strongly related* groups.

9.4.5   Analysis of the data

The analysis phase involved three steps: summarizing the relevant data obtained from ETS, calculating the reliability of the content analysis results, and hypothesis testing. Summarizing the data in the files from ETS provided a profile of the multiple-choice questions as well as a profile of the respondents.

The reliability of the content analysis results was evaluated using procedures derived from Krippendorff's presentation (1980). In content analysis, reliability is expressed as the amount of agreement that exists among the ratings given by all of the judges. Agreement is calculated using the formula $\alpha = 1 - D_o/D_e$ where α is the agreement coefficient, D_o is the observed disagreement, and D_e is the expected disagreement. Expected disagreement, which is based on the null hypothesis that any differences in ratings are attributable only to chance, is calculated as the average difference within all possible pairings of ratings, both across judges and across items. The agreement coefficient is interpreted as the reliability of the rating, where a value of 1.0 means "perfect agreement", 0.0 means "agreement entirely due to chance", and -1.0 means "perfect disagreement". Because no pre-existing software was found for calculating the reliability figures in a straightforward and easily interpretable fashion, the author designed and implemented her own software package. The statistics from this package included overall reliability, the reliability of each category in the classification system, and individual judge reliability.

As the basis for hypothesis testing, two research questions were investigated:

(a) In considering student performance on the test questions, was the distribution of performance for questions strongly related to logic different than for questions not strongly related to logic?

(b) Was there a relationship between individual performance on the set of questions whose content was strongly related to logic and on the set of questions whose content not strongly related to logic?

Question (a) was addressed in terms of the difficulty distribution of the questions allocated to each group. The questions were partitioned into categories of difficulty based on the proportion of students who answered correctly: "very difficult", "somewhat difficult", "average", "somewhat easy", and "very easy". The null hypothesis was then stated as:

H_a The difficulty distributions for the groups of questions strongly related and not strongly related to logic are the same.

To test this hypothesis, the difficulty distributions defined by the two groups of questions were compared. This comparison was accomplished using a hierarchical log-linear test of homogeneity, which is described in Section 9.5.3.

Research question (b) was addressed by the null hypothesis:

H_b The correlation between individual performance on questions in the *strongly related* group and questions in the *not strongly related* group is zero.

This hypothesis was tested by calculating the Pearson product-moment coefficient of correlation, treating individual cumulative score on questions in the *strongly related* group as the first variable and individual cumulative score on questions in the *not strongly related* group as the second variable.

9.5   Findings

This section begins with a description of the performance statistics for the Advanced Placement Examination in Computer Science (APCS exams). Next, the outcome of the content analysis procedure is considered from several points of view: the instruments under study (the APCS exams), the judges, the groups of multiple-choice questions, and the reliability of the content analysis results. The last subsection presents the results of hypothesis testing.

9.5.1   Performance statistics for the APCS exams

Based on the information in the individual data files from Educational Testing Services (ETS), it is possible to develop two contrasting views of performance. The first view considers the proportion of respondents from the total sample who answered each question correctly, while the second view considers the proportion of respondents who correctly answered each question among those who attempted the question. Each view has certain advantages; the research reported here used the first view. This choice was made for two reasons: (i) analyses for a particular exam were based on a constant sample size across all questions from that exam and (ii) the fact that a question was not attempted provided information about the perceived difficulty of the question. In contrast, ETS used the second view of performance, the proportion of respondents who answered the question correctly among those who attempted the question. Because ETS assesses a "guessing penalty" on the multiple-choice section, many students undoubtedly skipped questions about which they were unsure in order to avoid losing points. In addition, since each section of the exam was given during a fixed period of time, some students may have run out of time before completing all questions on a section. Thus, students who worked more slowly may not have had sufficient time to answer some questions even though in other circumstances they could have answered correctly. The second view takes this time constraint into consideration.

Table 9.2: Descriptive statistics for number of multiple-choice questions attempted and number of multiple-choice questions answered correctly on each APCS exam

APCS exam and version	number of questions	Proportion of questions attempted		Proportion of questions answered correctly		Sample size (N)
		mean	standard deviation	mean	standard deviation	
1984	44	0.94	0.08	0.58	0.19	4227
1988A	35	0.77	0.16	0.37	0.15	3369
1988AB	50	0.84	0.13	0.52	0.18	7375
1992A	40	0.88	0.12	0.49	0.18	5231
1992AB	40	0.86	0.14	0.54	0.19	4658

Table 9.2 summarizes the descriptive statistics for each of the five samples of students who took the APCS exams. Both the proportion of multiple-choice questions attempted and the proportion of multiple-choice questions answered correctly are considered, with the proportions scaled to the range $[0.0, 1.0]$ (where 0.0 means "none correct" and 1.0 means "all correct"). The descriptive statistics include the number of questions under consideration on each exam, the mean values of the proportion variables across all respondents, the standard deviations, and the number of respondents in the sample.

9.5.2 Content analysis procedure results

The instruments under study
Four distinct exams were considered during the content analysis procedure (1984, 1988, 1992A, and 1992B). Although the 1988 exam was administered in two versions to two different samples of students, the students taking the AB version began by taking the 35 questions of the A version, followed by an additional 15 questions specific to the AB version. As a result, the content analysis procedure considered only one exam packet for 1988 (the full AB version). On the 1992 exam, 15 questions on the A and AB versions were identical, although the order in which these questions appeared was different for the two exams. In order to give a basis for test-retest analysis (which indicates the consistency with which a judge rated an item), the packets were not modified to remove this redundancy.

The judges
The content analysis procedure was completed by 38 computer science educators during the period June through November, 1993. Two of the judges did not rate

Table 9.3: Number of questions in each group, the number of questions eliminated from consideration, and the total number of questions

APCS exam and version	Strongly related group	Not strongly related group	eliminated from consideration	total
1984	4	30	11	45
1988A	4	17	14	35
1988AB	5	29	16	50
1992A	8	13	19	40
1992AB	9	18	13	40

the questions from the 1988 exam, so the number of judges for that exam was 36. At the time of the content analysis, 10 of the judges were high school teachers, 25 were instructors at a college or university, 6 completed the rating task during both the pilot and final phases, 21 had served as readers in grading the 1992 APCS free-response questions, 11 had participated in an NSF-sponsored workshop on the use of formal methods in the undergraduate curriculum during summer 1993, and several had written introductory textbooks on various subjects in the field of computer science. In addition, two judges had been recognized as "Outstanding Educator of the Year" by the Association for Computing Machinery's Special Interest Group on Computer Science Education (ACM SIGCSE) and one judge had received the Turing Award, the highest honor available in the computing field.

Outcome of the grouping algorithm
The grouping algorithm, which resulted in three disjoint sets of multiple-choice questions, depended on the cumulative ratings from the content analysis procedure. A question was placed in the *strongly related* group if at least 75% of the judges had rated it as either "main concept" or "vital subconcept". The question belonged to the *not strongly related* group if at most 25% of the judges had rated it as either "main concept" or "vital subconcept" (in other words, more than 75% of the judges had rated it as either "trivial subconcept" or "not used"). Questions classified as "main concept" or "vital subconcept" by only 25% to 75% of the judges were eliminated from consideration. Table 9.3 summarizes the outcome of the grouping algorithm.

Content analysis reliability results
The content analysis reliability procedures were run for each of the four exam packets. For each packet, these calculations resulted in an overall reliability value, a single-category reliability value for each of the four classification categories, and individual judge reliability.
Overall reliability provides an indication of quality for the outcome of the

Table 9.4: Agreement coefficients showing overall reliability of the content analysis procedure

APCS exam and version	With all four categories	With collapsed categories
1984	0.290	0.473
1988 A & AB	0.303	0.496
1992A	0.458	0.704
1992AB	0.391	0.694

Table 9.5: Agreement coefficients for single-category reliability of the content analysis procedure

APCS exam and version	Main concept	Vital subconcept	Trivial subconcept	Not used
1984	0.415	0.156	0.130	0.419
1988 A & AB	0.421	0.198	0.116	0.434
1992A	0.645	0.161	0.164	0.602
1992AB	0.704	0.101	0.147	0.452

content analysis. In producing the overall reliability figures two different models were considered, a four-category model and a two- category model. In the four-category model, the distinct classification categories were maintained. The two-category model was based on two collapsed categories: *strongly related* (which included "main concept" and "vital subconcept") and *not strongly related* (which included "trivial subconcept" and "not used"). The agreement coefficients for the overall reliability of the content analysis results are given in Table 9.4. The two-category interpretation consistently resulted in much higher agreement. The best reliability was for both versions of the 1992 exam using the two-category model, where the agreement coefficient was approximately 0.70. For the 1984 and 1988 exams, the reliability under this same combination was less than 0.50.

Single-category reliability indicates the extent to which a category tends to distinguish itself from the other categories. A low agreement coefficient for a particular category means that judges tended to confuse that category with the remaining categories. Table 9.5 gives the agreement coefficients for the four classification categories. The categories "vital subconcept" and "trivial subconcept" tended to be highly unreliable, with agreement coefficients that were at most 0.20. The "not used" and "main concept" categories had the highest reliability, with agreement coefficients ranging from 0.41 to 0.70.

Individual judge reliability indicates the extent to which individual judges are the source of unreliable data. Judge reliability was calculated as the agreement between a particular judge and the pooled set of all other judges. Differences among judges can be explained by any of several factors, including work style (organized, neat, hurried), how well each judge understood the instructions, how consistently the concepts under consideration were understood, and the way in which the questions themselves were perceived. An important issue is whether judges whose individual reliability deviated greatly from that of the other judges should have been eliminated from further consideration. Krippendorff (1980) cautions against this practice. Since variability in ratings implies nothing about which judges are "right" and which are "wrong", forcing agreement by taking averages or considering only majority judgements may conceal the very phenomena under study. In addition, if only data for which the judges achieve perfect agreement is allowed, it is possible that the data will reflect chance agreements. Finally, basing the analysis on high agreement may introduce a bias toward that which can be easily coded. Krippendorff does concede that, if a particular judge proves to be very unreliable, the data contributed by that judge "could be removed, checked, or recoded by the other [judges and] data reliability would improve . . ." (p. 150). For this study, all judges were retained in spite of wide variations by some individuals.

This research provided some insight into differences in the way the multiple-choice questions were perceived by the judges. There was a great deal of variation among the judges in their perceptions of which questions included mathematical logic concepts and to what degree. This observation underscores the lack of consensus within the field of computing regarding the relationship between mathematical logic and other computer science concepts. While it would have been possible to train the judges to rate questions more consistently than they did in this study, such training was deemed undesirable. An explicit decision was made to allow judges to use their expertise and the taxonomy in doing the classification task. This freedom of interpretation and feedback from the judges assisted the researcher in refining the taxonomy of concepts.

9.5.3   Hypothesis Testing

Descriptive statistics for performance differential between groups
Descriptive statistics for each of the five samples that took the APCS exams are reported in Table 9.6. The delta value for the mean and the standard deviation was calculated as the difference between corresponding values for the *strongly related* group and the *not strongly related* group. A negative delta value indicates that the value in the *strongly related* group was less than the corresponding value in the *not strongly related* group.

In general, each *strongly related* group had a lower mean and smaller standard deviation than for the corresponding *not strongly related* group. Thus, the average number of respondents who correctly answered the questions in a group was consistently lower for the *strongly related* than for the *not strongly related* group. This means that there was less variability in the number of respondents who

Table 9.6: Number of multiple-choice questions, mean and standard deviation of proportion answering correctly, and delta for mean and standard deviation

APCS exam and version	Proportion in *strongly related* group answering correctly			Proportion in *not strongly related* group answering correctly			Delta between groups	
	num. Qs	mean	std. dev.	num. Qs	mean	std. dev.	mean	std. dev.
1984	4	0.42	0.26	30	0.60	0.15	-0.18	+0.11
1988A	4	0.33	0.08	17	0.44	0.27	-0.11	-0.19
1988AB	5	0.48	0.11	29	0.57	0.25	-0.09	-0.14
1992A	8	0.39	0.09	13	0.47	0.26	-0.08	-0.17
1992AB	9	0.48	0.13	18	0.53	0.18	-0.05	-0.05

correctly answered the questions in the *strongly related* group than in the number who correctly answered the questions in the *not strongly related* group. The exception was the 1984 sample, where the standard deviation of the *strongly related* group was larger than the standard deviation of the *not strongly related* group. This difference could be related to the fact that 1984 was the first year in which the APCS exam was offered.

Differences in difficulty distributions between groups
Research question (a) asked: *In considering student performance on the multiple-choice questions, was the distribution of performance for questions strongly related to logic different than for questions not strongly related to logic?* This was tested using the following null hypothesis:

H_a The difficulty distributions for the groups of questions strongly related and not strongly related to logic are the same.

If it was possible to show that the difficulty distributions were statistically different (or non-homogeneous), this would lead to the conclusion that one group of questions was, in general, more difficult than the other group of questions. The analysis considered one dependent variable and two independent variables. The dependent variable was the number of questions in each group. The first independent variable was the artificial dichotomy that divided the questions into the *strongly related* and *not strongly related* groups. The second independent variable stratified the questions according to difficulty. The operational definition for difficulty of a multiple-choice question depended on the proportion of students who correctly answered the question. The difficulty categories, which were mutually exclusive, were defined in terms of the proportion of respondents who answered correctly: "very difficult" for the interval $[0.0, 0.2)$, "somewhat difficult" for the interval $[0.2, 0.4)$, "average" for the interval $[0.4, 0.6)$, "somewhat easy" for the interval $[0.6, 0.8)$, and "very easy" for the interval $[0.8, 1.0]$.

Table 9.7: Number and proportion of questions at each difficulty level in the *strongly related* and *not strongly related* groups

	Strongly related group	Not strongly related	Totals
Very difficult	1	9	10
Somewhat difficult	10	20	30
Average difficulty	16	33	49
Somewhat easy	3	29	32
Very easy	0	16	16
Totals:	30	107	137

Because the number of questions in some categories was small, the results from the five exams were pooled for this analysis. Table 9.7 presents the number of questions at each level of difficulty in each group. Figure 9.2 presents the same data in the form of a graph, where the *x*-axis is the difficulty category and the *y*-axis is the proportion of questions that fell into each group. The graph in Figure 9.2 reveals that the skew of the difficulty distribution for the *strongly related* questions is towards the "very difficult" end of the scale while the difficulty distribution for *not strongly related* distribution has more of a bell shape.

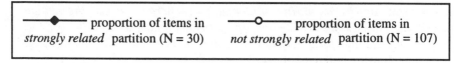

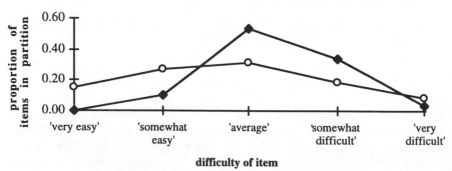

Figure 9.2: Difficulty distribution of questions in the *strongly related* and *not strongly related* groups, with questions pooled across all exams

To further compare the difficulty distributions of the multiple-choice questions in the *strongly related* and *not strongly related* groups, hierarchical log-linear tests of homogeneity were run on the data in Table 9.7. These tests considered whether the distributions were homogeneous with respect to the five levels of question difficulty, that is, whether the number of questions from each group at each level of difficulty was statistically similar. The test of fit resulted in $G^2 = 17.507$ with 4 df ($p \leq 0.002$) and the null hypothesis was rejected. This means that the difficulty distributions of the *strongly related* and *not strongly related* groups were not homogeneous. This result, coupled with the direction of skew in Figure 9.2, leads to the conclusion that the questions in the *strongly related* group were generally more difficult that the questions in the *not strongly related* group.

Correlation between number correct in each group
Research question (b) asked: *Was there a relationship between individual perfor-mance on the set of multiple-choice questions whose content was strongly related to logic and the set of questions whose content was not strongly related to logic?* The following null hypothesis was tested:

H_b The correlation between individual performance on questions in the *strongly related* group and questions in the *not strongly related* group is zero.

To test this hypothesis, the correlation coefficient was developed for each of the five samples (1984, 1988 version A, 1988 version AB, 1992 version A, and 1992 version AB). The correlation coefficient expresses in mathematical terms the degree of relationship between the two variables. To find the correlation coefficient, the two groups of questions were treated as distinct subtests and Pearson's product–moment correlation calculated for the cumulative scores for the *strongly related* and *not strongly related* groups for each sample. The coefficient of determination was also calculated for each of the five samples. The coefficient of determination, which is calculated as the square of the correlation coefficient, describes the shared variance in the two-score distribution. More specifically, it expresses the amount of variance in the dependent score (in this case, the score on the *not strongly related* questions) that could be predicted by the score on the independent variable (here, on the *strongly related* questions). The correlation coefficients and coefficients of determination for the five samples are reported in Table 9.8.

All correlation coefficients were significant ($p \leq 0.01$), so the null hypoth-esis H_b was rejected in all cases. This indicates there is, indeed, some sort of relationship between performance on questions in the *strongly related* group and performance on questions in the *not strongly related* group. However, the shared variance between the two groups was fairly low. The coefficients of determination were highest for version AB of the 1992 exam, at 41%. For version A of the 1988 exam, only 18% of the variance was shared. In all cases, less than 50% of the variability in performance was shared variance. This suggests that the cognitive abilities required to answer correctly the questions in the two groups are rather different.

A number of different factors could have influenced the value of the correlation coefficients. First, there is a direct relationship between the number of questions per group and the scores. Thus, if these values increase, the correlations will tend

Table 9.8: Correlation between number correct in the *strongly related* and *not strongly related* groups

APCS exam and version	Correlation coefficient	Coefficient of determination
1984	0.60	0.36
1988A	0.42	0.18
1988AB	0.60	0.36
1992A	0.56	0.31
1992AB	0.64	0.41

to be higher. In this study, because questions for which agreement was below a certain threshold were eliminated from consideration, the correlations were smaller than they would have been had all questions been included. A second aspect that could have affected the correlation coefficient was the elimination of specific questions under the grouping algorithm. The eliminated questions may have had something in common with one another, perhaps to the extent that they were measuring some of the same abilities. A third factor that can influence the value of the correlation coefficient is sample size. As sample size increases, the correlation coefficient becomes more reliable. In fact, for very large N, very small correlation coefficients can be statistically significant. In this study, the sample sizes were very large, ranging from 3369 to 7375.

9.6 Conclusions

This section provides a summary of the research results. We also consider directions for future research and consider the conclusions we can draw from this study.

9.6.1 Summary of results

This research sought objective evidence as to whether novice computer science students have more difficulty understanding mathematical logic concepts in the domain of computer science than they generally have in understanding other computer science concepts. The results reported here support this conjecture.

A content analysis procedure was developed for reliable and valid classification of content-area test questions according to their degree of relationship to a pre-defined set of logic concepts. Reliability results showed that, in general, the classification that emerged from the content analysis was consistent and reliable. Content validity was established for the classification results based on the agreement of nearly 40 computer science educators.

Given the results of the classification process during the final content analysis procedure, the test questions under consideration were divided into groups of questions that were strongly related and not strongly related to logic. As the basis for hypothesis testing, the first research questions that was investigated was "In considering student performance on the test questions, was the distribution of performance for questions strongly related to logic different than for questions not strongly related to logic?" The second research question asked "Was there a relationship between individual performance on the set of questions whose content was strongly related to logic and on the set of questions whose content not strongly related to logic?"

In general, the questions in the *strongly related* group were more difficult for the five samples of students who took the APCS exams that were considered in this research. With regard to question (b), the study revealed some systematic relationships between the patterns of responses to questions in the two groups, suggesting a relationship between some constructs being tested by questions in each group. However, the variability of individual responses to questions in the *not strongly related* group explained only a small amount of the variability of individual responses to questions in the *strongly related* group, which means that there are other factors that explain these differences.

9.6.2   Generalizability of results

In this subsection, we consider several factors that address whether these results are generalizable beyond the current setting. Because individuals who take the APCS exams are high school students, the generalizability of these results to novice computer science students at post-secondary institutions comes into question. However, advanced placement students tend to be enrolled in advanced or honors high school courses and are generally more successful academically than the average high school student. In addition, secondary students and first-year undergraduates tend to be near one another in age and attitude. The similarities between these two groups argue that conclusions about individual performance for the students taking the APCS exam are generalizable to the results for novice post-secondary students taking the same exams.

The educators who participated as judges in the content analysis procedure and who reviewed the taxonomy of concepts were all actively engaged in undergraduate instruction and in research about computer science education. Thus, they represented an informed sample of the total population of computer science instructors. At least 36 judges rated the questions in each exam packet, so that their pooled ratings ensured the validity of the way in which the questions were grouped. We predict, therefore, that repeating the content analysis procedure on the same pool of questions with another set of judges would produce essentially the same groups of questions.

While the subdomain of logic does cause difficulties for novice computer science students, there may be other subdomains that include concepts that are equally or more difficult for novices to understand. This study focused only on the concepts of logic, grouping all other questions together, irrespective of consideration of the relative simplicity or difficulty of the concepts they covered. The difficulty of logic relative to other specific concepts within computer science was not addressed.

9.6.3 Suggestions for future research

The research presented here suggests a number of follow-up studies. In order to verify or refute these results, the procedure can be replicated with other sets of data or with a different set of judges looking at the same data. The results from the current study can also be extended.

For example, the existing data can be evaluated to determine the relationship between performance on the free-response section and performance on each group of multiple-choice questions. Bennett *et al.* (1991) found that the free-response and multiple-choice questions on the APCS exams measure approximately the same constructs in different ways, so that relationships in performance could provide insights into differential performance on the *strongly related* and *not strongly related* groups of questions.

Another issue that can be considered with these data is whether there is a significant difference in performance by different demographic groups across the groups of questions. For the data sets used in this study, gender and ethnicity were reported, so group performance statistics could be developed. The results could then be contrasted with what other studies have reported regarding performance differential based on ability in logic (Stager-Snow, 1985; Stofflett and Baker, 1992).

The current study has shown that, for the samples of novice students who took the Advanced Placement Examinations in Computer Science, questions that included logic as a main concept or vital subconcept were generally more difficult. Curricular guidelines for computer science (such as Tucker, 1990) include mathematical logic as a topic in the discrete mathematics course that is recommended for all computer science majors. Anecdotal reports suggest that novice computing students at the post-secondary level have similar problems. Warford (1994) has described his experiences teaching a discrete mathematics course that had as its foundation the skillful manipulation of expressions in propositional and predicate calculus. Research should be designed to compare and contrast the effectiveness of this approach and other approaches to teaching discrete mathematics and formal methods.

Saiedian (1992) surveyed the mathematics of computing and predicted that the integration of courses in discrete mathematics and mathematical logic will "increase our students' level of reasoning, prepare them for courses in formal models, improve their theoretical foundation, and prepare them for career growth and/or advanced studies" (p. 220). Unfortunately, little objective evidence exists that supports a direct link between students' enrollment in courses in discrete mathematics or mathematical logic and subsequent improvement in their levels of reasoning. Future research must be designed to provide objective evidence of such claims — claims that too many computer science educators currently take as "self-evident".

9.6.4 Epilogue

The results of this study indicate that novice computer science students do experience more difficulty with the concepts of mathematical logic than they do, in general, with other computer science concepts. No attempt was made to establish logic as "the most difficult" subdomain of computer science. However, the evidence presented here does show that the Advanced Placement Examination multiple-choice questions judged to be strongly related to logic were more difficult than the questions that were judged not strongly related to logic.

Two important questions to be considered in continued research are: (1) What can be done to improve beginning students' likelihood of learning the concepts in this content domain well? and (2) How can one provide remediation for novice students who have learned the concepts of logic poorly?

The answers to these questions have strong potential for positively influencing the future success of computer science students, especially in the area of formal methods. In particular, this study has implications for pre-college instruction in mathematical logic and for the college-level discrete mathematics course(s) taken by beginning and novice computing students.

Acknowledgments

Personal communications with David Naumann, Nic McPhee, and David Gries helped shape the discussion of "first class" status for data types in Section 9.2.2. The historical description of the development of techniques of program verification in Section 9.2.3 is based in part on discussions with E.W. Dijkstra.

I want to reiterate my gratitude to everyone mentioned in the acknowledgments section of my thesis (Almstrum, 1994). Thank you to Anders Berglund and Mats Daniels for extensive comments and stimulating discussions during my time at Uppsala University. Suggestions from David Gries helped crystallize the presentation at several points. Christina Björkman, Hamilton Richards, and Barbara Owens have also influenced the final form of this chapter. Markus Kaltenbach gave invaluable assistance during the effort of converting into LaTeX. Finally, many thanks to Neville Dean, Mike Hinchey, and Torgny Stadler for their patience and their support.

9.7 References

Almstrum, V.L. (1994) *Limitations in the understanding of mathematical logic by novice computer science students*, Doctoral dissertation, The University of Texas at Austin, Dissertation Abstracts International, 55, 06A, p. 1496, December, 1995.

Anderson, J.R. (1980) *Cognitive Psychology and Its Implications*, W. H. Freeman, San Francisco, CA.

ASL Committee on Logic and Education (1995) Guidelines for logic education, *Bulletin of Symbolic Logic*, 1(1):4–7.

Atchison, W.F. (chair) (1968) Curriculum '68: Recommendations for academic programs in computer science, *Communications of the ACM*, 11(3):151–197, March.

Austing, R.H. (chair) (1979) Curriculum '78: Recommendation for the undergraduate program in computer science, *Communications of the ACM*, 22(3):147–166, March.

Berztiss, A. (1987) A mathematically focused curriculum for computer science, *Communications of the ACM*, 30(5):356–365.

College Board (1986) The Entire 1984 AP Computer Science Examination and Key. College Entrance Examination Board.

College Board (1989) The 1988 Advanced Placement Examinations in Computer Science and their grading. College Entrance Examination Board.

College Board (1990) Advanced Placement Course Description: Computer Science. College Entrance Examination Board. May 1991 version.

College Board (1993) The 1992 Advanced Placement Examinations in Computer Science and their grading. College Entrance Examination Board.

Cooke, J. (1992) Formal methods — mathematics, theory, recipes, or what?, *The Computer Journal*, 35(5):419–423.

Copi, I M. (1979) *Symbolic Logic*, 5th edition, Macmillan, New York.

Dale, N. and Walker, H. (1996) *Abstract data types: Specification, implementation, and application*, D.C. Heath, Lexington, MA.

Denning, P.J. (chair) (1989) Computing as a discipline, *Communications of the ACM*, 32(1):9–23, January.

Dijkstra, E.W. (1968) A constructive approach to the problem of program correctness, *BIT*, 8:174–186.

Dijkstra, E.W. (1976) *A Discipline of Programming*, Prentice Hall, Englewood Cliffs, NJ.

Dijkstra, E.W. (1989) On the cruelty of really teaching computing science, *Communications of the ACM*, 32(12):1398–1404.

Dijkstra, E.W. and Feijen, W.H.J. (1988) *A Method of Programming*, Addison-Wesley, Menlo Park, CA.

Dijkstra, E.W. and Scholten, C.S. (1990) *Predicate Calculus and Program Semantics*, Springer Verlag, New York.

Floyd, R.W. (1967) Assigning meaning to programs. In Proceedings of the American Mathematical Society Symposia in Applied Mathematics, 19:19–32.

Franzblau, D. (1993) New models for courses in discrete mathematics, *SIAG DM News*, 15 November.

Galton, A. (1992) Logic as a Formal Method, *The Computer Journal*, 35(5):431–440.

Gardner, H. (1985) *Frames of Mind: The Theory of Multiple Intelligences*, Basic Books, New York.

Gardner, H. and Hatch, T. (1989) Multiple Intelligences go to school: Educational implications of the theory of multiple intelligences. *Educational Researcher*, November.

Gibbs, N.E. and Tucker, A.B. (1986) A model curriculum for a liberal arts degree in computer science, *Communications of the ACM*, 29(3):202–210, March.

Goldson, D., Reeves, S. and Bornat, R. (1993) A review of several programs for the teaching of logic, *The Computer Journal*, 36(4):373–386.

Gries, D. (1981) *The Science of Programming*, Springer Verlag, New York.

Gries, D. (1990) Calculation and discrimination: A more effective curriculum, *Communications of the ACM*, **34**(3):44–55.

Gries, D. and Schneider, F.B. (1993a) *A Logical Approach to Discrete Math*, Springer Verlag, New York.

Gries, D. and Schneider, F.B. (1993b) *Instructor's Manual: A Logical Approach to Discrete Math*, Computer Science Department, Cornell University, Ithaca, NY.

Gries, D. and Schneider, F.B (1994) *A New Approach to Teaching Mathematics*, Unpublished manuscript, Cornell University, Computer Science Department, Ithaca, NY.

Guilford, J.P. (1967) *The Nature of Human Intelligence*, McGraw-Hill, New York.

Hoare, C.A.R. (1969) An axiomatic basis for computer programming, *Communications of the ACM*, **12**:576–583. (Reprinted in *Communications of the ACM*, **26**(1):53–56, January 1983).

IEEE Computer Society Education Committee (1976) *A Curriculum in Computer Science and Engineering*, IEEE Computer Society, Model Curriculum Subcommittee.

IEEE Model Program Committee (1983) *The 1983 IEEE Computer Society Model Program in Computer Science and Engineering*, IEEE Computer Society, Educational Activities Board.

International Standards Organization (1994) *Information Technology — Language-Independen Datatypes*, ISO/IEC draft International Standard 11404, Geneva.

Koffman, E.B., Miller, P.L. and Wardle C.E. (1984) Recommended Curriculum for CS1, *Communications of the ACM*, **27**(10):998–1001, October..

Koffman, E.B., Stempel, D. and Wardle C.E. (1985) Recommended Curriculum for CS2, *Communications of the ACM*, **28**(8):815–818, August.

Krippendorff, K. (1980) *Content Analysis: An Introduction to Its Methodology*, Sage Publications, Beverly Hills, CA.

Lockwood, W., Pallrand, G. and VanHarlingen, D. (1980) The relationship between logical operators and achievement in university physics. Paper presented at the meeting of the National Association for Research in Science Teaching, Boston, MA (abstract), April.

Lockwood, W., Pallrand, G. and VanHarlingen, D. (1982) Logical ability and achievement in high school level physics. Paper presented at the meeting of the National Association for Research in Science Teaching, Lake Geneva, WI (abstract), April.

Myers, Jr., J.P. (1990) The central role of mathematical logic in computer science, *SIGCSE Bulletin*, **22**(1):22–26, January.

Piburn, M.D. (1989) Reliability and validity of the propositional logic test, *Educational and Psychological Measurement*, **49**:667–672.

Piburn, M.D. (1990) Reasoning about logical propositions and success in science, *Journal of Research in Science Teaching*, **27**(9):887–900.

Piburn, M.D. and Baker, D. (1988) Reasoning about logical propositions and success in science. Paper presented at the meeting of the American Educational Research Association, New Orleans, LA, April.

Pollack, S.V. (1982) The development of computer science. In S.V. Pollack, editor, *Studies in Computer Science*, The Mathematical Association of America.

Powers, D.E. and Enright, M.K. (1987) Analytic reasoning skills involved in graduate study: Perceptions of faculty in six fields, *Journal of Higher Education*, **58**:658–682.

Ralston, A. (editor) (1989) Discrete mathematics in the first two years, *MAA Notes*, **15**, Mathematical Association of America.

Ralston, A. and Shaw, M. (1980) Curriculum '78 — Is computer science really that unmathematical?, *Communications of the ACM*, **23**(2):67–70.

Rothaug, W. (1984) *Logical Connectives and Community College Science Course Achievement*, Unpublished doctoral dissertation, Rutgers University, New Brunswick, NJ.

Rothaug, W. and Pallrand, G. (1982) Reasoning skills and science course achievement. Paper presented at the meeting of the National Association for Research in Science Teaching, Lake Geneva, WI (abstract), April.

Rothaug, W., Pallrand, G. and VanHarlingen, D. (1981) Logical operations and achievement in community college students. Paper presented at the meeting of the National Association for Research in Science Teaching, Grossingers, NY (abstract), April.

Saiedian, H. (1992) Mathematics of computing, *Computer Science Education*, 3(3):203–221.

Seeber, F., Pallrand, G., VandenBerg, G. and VanHarlingen, D. (1979) Logical ability, formal thought and achievement in physics. Paper presented at the meeting of the National Association for Research in Science Teaching, Atlanta, GA (abstract), April.

Shaw, M. (editor) (1985) *The Carnegie-Mellon Curriculum for Undergraduate Computer Science*, Springer Verlag, New York.

Sperschneider, V. and Antoniou, G. (1991) *Logic: A Foundation for Computer Science*, Addison-Wesley International Computer Science Series, Reading, MA.

Stager-Snow, D. (1985) *Analytical ability, logical reasoning and attitude as predictors of success in an introductory course in computer science for non-computer science majors*, Doctoral dissertation, Rutgers University, New Brunswick, NJ, Dissertation Abstracts International, 45, 08A, p. 2473, February, 1985.

Stofflett, R.T. and Baker, D.R. (1992) The effects of training in combinatorial reasoning and propositional logic on formal reasoning ability in high school students, *Research in Middle Level Education*, 16(1):159–177.

Tucker, A.B. (editor) (1990) *Computing Curricula 1991: Report of the ACM/IEEE-CS Joint Curriculum Task Force*, Final Draft, 17 December, ACM Order Number 201910, IEEE Computer Society Press Order Number 2220.

Warford, J.S. (1994) Book review of *A Logical Approach to Discrete Math* (1993) by D. Gries and F.B. Schneider, *Computing Reviews*, Review number 9407-0412, Section G.2.0.

Wing, J. M. (1990) A specifier's introduction to formal methods, *IEEE Computer*, 23(9):8–24.

An executable course in the algebraic semantics of imperative programs

10.1 Introduction

This chapter describes a novel approach to teaching formal methods in computing science through an *executable* course on the semantics and verification of imperative programs. This approach allows students to learn both formal semantics and techniques for formal reasoning about programs by experimenting at a computer. Our experience teaching a course titled *Algebraic Semantics of Imperative Programs* suggests that this can significantly enhance learning.

This course has developed over the last seven years, during which some form of it was taught once each year; this development has recently culminated in a textbook (Goguen and Malcolm, 1996). The course is taught to graduate students from a variety of academic backgrounds beginning their serious study of computing science through the "conversion" M.Sc. in Computation programme at Oxford; it could equally well be taught to undergraduates as early as their second year. The philosophy of our course and of the programme of which it is part is captured in the following quote from Christopher Strachey, founder of the Programming Research Group at Oxford:

> It has long been my personal view that the separation of practical and theoretical work is artificial and injurious. Much of the practical work done in computing, both in software and in hardware design, is unsound and clumsy because the people who do it have not any clear understanding of the fundamental design principles of their work. Most of the abstract mathematical and theoretical work is sterile because it has no point of contact with real computing. One of the central aims of the Programming Research Group as a teaching and research group has been to set up an atmosphere in which this separation cannot happen.

Specific goals of our course include the following:

1. Improve intuition and ability in imperative programming, through understanding the semantics of programs and seeing numerous examples.

2. Teach how to prove properties of programs.

3. Develop relevant mathematical background.

4. Present the OBJ system and use it for all proofs.

5. Show that all this can be done in a way that is completely rigorous, yet not too difficult or too abstract, by using equational logic, which is simply the logic of substituting equals for equals.

Our semantic approach gives an equational specification for a class of abstract machines and specifies programming language features by their effect on these machines. The features treated in the course are assignment, sequential composition, conditional, while-loop, procedure definition, and procedure call; we also give semantics for the array data structure and for programs that manipulate arrays. The equational axioms describing these features are used in proving program correctness.

Thus, this course both presents a rigorous semantics for imperative programs, and uses that semantics to prove properties of programs. Most comparable courses concentrate on one or the other of these aims, either presenting mathematical theories of semantics of programming languages, or presenting a logical calculus (such as Hoare-triples or weakest preconditions) and using this to prove properties of programs. In both cases, the course work is done on paper, since the semantics of programs and proofs of their properties are presented on paper.

By contrast, our Algebraic Semantics of Imperative Programs course uses an *executable* presentation of program semantics in OBJ (Goguen *et al.*, 1996), an implemented specification language that can be used for theorem proving and rapid prototyping, and which itself has a formal semantics based on equational logic. OBJ is not just another functional programming language, although it does have an executable functional sublanguage. OBJ was designed for algebraic semantics; its declarations introduce symbols for sorts and functions, its statements are equations, and its computations are equational proofs. OBJ also has a sublanguage of "theories" for declaring properties. Thus, an OBJ "program" actually *is* an equational theory, and every OBJ computation actually *proves* some theorem about such a theory. This means that an OBJ program used for defining the semantics of a program already has a precise mathematical meaning. Moreover, standard techniques for mechanising equational reasoning can be used for verifying programs.

This novel approach has several advantages:

♦ because OBJ has a formal semantics, our presentation of the semantics of imperative programs is mathematically rigorous;

♦ because OBJ's semantics is based on equational logic, which is simply the logic of substituting equals for equals, our presentation of the semantics of imperative programs is simple and readily understandable;

♦ because OBJ supports the specification of abstract data types, we can present the semantics of imperative programs that manipulate a variety of data structures.

However, the chief advantages of this approach stem from the most innovative aspect of the course: that the semantics is executable. This means that students can:

♦ acquire a feeling for the semantics of imperative programs by experimentation – they can use OBJ to "step through" a computation and examine its results;

♦ acquire a feeling for the semantics of correctness proofs by experimentation – they can use OBJ and its semantics to construct and execute such proofs; and

♦ experiment with extensions of the semantics to treat features of imperative programs not directly covered in the course.

The next-to-last point represents the bulk of the course work for the students; each week they are given practical exercises which require them to construct proofs in OBJ. As new features of imperative programs are introduced in the lectures, they are encouraged to experiment with the semantics to consolidate their grasp of the material. This seems to be especially useful in learning the semantics of programs that manipulate unfamiliar data structures such as arrays (in previous years, the course has covered stack-based programming); students can gain insight into a data structure by observing the effect of running simple programs. Some of the exercises also introduce new language features and/or data structures, and ask the students to use them in programs and proofs.

We have found that this novel approach appeals to students, and that executability can greatly facilitate teaching an introductory course on formal semantics and formal reasoning about programs.

The following section gives a more detailed account of the background and goals of the course, and Section 10.3 gives an example of the material taught in the course so that readers can evaluate the claims we have made. The example consists of an OBJ theory for a class of abstract machines, the syntax and semantics of a simple programming language with while loops, and a correctness proof for a program that computes the exponential of two numbers. In fact, this example, which fits into a handout of three pages, constitutes the bulk of the introductory lecture to the course! Students are generally impressed that so much can be done so rigorously in so little space, and we hope the reader will share something of the excitement we still feel in presenting this material.

10.2   Some goals and issues in algebraic semantics

All formal methods rely on some semantics of computation. In recent years, many promising formal methods have arisen from algebraic approaches to semantics. We believe that algebraic approaches tend to be simpler and more tractable, in the sense that they lend themselves readily to formal reasoning, for example in proving the correctness of refinement or implementation (Goguen and Malcolm,

1994; Malcolm and Goguen, 1994), or, as in our course on algebraic semantics, in providing a simple yet rigorous foundation for proving correctness of imperative programs. In this section we sketch the main differences between our algebraic semantics, which might be called *algebraic denotational semantics* (*ADS*), and other well-established approaches.

Roughly speaking, the most popular approaches to the semantics of imperative languages divide into three groups: operational, axiomatic and denotational. An *operational semantics* describes the meaning of a programming language by describing a way of executing its programs. Often this is done by giving an interpreter or compiler for the language. So-called *structured operational semantics* (also called *natural semantics*) (Plotkin, 1981) describes computations by giving formal rules of deduction for steps of computation; this may be considered an abstract interpreter.

In *axiomatic* approaches, programming language features are defined by writing axioms in some logical system. First order logic, or some variant of it, is the most popular, since this is the logical system most widely used in mathematics and its foundations. An axiomatic approach using assertions and invariants was pioneered by Turing (1949) and Goldstine and von Neumann (1949), and later made more formal by Floyd (1967) and Hoare (1969).

By contrast, *denotational* approaches build mathematical models of programming language features; these models are called *denotations*. For example, the denotation of a program might be a partial function from inputs to outputs. Usually set theory is used in constructing these denotations, perhaps with some technical constraints, such as continuity. In this approach, the denotation of a program is constructed by composing the denotations of its parts. Denotational semantics was pioneered by McCarthy (1962), and greatly extended by Scott and Strachey (1971).

In classical denotational semantics (often called *Scott–Strachey semantics*, see Gordon, 1979 and Stoy, 1977), the model of storage can be criticized for being too concrete. However, ADS *axiomatizes* the notion of storage, so that any model satisfying the axioms can be used, thus avoiding the need to select one particular model; that is, ADS uses so-called "loose" algebraic semantics to specify a *class* (i.e., "variety") of models for storage. For example, the algebra modeling storage may involve cache and/or disk memories.[1] Another criticism of classical denotational semantics is that it can be very difficult to prove properties of programs in this framework. We will see that proofs in the ADS framework can be surprisingly easy.

So-called *weakest precondition semantics* is a well-known variety of axiomatic semantics developed by Dijkstra (1975, 1976). Standard textbooks using this approach have been written by Gries (1981) and Backhouse (1986). In this approach, the semantics of programming language constructs is given by axioms which prescribe how those constructs transform predicates on states; thus, this semantics also has a denotational aspect, in that programs denote functions from sets of states to sets of states. A difficulty with weakest preconditions is that the semantics of iteration is rather complicated: in fact, Dijkstra, Gries and others assume that first-order logic is adequate, but it seems that *infinitary logic* (i.e., the logic of infinitely long sentences!) is needed for the weakest preconditions of general iterations (see Engeler, 1971); alternatively, one might use second order logic, or abandon predicates in favor of sets defined by infinite least upper bounds. In contrast, first order equational logic is sufficient for ADS.

Iteration also raises the issues of termination and well-defined values. In Gries's (1981) approach to weakest preconditions, a 3-valued logic is used to handle non-termination (VDM (Jones, 1986) also uses a 3-valued logic); however, ADS uses only ordinary 2-valued logic. We believe that ADS gives a simpler treatment of iteration because it distinguishes between the semantics of programs and other properties of programs, such as termination and correctness. The semantics of iteration is given by two very simple OBJ equations that describe the effects on states in possible models of storage; moreover, because OBJ itself has a simple, precise semantics in equational logic, we can use the semantics of OBJ to reason about properties of such models, and hence about properties of programs. The result is that ADS provides a simple semantics, unclouded by issues of correctness or termination of programs; and in addition, we are able to use equational logic for a separate, simple treatment of correctness and termination (Goguen and Malcolm, 1996). The use of order sorted algebra plays a key role in our treatment of non-terminating programs; see Goguen and Malcolm (1996) for details.

Another issue raised by various axiomatic approaches to the semantics of imperative programs, including weakest preconditions and Hoare *et al.*'s "Laws of Programming" (1987), is nondeterminism. Although programming languages are necessarily deterministic, a "nondeterministic" algorithm can be viewed as an equivalence class of procedures, where each procedure is a refinement, or possible implementation, of the algorithm; this is what we call loose semantics. Alternatively, nondeterminism can be seen as a property of specifications in a specification language with a formal notion of one specification being more deterministic than another, as in (Hoare *et al.*, 1987). For simplicity, we avoid both these senses of nondeterminism and give a deterministic treatment of deterministic languages. However, ADS can be enriched with additional operations to support a loose semantics for nondeterminism, as shown in (Malcolm and Goguen, 1995).

The main motivations for nondeterministic specification are that it allows post-poning design decisions, and that it leads to simple proofs of program correctness. There are even claims that, with the right semantics, algorithm development becomes an easy, near-mechanical process of looking for simple proofs. While we agree that a clear and simple formalism should lead to clarity of proof, we steer clear of any claims about the easy automatic development of algorithms; actually, there are good reasons to believe the contrary. However, in simpler cases, one can use proof construction as an aid to program construction, and we think it may be easier to do this in ADS than in more complex settings.

Our approach to properties of programs is traditional, in that we use first-order logic for preconditions, postconditions, and invariants. This raises the issue of how to handle first-order sentences in the context of an algebraic semantics. Our approach is to use standard rules of deduction to translate first-order sentences into sequences of declarations and reductions.[2] Predicates are represented as `Bool`-valued operations. Assumptions and goals must be treated differently: assumptions become declarations, while goals become reductions (generally in the context of some specifically constructed declarations). For example, an assumption that is a conjunction of sentences is represented by giving one declaration for each sentence. Universal quantifiers in goals are handled by introducing new constants (this is valid by the so-called "theorem of constants"). Existential quantifiers in assumptions are handled by introducing so-called Skolem functions. The result of all this is what we call an OBJ *proof score*, that is, an OBJ program such that if its reductions all produce `true` when expected, then the desired theorem has in fact been proved.

A particular pitfall for those who wish to develop a formal semantics for imperative programming lies in the surprising variety of different kinds of variable that are involved. In fact, one must distinguish among at least the following:

1. variables that occur in programs (such as X in X := X + 1);

2. variables that range over data types used in programs (such as integers and Booleans);

3. variables that range over programs and program parts (such as expressions); and

4. variables that range over meta-logical entities used in reasoning about programs (such as computation sequences).

Furthermore, each kind of variable may have many different types. In general, textbooks on program semantics have not been very rigorous about all this. An exemplary exception is the book by Reynolds (1981). However, such rigor is necessary for our use of OBJ as a meta-language, and also for any discussion of the semantics of procedures with parameters. The formal parameters to a procedure are variables that range over program variables; if this point is not clearly made in the semantics of procedure calls, much confusion can arise.

In summary, our algebraic denotational semantics combines aspects of denotational, axiomatic and operational semantics. The denotational aspect arises because everything we specify has a denotation in an algebra; the axiomatic aspect arises from the fact that we specify these algebras using equations; and the operational aspect arises from the fact that we can symbolically execute programs using the term-rewriting facility of OBJ.

10.3 An example of algebraic denotational semantics

Because the semantics is presented in the algebraic specification language OBJ, the first two or three weeks of the course necessarily include an introduction to that language and its semantics. We have adopted the policy of throwing students in at the deep end: in the first lecture, after explaining the goals of the course and giving a brief introduction to formal methods and semantics, we present a simple language of while programs, its semantics, and a correctness proof of a short program; the OBJ code for this example, which fits onto a handout of just three pages, is given below. To give the reader an idea of the issues raised and how the material is taught, we also include brief explanations of the most important points in the OBJ specification. These explanations are along the lines of what we actually say in the lecture. We stress that students are not expected to understand all the details of this example; the goal is simply to give the flavor of the rest of the course. We find that students manage very well to follow the gist of the example, which provides a good opportunity to illustrate important concepts such as syntax, semantics, and loop invariants, which all play a key role later in the course.

The example divides naturally into three parts. The first part specifies the data types that are manipulated by the program, in this case the natural numbers. The second part specifies a theory of abstract computing machines that we call "stores", and the syntax and semantics of while programs. The semantics is given by equational axioms that specify the effect of programs on stores. Finally, the third part defines a particular program to compute exponentiation and proves that this program is correct. The correctness proof uses the notion of loop invariant; a particular invariant for the exponentiation program is proposed, and then OBJ is used to prove that it is indeed an invariant of the program. Once the invariant is given, the correctness proof is performed entirely mechanically in OBJ: in fact, the correctness proof is *executed* in OBJ. The output produced during this execution is shown in the appendix.

The specification of the natural numbers with some basic operations requires little explanation. The students have already had some experience with declarative definitions of data structures in a course on functional programming. The basic data structure is very simply set out in the following OBJ module:

```
obj NAT is
  sort Nat .
  op 0 : -> Nat .
  op s_ : Nat -> Nat [prec 1] .
endo
```

The chief issue here is simply to introduce OBJ's notation for declaring data structures: these modules begin and end with the keywords obj and endo; names for sorts (or data types, if you prefer) are introduced after the keyword sort; and names for operations are introduced after the keyword op. We also stress, without going into details, that OBJ's denotational semantics gives a precise meaning to such declarations; in this case, it so happens that the denotational semantics gives us the 'obvious' denotation, i.e., the natural numbers. Some operations on numbers are specified in the next OBJ module:

```
obj NATOPS is pr NAT .
  op 1 : -> Nat .
  eq 1 = s 0 .
```

```
op _+_ : Nat Nat -> Nat [assoc comm prec 3] .
vars M N : Nat .
eq  M + 0  =  M .
eq  M + s N  =  s(M + N) .
op _*_ : Nat Nat -> Nat [assoc comm prec 2] .
eq  M * 0  =  0 .
eq  M * s N  =  M * N + M .
op _**_ : Nat Nat -> Nat [prec 4] .
eq  M ** 0  =  1 .
eq  M ** s N  =  (M ** N) * M .
op _-_ : Nat Nat -> Nat .
eq  M - 0  =  M .
eq  0 - M  =  0 .
eq  s M - s N  =  M - N .
op _%2 : Nat -> Nat [prec 10] .
eq  0 %2  =  0 .
eq  s 0 %2  =  0 .
eq  s s N %2  =  s(N %2) .
op even_ : Nat -> Bool  [prec 10] .
eq  even 0  =  true .
eq  even s 0  =  false .
eq  even s s M  =  even M .
op pos_ : Nat -> Bool .
eq  pos 0  =  false .
eq  pos s N  =  true .
[lemma1] cq (N * N)**(M %2) = N ** M if even M .
[lemma2] cq N *(N **(M - s 0)) = N ** M if pos M .
endo
```

Again, this requires little explanation. Modules are imported using the keyword pr (for "protecting", in the sense that the declarations in the module do not add any new numbers to the specification in NAT, nor do they identify distinct numbers). The operation %2 is integer division by two. We point out that in OBJ's denotational semantics, equational axioms, introduced by the keyword eq (or cq for conditional equations), assert equalities, while in OBJ's operational semantics, they are used left-to-right to rewrite terms. For example,

```
((s 0)+(s 0))**(s s s 0)
```

is rewritten in the obvious way to

```
s s s s s s s s 0 .
```

The two labelled equations at the end of the NATOPS module are lemmas that are needed for executing the correctness proof of the exponentiation program in OBJ. They were obtained by looking at OBJ's output when it failed to complete the proof: instead of returning the result true, it returned a term containing instances of the lefthand sides of the given lemmas. This enabled us to see that these particular additional properties were needed.[3] In a similar way, the fact that OBJ returns subexpressions that it cannot yet reduce is of considerable help with the task of strengthening invariants that is so often necessary in construcing correctness proofs of imperative programs.

The real business of algebraic denotational semantics begins with the next module, STORE, which defines a class of abstract machines that associate natural number values with variables in the programming language. For these variables, we use OBJ's built in sort Id of "quoted identifiers". The declaration

```
pr QID *(sort Id to Var) .
```

imports this built in sort and renames it to Var. We stress that program variables of sort Var are very different from the variables used in OBJ equations (these are introduced after the keyword var, with a small "v").

```
th STORE is pr NATOPS .
              pr QID *(sort Id to Var) .
   sort Store .
   op initial : -> Store .
   op _[[_]] : Store Var -> Nat .
   op (_;_:_) : Store Var Nat -> Store .
   vars X Y : Var .
   var  S : Store .
   var  N : Nat .
   eq  initial [[X]]  =  0 .
   eq  S ; X : N [[X]]  =  N .
   cq  S ; X : N [[Y]]  =  S[[Y]] if X =/= Y .
endth
```

This module begins and ends with the OBJ keywords th and endth, which indicates that the module defines a *theory* of abstract machines: anything that associates values with variables in the way described by the equations is acceptable as a model of this theory, whereas the previous modules, which begin and end with the keywords obj and endo, are intended to denote the 'obvious' or 'standard' (i.e., technically, the initial (Goguen *et al.*, 1978)) model; that is, they are intended to specify the data type of natural numbers. A Store is therefore anything which has a distinguished constant initial, an operation

```
_[[_]] : Store Var -> Nat
```

(which allows examining the value a store associates with a given program variable), and an operation

```
(_;_:_) : Store Var Nat -> Store
```

(which updates the value associated with a given program variable) satisfying the equations given in the module. In a similar way, a theory of monoids could be given by declaring a sort with a constant and a binary operation which satisfy identity and associativity equations. The semantics of imperative programs will be given by equations that specify the effect of programs on stores.

The syntax of our programming language is defined simply by declaring the constructs of the language as operations. The module EXP defines integer and boolean expressions for a simple programming language. The equations of the module give the semantics of these expressions, relative to a given Store, in the following:

```
obj EXP is pr STORE .
  sorts Exp Bexp .
  subsorts Nat Var < Exp .
  subsorts Bool < Bexp .
  op _*_ : Exp Exp -> Exp .
  op _-_ : Exp Exp -> Exp .
  op _%2 : Exp -> Exp .
  op even_ : Exp -> Bexp .
  op pos_ : Exp -> Bexp .
  op _[[_]] : Store Exp -> Nat .
  op _[[_]] : Store Bexp -> Bool .
  var  S : Store .
  var  N : Nat .
  var  B : Bool .
  vars E E' : Exp .
  var  BX : Bexp .
  eq  S[[N]]  =  N .
  eq  S[[B]]  =  B .
  eq  S[[E * E']]  =  S[[E]] * S[[E']] .
  eq  S[[E - E']]  =  S[[E]] - S[[E']] .
  eq  S[[E %2]]    =  S[[E]] %2 .
  eq  S[[even E]]  =  even(S[[E]]) .
  eq  S[[pos E]]   =  pos(S[[E]]) .
endo
```

The key point is that expressions in the language "look like" natural numbers, except that they may contain variables; if we can assign natural number values to these variables (by means of a Store), then we can assign natural number values to the expressions which contain those variables. The equations in this module demonstrate the difference between syntax and semantics: for example, the operation _+_, which takes two expressions as arguments and returns an expression as result, is purely syntactic, but the equations which describe semantics of expressions relative to a given Store state that it is *interpreted* as addition on the semantic domain of natural numbers.

Similarly, the module PGM defines the syntax and semantics of a simple programming language. As in EXP, the operations declared in the module specify the syntax of the language, and the equations specify its semantics.

```
obj PGM is pr EXP .
            pr STORE .
    sort Pgm .
    op _:=_ : Var Exp -> Pgm .
    op _;_ : Pgm Pgm -> Pgm [assoc prec 50] .
    op if_then_else_fi : Bexp Pgm Pgm -> Pgm .
    op while_do_od : Bexp Pgm -> Pgm .
    op _;_ : Store Pgm -> Store .
    var  S : Store .
    var  X : Var .
    var  E : Exp .
    var  BX : Bexp .
    vars P P' : Pgm .
    eq  S ; (X := E)  =  S ; X : S[[E]] .
    eq  S ; (P ; P') =  (S ; P); P' .
    cq  S ; if BX then P else P' fi  =  S ; P
        if  S[[BX]] .
    cq  S ; if BX then P else P' fi  =  S ; P'
        if  not(S[[BX]]) .
    cq  S ; while BX do P od  =  S ; P ; while BX do P od
        if  S[[BX]] .
    cq  S ; while BX do P od  =  S
        if  not(S[[BX]]) .
    endo
```

The first four operations declared in the module give the constructs of our simple programming language: assignment, sequential composition, conditional, and iteration. The fifth operation,

```
    _;_ : Store Pgm -> Store ,
```

allows evaluating a given program in a given store; the modified store is returned as result. It is by means of this operation that we define the semantics of the language, by specifying the effect of each construct on a given store. The first equation in this module defines the semantics of assignment, the programming construct that underlies all imperative programming languages. The equation states that the effect of an assignment on a store is to update the value associated with the given variable. The remaining equations specify the effect of the other constructs in the programming language on stores.

Note that it is possible to specify in a very short time a semantic domain (the natural numbers), a theory of abstract machines, the syntax of a programming language, and the semantics of that language. Moreover, while the specification has an abstract algebraic denotation, the operational semantics of OBJ provides an operational semantics for the example programming language! OBJ evaluates terms by rewriting them according to the given equations, from left to right; the equations in our specification allow OBJ to evaluate programs written in the example programming language. For example, the module POW defines a program that computes exponentiation:

```
th POW is inc PGM .
  ops a0 b0 : -> Nat .
  let init  = 'A := a0 ; 'B := b0 ; 'C := 1 .
  let step  = 'B := 'B - 1 ; 'C := 'C * 'A .
  let inner = 'A := 'A * 'A ; 'B := 'B %2 .
  let outer = while even 'B do inner od ; step .
  let pow   = init ; while pos 'B do outer od .
endth
```

Here, the operations a0 and b0 are used to represent the initial values[4] given to the program, which sets the variable 'C to a0 to the power of b0. The keyword let introduces an abbreviation. Such abbreviations are treated by OBJ in the same way as equations, so the command

```
red pow .
```

causes OBJ to reduce the term pow using the given equations, giving the following result:

```
'A := a0 ; 'B := b0 ; 'C := 1 ;
while pos 'B
do while even 'B
   do 'A := 'A * 'A ; 'B := 'B %2 od ;
   'B := 'B - 1 ; 'C := 'C * 'A
od
```

The equations defining the semantics of the programming language can also be used to evaluate the results of running the program pow. For example,

```
open POW .
eq a0 = s s 0 .
eq b0 = s s s 0 .
red initial ; pow [['C]] .   ***> should be: 8
close
```

sets the initial values of a0 and b0 to 2 and 3, respectively, and asks for the value of the variable 'C after running the program in the initial state (in which all variables have the value 0). The result returned is, as it should be, 8 (of course, in the form of 8 ss followed by a 0). The command ***> indicates that what follows it (on the same line) is a comment that should be printed in the output when it is executed.

The remainder of the OBJ code presents a proof that the program is correct. The proof uses the notion of invariant, which is central to the course, and can be explained at a very intuitive level by drawing a flow chart to give a graphic representation of the nested loop structure.[5] An invariant of the program is a property that holds before the loop is entered, and is preserved by each iteration of both the inner and outer loop, and it therefore holds when (or if!) the loop is exited. An appropriate invariant for the correctness proof of POW is given in the following:

```
obj PROOF is pr POW .
  op inv : Store -> Bool .
  var S : Store .
  eq  inv(S)  =  ((S[['A]]) ** (S[['B]]))
                               * (S[['C]]) == a0 ** b0 .
  op s : -> Store .
  ops a b c : -> Nat .
  eq s[['A]] = a .
  eq s[['B]] = b .
  eq s[['C]] = c .
endo
```

As well as defining the invariant for the proof, this module introduces an arbitrary store s, and abbreviations a, b and c for the values of 'A, 'B and 'C in this store. The program is proved correct by showing that init establishes the invariant, and that the truth of the invariant is preserved by the bodies of the inner and outer loops. Each part of the proof is achieved by an OBJ reduction. The reduction

```
open PROOF .
red inv(s ; init) .  ***> should be: true
close
```

shows that the invariant holds initially before the loop is entered, and the two reductions below show that if the invariant holds before the body of the loop is evaluated, then it also holds after the body is evaluated. The assumption that the invariant holds before the body is evaluated is made by asserting the equations that precede the final two reductions.

```
open PROOF .
eq (a ** b)* c = a0 ** b0 .
eq pos b = true .
eq even b = true .
red inv(s ; inner).  ***> should be: true
close

open PROOF .
eq (a ** b)* c = a0 ** b0 .
eq even b = false .  ***> therefore by [lemma3]:
eq pos b = true .
red inv(s ; step) .  ***> should be: true
close
```

The program pow terminates when the guard of the loop fails, that is, when 'B finally becomes zero, assuming the precondition that the value of 'B is initially non-negative. In this case, the invariant still holds, and it says that 'C has the value a0 ** b0, as desired. (Later in the course, this method is stated as a formal theorem.) This proof of partial correctness extends to a proof of total correctness by showing that the program actually terminates, and this is done in our course and in our book, again using simple reductions that are performed in OBJ.

It is worth pausing to notice that all we had to do was set up the proof and let OBJ do all the tedious computations, and OBJ even provided hints for the non-routine parts, including the lemmas that were needed. The entire example took only three pages of OBJ code, including defining the numbers, giving the syntax and semantics of a simple imperative programming language, and using that semantics in a correctness proof for an exponentiation program. Moreover, both the semantics of the language and the correctness proof are executable.

The course and the book that developed from it (Goguen *et al.*, 1996) give a more encompassing semantics for numbers, as well as for arrays and procedures, and of course, there are many more examples using these and other features. Termination and total correctness proofs are also treated.

10.4   Discussion and conclusions

The example of algebraic denotational semantics given in the previous section illustrates the advantages of using OBJ to express the semantics of imperative programs. The example is sufficiently short, intuitive and readable to be used in an introductory lecture, yet because OBJ is a formal, implemented notation, an extremely high level of formality and mathematical rigor is achieved. OBJ's algebraic semantics gives a precise meaning to the specification, while OBJ's operational semantics gives a way to execute programs and proofs. The operational component allows students to gain insight into the constructs of our programming language, and the nature of correctness proofs. This course is, we believe, unique in computing science education in that it is *executable*. Its success arises in large measure from the simplicity and efficiency of equational logic, with its armory of powerful theorems and algorithms.

Contrary to claims in many books on formal methods, we believe that programming is not purely formal. Programming is a skill, and to be really good at it can take years of hard work. One must learn how to use tools like configuration managers and debuggers. For large programs, one must learn how to work in a team; and for really large projects, management and other social issues are often dominant (Goguen and Luqi, 1995). One must learn discipline and organization, and how to read and write documentation. One must keep learning new languages, tools, concepts, algorithms, and skills; sometimes one must even invent these things. Software engineering is a difficult area requiring diverse skills and knowledge, and the material taught in our course provides little help with those aspects that are not formal and cannot be formalized.

It is unhealthy to confuse a formal notation with a formal method. A *method* should say how to do something, whereas a *notation* allows one to say something (Goguen and Luqi, 1995). Thus, OBJ is only a notation, but using it as described in our course and book gives a method for proving properties of imperative programs. This method is not completely mechanical, because some of the problems involved are uncomputable (such as finding loop invariants), although of course, the OBJ3 implementation[6] is completely mechanical. Nevertheless, the method is surprisingly effective, in part because OBJ does all the routine work, and even provides hints to help with doing much of the non-routine work.

The problems that arise for large programs are qualitatively very different from those that arise for small programs. The student should not be led into believing that it is just as easy to find specifications and invariants for the flight control software of a real aircraft as it is for a sorting algorithm, or indeed that finding specifications and invariants will be a major activity in real industrial work. On the contrary, it turns out that finding requirements (i.e., determining what kind of system to build), structuring the system (modular design), understanding what has already been done (reading documentation and talking to others), and organizing the efforts of a large team, are all much more important for a large system development effort.

Nevertheless, we hope that having a precise understanding of programming constructs and of what programs mean will be a good basis for further professional development. In particular, we hope that the way we use OBJ for specification can be an inspiration for documentation, and that the way we use OBJ modules can be an inspiration for structuring large programs. We also hope that the material covered in the course will be useful to those who wish to design new languages, new computers, new operating systems, etc., or to develop new theories and formal methods that support such endeavours in software engineering. We believe that the sort of algebraic approach developed in the course is particularly promising for such efforts, and we hope to provide a foundation for approaching the large literature that applies algebraic techniques in computing science in general and to formal methods in particular.

Notes

1. Meseguer's so-called "logical semantics" for the λ-calculus (Meseguer, 1991) is abstract in a similar way.

2. Although it is not discussed in the course, it is possible to mechanise this translation using OBJ itself; see Goguen (1996).

3. These properties can also be proved using OBJ, since inductive proofs of properties of data types are very similar to proofs of invariants of programs. This is not emphasized in our course, but it is discussed in Goguen (1996).

4. Such variables are sometimes called "ghost variables".

5. Indeed, this is how it was historically introduced (independently) by Turing and von Neumann.

6. "OBJ" refers to the general design, while "OBJ3" refers to a specific implementation.

References

Backhouse, R. (1986) *Program Construction and Verification*, Prentice Hall International Series in Computer Science, Hemel Hempstead.

Dijkstra, E.W. (1975) Guarded commands, nondeterminacy and formal derivation of programs, *Communications of the ACM*, **18**:453–457.

Dijkstra, E.W. (1976) *A Discipline of Programming*, Prentice Hall, Englewood Cliffs, NJ.

Engeler, E. (1971) Structure and meaning of elementary programs. In E. Engeler, editor, *Symposium on Semantics of Algorithmic Languages*, pp 89–101, Lecture Notes in Computer Science **188**, Springer Verlag, New York.

Floyd, R.W. (1967) Assigning meanings to programs. In J. Schwartz, editor, *Proceedings, Symposia Applied Mathematics* **19**:19–32, American Mathematical Society.

Goguen, J.A. (1996) *Theorem Proving and Algebra*, MIT Press, Cambridge, MA, to appear.

Goguen, J.A. and Luqi (1995) Formal methods and social context in software development. In P. Mosses, M. Neilsen and M. Schwartzbach, editors, *Proceedings, Sixth International Joint Conference on Theory and Practice of Software Development*, pp 62–81, Lecture Notes in Computer Science **915**, Springer Verlag, New York.

Goguen, J.A. and Malcolm, G. (1994) Proof of correctness of object representations. In A.W. Roscoe, editor, *A Classical Mind: Essays in Honour of C.A.R. Hoare*, pp 119–142, Prentice Hall International Series in Computer Science, Hemel Hempstead.

Goguen, J.A. and Malcolm, G. (1996) *Algebraic Semantics of Imperative Programs*, MIT Press, Cambridge, MA, to appear.

Goguen, J.A., Thatcher, J. and Wagner, E. (1978) An initial algebra approach to the specification, correctness and implementation of abstract data types. In R. Yeh, editor, *Current Trends in Programming Methodology IV*, pp 80–149, Prentice Hall, Englewood Cliffs, NJ. Previously published as Technical Report RC 6487, IBM T.J. Watson Research Center, October 1976.

Goguen, J.A., Winkler, T., Meseguer, J., Futatsugi, K. and Jouannaud, J.-P. (1996) Introducing OBJ. In J.A. Goguen and G. Malcolm, editors, *Case Studies in Algebraic Specification using OBJ*, Cambridge University Press, Cambridge, to appear.

Goldstine, H. and von Neumann, J. (1949) Planning and coding of problems for an electronic computing instrument. In A. Traub, editor, *Collected Works of J. von Neumann*, pp 80–151, Pergamon Press, Oxford. Previously published as a report of the US Ordinance Department.

Gordon, M.J.C. (1979) *The Denotation Description of Programming Languages*, Springer Verlag, New York.

Gries, D. (1981) *The Science of Programming*, Springer Verlag, New York.

Hoare, C.A.R. (1969) An axiomatic basis for computer programming, *Communications of the ACM*, **12**(10):576–580, October.

Hoare, C.A.R., Spivey, J.M., Hayes, I., He., J., Morgan, C.C., Roscoe, A.W., Saunders, J., Sorenson, I. and Sufrin, B. (1987) Laws of programming, *Communications of the ACM*, **30**(8):672–686, August.

Jones, C.B. (1986) *Systematic Software Development using VDM*, Prentice Hall International Series in Computer Science, Hemel Hempstead.

Malcolm, G. and Goguen, J.A. (1994) *Proving Correctness of Refinement and Implementation*, Technical Monograph PRG-114, Programming Research Group, Oxford University Computing Laboratory.

Malcolm, G. and Goguen, J.A. (1995) *Algebraic Semantics of Nondeterministic Choice*, Technical Report PRG-TR-5-95, Programming Research Group, Oxford University Computing Laboratory.

McCarthy, J. (1962) Towards a mathematical science of computation. In *Information Processing ù62*, pp 21–28, North-Holland, Amsterdam.

Meseguer, J. (1991) Conditional rewriting logic: deduction, models and concurrency. In S. Kaplan and M. Okada, editors, *Conditional and Typed Rewriting Systems*, pp 64–91, Lecture Notes in Computer Science **516**, Springer Verlag, New York.

Plotkin, G. (1981) *A Structural Approach to Operational Semantics*, Technical Report DAIMI FN-19, Computer Science Department, Aarhus University, September.

Reynolds, J.C. (1981) *The Craft of Programming*, Prentice Hall, Englewood Cliffs, NJ.

Scott, D. and Strachey, C. (1971) Towards a mathematical semantics for computer languages. In *Proceedings, 21st Symposium on Computers and Automata*, pp 19–46, Polytechnic Institute of Brooklyn. Also available as Technical Monograph PRG-6, Programming Research Group, Oxford University Computing Laboratory.

Stoy, J. (1977) *Denotational Semantics of Programming Languages: The Scott-Strachey Approach to Programming Language Theory*, MIT Press, Cambridge, MA.

Turing, A.M. (1949) Checking a large routine. In *Report of a Conference on High Speed Automatic Calculating Machines*, pp 67–69, University Mathematical Laboratory, University of Cambridge.

Appendix
Executing the proof score

In a certain sense, not only our course, but also this paper is executable! OBJ3 has a facility that extracts OBJ code from an arbitrary text file and then executes it. The (unedited) result of using this facility on the LaTeX source file for this paper is given below. It shows OBJ3 executing the correctness proof given in the body of this paper, and outputting `true` for the initialization and loop subproofs of invariance, as expected.

```
            \|||||||||||||||||||/
            --- Welcome to OBJ3 ---
            /|||||||||||||||||||\
        OBJ3 version 2.02 built: 1992 May 18 Mon 9:57:30
          Copyright 1988,1989,1991 SRI International
                 1995 Nov 5 Sun 16:59:11
OBJ>
==============================================
obj NAT
Warning: redefining module NAT
==============================================
obj NATOPS
==============================================
th STORE
==============================================
obj EXP
==============================================
```

```
obj PGM
============================================
th POW
============================================
reduce in POW : pow
rewrites: 7
result Pgm: 'A := a0 ; 'B := b0 ; 'C := s 0 ;
    while pos 'B do while even 'B do 'A := ('A * 'A) ;
    'B := ('B %2) od ; 'B := ('B - s 0) ;
    'C := ('C * 'A) od
============================================
open POW
============================================
eq a0 = s s 0 .
============================================
eq b0 = s s s 0 .
============================================
reduce in POW : (initial ; pow)[['C]]
rewrites: 223
result Nat: s (s (s (s (s (s (s (s 0)))))))
============================================
***> should be: 8
============================================
close
============================================
obj PROOF
============================================
open PROOF
============================================
reduce in PROOF : inv(s ; init)
rewrites: 27
result Bool: true
============================================
***> should be: true
============================================
close
============================================
open PROOF
============================================
eq ( a ** b ) * c = a0 ** b0 .
============================================
eq pos b = true .
============================================
eq even b = true .
============================================
```

```
reduce in PROOF : inv(s ; inner)
rewrites: 27
result Bool: true
===========================================
***> should be: true
===========================================
close
===========================================
open PROOF
===========================================
eq ( a ** b ) * c = a0 ** b0 .
===========================================
eq even b = false .
===========================================
***> therefore by [lemma3]:
===========================================
eq pos b = true .
===========================================
reduce in PROOF : inv(s ; step)
rewrites: 31
result Bool: true
===========================================
***> should be: true
===========================================
close
OBJ> Bye.
```

Improving the curriculum through the teaching of calculation and discrimination

11.1   The current state of programming

There is real concern, and not only on the part of computer scientists, with the lack of rigor and accountability in software engineering.

For example, consider the report (GPO, 1989) by the subcommittee on Investigations and Oversight of the House of Representatives Committee on Science, Space, and Technology, which addresses problems of software system safety, reliability, and quality. This report, in part, criticizes the universities for providing inadequate education for software engineers both in their discipline and in ethical training related to their discipline. Cherniavsky, in commenting and summarizing this report in an article in *Computing Research News* (Cherniavsky, 1990), says the following:

> ... [there is] a fundamental difference between software engineers and other engineers. Engineers are well trained in the mathematics necessary for good engineering. Software engineers are not trained in the disciplines necessary to assure high quality software. ... The problem is not so much not having the mathematics necessary to solve the software problem, but instead having the trained software engineers.

As another example, a report on the research agenda for software engineering (Computer Science and Technology Board, 1990) indicates the need for strengthened mathematical foundations in the work force:

> In the absence of a stronger scientific and engineering foundation, complex software systems are often produced by brute force. ... As software engineers begin to envision systems that require many thousands of person-years, current pragmatic or heuristic approaches begin to appear less adequate to meet application needs. In this environment, software engineering leaders are beginning to call for more systematic approaches: More mathematics, science, and engineering are needed.

TEACHING AND LEARNING FORMAL METHODS   ISBN 0-12-349040-5

This program, instruction manual, and reference materials are sold "as is" without warranty as to their performance, merchantability, or fitness for any particular purpose. The entire risk as to the results and performance of this program is assumed by you.

However, to the original purchaser only, the publisher warrants the magnetic media on which the program is recorded to be free from defects in materials and faulty workmanship under normal use for a period of ninety days from the date of purchase.

Figure 11.1: A statement on a software product

In the face of the growing problems of developing and managing more and more complex software systems, the report calls for a more rigorous use of mathematical techniques, in the hope that this can help researchers manage and diminish complexity. Promising directions, the report says, include the application of formal methods, which involve mathematical proofs.

One symptom of the problem with software production is the lack of professionalism in the field. Few software products are guaranteed, and many products contain statements like the one in Figure 11.1. Note that this statement refuses even to refund the price of the software, should it not live up to expectations, yet there is a guarantee for the hardware!

The lack of professionalism is not isolated to software firms that develop programs for the PC market. In large corporations, one can find many instances of software written from poorly prepared requirements and specifications, where a more professional engineering practice would have been to rewrite the specification completely before beginning design and development. No professional architect, bridge builder, or car designer would work with specifications of the same shoddy nature that one finds in software engineering. Many software engineers lack the judgement to determine whether their task is well defined, or at least the sense of responsibility and confidence to complain when it isn't. One hears that software projects are larger and more complex than other classical engineering projects, but that is even more — and not less — reason to be more professional in software engineering

The maintenance of programs is another area where lack of rigor, precision, clarity, and professionalism exhibits itself. Many programs are difficult to modify in order to reflect changing specifications only because they are poorly organized, poorly written, and poorly documented.

The problem with software is not limited to the software engineering profession. As editor of several journals, most notably *Information Processing Letters*, I have read far too many papers submitted by computing scientists that contained poorly presented algorithms, which if published would force each reader to waste far too much time. I have critiqued many papers myself, showing how the algorithms could be presented more effectively. Generally, the authors have been grateful for the help, and in at least five instances I have been asked to be a co-author, simply because I made an algorithm presentable! In general, computing scientists and engineers show amazingly little ability to present algorithms effectively and are setting appallingly low standards for the next generation to follow.

Moreover, poor presentations of algorithms in texts and lectures cause a great a great waste of time and effort in courses on data structures, operating systems, compiling, and the like.

In summary, software engineering, computing, and computing education all suffer from a lack of basic mathematical skills that are needed in dealing with algorithmic concepts.

11.2 A common perception of formal methods

The formal techniques that I am discussing involve a *calculational* style of working, in which, at least part of the time, formulas of a calculus are manipulated according to the rules of that calculus. The techniques are not restricted to programming, but can be beneficial in parts of mathematics as well. (Also, they are not the only techniques needed in programming or mathematics.)

Currently, formal techniques and their application in programming are taught too late (if at all) — to programmers and software engineers in industry, to graduate students, and to upper-level undergraduates. Since these people don't have the basic skills needed to apply the techniques with any degree of success, attention has to be divided between teaching basic skills and discussing their advanced applications. Consequently, both topics suffer. To put it bluntly, graduate software engineering programs, like that at the Software Engineering Institute in Pittsburgh, are forced to spend time introducing material at the Masters degree level that should have been taught at the freshman or even high school level.

A great deal of the problem lies in the typical perception of logic as an object of study. For example, while texts on discrete mathematics for computer science students have a chapter on logic, the material is rarely used in the rest of the text. Hence, the student and the instructor come away with the feeling that the mathematical tools are of academic interest only. They have seen some of the techniques but lack skill in their use and question their applicability. Certainly, most programmers and software engineers feel this way. So much so that they vociferously voice the opinion that their problems are too big and complex to be handled by those formal, mathematical methods. The retort "We know what we want to do, and it's too big a task to formalize" is heard far too often.

Contrast this with scientists in most other fields. Have you ever heard a physicist say that their problems are too big and complex to be handled by mathematical techniques? On the contrary! The size and complexity of their problems force them to turn to mathematics for help!

The negative perception of the role of mathematical techniques in programming is not limited to programmers and software engineers. It can be heard in many computer science graduate courses and industrial short courses given by academic faculties. It is passively voiced by the authors of the far-too-many introductory programming texts that teach programming in a clumsy and awkward manner and by every algorithmicist who presents an algorithm in a less-than-effective operational style.

Chandy and Misra (1988) in their book on foundations of parallel programming, have an insightful essay on the interplay of formalism and intuition. Much programming and mathematics is inspired by intuition, they say, and that will continue. Formalism does not supplant intuition; it complements and supports intuition. Formal reasoning is not merely intuitive argument couched in mathematical notation; indeed, formal reasoning often allows us to take short cuts that have no counterparts in an informal argument. Formal reasoning also provides a degree of rigor and precision that is almost impossible to obtain using intuition alone. On the one hand, Chandra and Misra say, we should not hesitate to rely on intuition to propose programs and theorems; on the other hand, we should not hesitate to dispense with intuition in our proofs.

However, we can only make substantial use of formalisms if we have had proper education and training, and this education and training has been lacking in our undergraduate curricula.

A few years ago, I reviewed a Ph.D. thesis whose author had used a great deal of mathematical notation, but in a rather strange way. As I studied it, it dawned on me that mathematical notation was used *only to abbreviate English*. For example, a theorem would read, "$\forall$ elements $\in$ the set, $\exists$ a value satisfying property P." The proof would be in the same style, with no attempt at using the mathematics to aid in reasoning. When asked about it, the author readily admitted using mathematical notation only for abbreviating and not for helping him reason. It was quite clear to me that his education was inadequate.

Overcoming the perception that formal methods are not applicable requires a change in how and what we teach, early in the curriculum. We should be giving the students a real skill with formal methods, so that the methods become as ingrained as the techniques learned in elementary school for manipulating arithmetic expressions.

11.3   We should be teaching calculational skills

Every high school student is taught to solve word problems, like the following one.

> Mary has twice as many apples as John. Mary eats two. John throws
> half of his away because they are rotten. Mary still has twice as as
> many apples as John. How many did each have initially?

We solve this problem as follows. We first *translate the statement into a formal, mathematical notation*, in this case, into two equations. Using M and J to denote the number of apples Mary and John have initially, we write the equations

$$M \;=\; 2 * J \text{ and } M - 2 \;=\; 2 * (J/2).$$

We then *solve these equations, using methods that have been taught in class.* In this case, we can substitute $2 * J$ for M in the second equation, yielding

$$2 * J - 2 = 2 * (J/2),$$

and then solve for J, yielding $J = 2$. Substituting 2 for J in the first equation yields M: $M = 4$.

The next step is to *check the answers.* We substitute the answers $M = 4$ and $J = 2$ in the second equation and check to see if it is true:

$$
\begin{aligned}
& \quad 4 - 2 = 2 * (2/2) \\
&= \quad 2 = 2 * 1 \\
&= \quad true
\end{aligned}
$$

If an error is found while checking the answer, *we go through the calculations performed earlier to determine where a mistake was made.*

In summary, part of the mathematical method that is taught in high school goes as follows:

> **Method.** Formalize the problem; solve the problem using known techniques; check the solution; and if the solution is wrong determine where a mistake was made in formalizing or solving the problem.

Now, consider the following related problem.

> Mary has an even number of apples. Twice the number of apples that Mary has plus the number of apples that John has is some (unknown) constant C. Suppose Mary throws half her apples away. What should be done with John's apples so that twice the number of apples that Mary has plus the number of apples that John has is still C?

This kind of problem occurs fairly frequently in programming. For example, the body of a loop typically makes progress towards termination (throw half of Mary's apples away), and some other statements are needed to maintain a loop invariant (what should be done with John's apples?). The problem can be formalized as the problem of finding an expression E that makes the following Hoare triple valid:

$$\{even(M) \land 2 * M + J = C\} \; M, J := M \, div \, 2, E \; \{2 * M + J = C\} \quad (11.1)$$

Instead of using the general method for solving this problem, most computing scientists would guess the answer, would test the answer by running on a computer or hand simulating, and, if a mistake were detected, would guess another answer. There would be no formalization, no calculation, and, upon finding an error, no attempt to determine the mistake made during the calculation.

This, we believe, is at the heart of the problem in software engineering. There is no attempt to teach methods for formalizing, for solving by calculation, and for checking calculations. The field relies far too much on intuition and guessing.

Problem (11.1) can actually be solved quite simply. It is equivalent to solving for E in

$$even(M) \land 2*M+J = C \Rightarrow wp(\text{``}M, J := M \, div \, 2, E\text{''}, \; 2*M+J = C) \, (11.2)$$

which can be solved by setting aside the antecedent and manipulating the consequent:

$$wp(\text{``}M, J := M \operatorname{div} 2, E\text{''}, \ 2 * M + J = C)$$
$$= \quad \langle \text{Use definition of} := \text{and textual substitution} \rangle$$
$$2 * (M \operatorname{div} 2) + E = C$$
$$= \quad \langle \text{Use antecedent to replace } C \rangle$$
$$2 * (M \operatorname{div} 2) + E = 2 * M + J$$
$$= \quad \langle \text{Solve for } E, \text{ using the fact that } M \text{ is even} \rangle$$
$$E = M + J$$

This example is only the tip of the tip of the iceberg with regard to calculation in programming. Many more examples could be given to show the use of formalizing and calculating, dealing with assignments, loops, recursive functions, and the like.

Here is another example of the use of calculation, due to Dijkstra, which deals with mathematical induction. Generally speaking, students are taught how to perform mathematical induction over the natural numbers. They are not taught *why* it works, and they are not taught how it generalizes to other sets and relations besides the natural numbers and operation $<$.

One can give the students a far better feel for mathematical induction, as well as some more education in formal manipulation, by proving to them that the validity of the principle of mathematical induction over a set U and relation $<$ is equivalent to the pair $(U, <)$ being well founded.

$(U, <)$ is well founded means that every nonempty subset of U contains a minimal element (according to $<$). Using S to denote an arbitrary subset of U, we write this formally as

$$\neg empty(S) \ \equiv \ (\exists y :: y \in S \land (\forall x : x < y : x \notin S)) \tag{11.3}$$

On the other hand, mathematical induction can be formalized as follows (P is a boolean function, or predicate, of one argument, and $P.x$ denotes its application to x):

$$(\forall x : x \in U : P.x) \ \equiv \ (\forall y : y \in U : (\forall x : x < y : P.x) \Rightarrow P.y) \tag{11.4}$$

which, by the laws of implication and De Morgan, is equivalent to

$$(\forall x : x \in U : P.x) \ \equiv \ (\forall y : y \in U : P.y \lor (\exists x : x < y : \neg P.x)) \tag{11.5}$$

In Figure 11.2, we prove using a calculational style that well foundedness and the principle of mathematical induction are equivalent. I can attest to the fact that this proof is well within the grasp of junior computer science majors, so much so that they can repeat it on a test. Further, my experience leads me to believe that, with proper education, freshmen will have little difficulty mastering it.

Consider another example, taken from a draft of a text on discrete mathematics, written for computer scientists by mathematicians. Figure 11.3 is a proof, from the text, that the composition of binary relations is associative. Note that the proof is given basically in English and that it requires *two* proofs, the so-called "if" and "only if" parts.

Theorem. Well foundedness and the validity of mathematical induction are equivalent.

Proof. We have

$$(11.3)$$
$$= \quad \langle \text{Definition} \rangle$$
$$\neg empty(S) \equiv (\exists y :: y \in S \wedge (\forall x : x < y : x \notin S))$$
$$= \quad \langle \text{Complement both sides, use Negation and De Morgan} \rangle$$
$$empty(S) \equiv (\forall y :: y \notin S \vee (\exists x : x < y : x \in S))$$
$$= \quad \langle \text{Define a predicate } P\text{: } P.x \equiv (x \notin S);$$
$$\quad \text{replace occurrences of } S \text{ by } P \rangle$$
$$(\forall x : x \in U : P.x) \equiv (\forall y : y \in U : P.y \vee (\exists (x : x < y : \neg P.x))$$
$$= \quad \langle \text{The above formula is 11.5} \rangle$$
$$(11.5)$$

Since one can argue that for every set S there exists a predicate $P.x \equiv (x \notin S)$, and for every predicate P one can define the corresponding set S, we have proved the theorem.

Figure 11.2: Proof of equivalence of well foundedness and math induction

---

Theorem. Composition of binary relations is associative: $\rho \circ (\sigma \circ \theta) = (\rho \circ \sigma) \circ \theta$.

Proof. Let $(a, d) \in \rho \circ (\sigma \circ \theta)$. Then there is a b such that $(a, b) \in \rho$ and $(b, d) \in \sigma \circ \theta$. This means that there exists c such that $(b, c) \in \sigma$ and $(c, d) \in \theta$. Therefore, we have $(a, c) \in \rho \circ \sigma$, which implies $(a, d) \in (\rho \circ \sigma) \circ \theta$. This shows that

$$\rho \circ (\sigma \circ \theta) \subset (\rho \circ \sigma) \circ \theta \tag{11.6}$$

Conversely, let $(a, d) \in (\rho \circ \sigma) \circ \theta$. There is a c such that $(a, c) \in \rho \circ \sigma$ and $(c, d) \in \theta$. This implies the existence of a b for which $(a, b) \in \rho$ and $(b, c) \in \sigma$. For this b we have $(b, d) \in \theta$, which gives $(a, d) \in \rho \circ (\sigma \circ \theta)$. We have proven the reverse inclusion

$$(\rho \circ \sigma) \circ \theta \subset \rho \circ (\sigma \circ \theta) \tag{11.7}$$

which gives the associativity of relation composition.

Figure 11.3: A mathematician's proof of associativity of relation composition

---

Theorem. Composition of binary relations is associative: $\rho \circ (\sigma \circ \theta) = (\rho \circ \sigma) \circ \theta$.

Proof. We show that (a, d) is in $\rho \circ (\sigma \circ \theta)$ exactly when it is in $(\rho \circ \sigma) \circ \theta$.

$$(a, d) \in \rho \circ (\sigma \circ \theta)$$
$$= \quad \langle \text{Definition of } \rho \circ (\sigma \circ \theta) \rangle$$
$$(a, b) \in \rho \text{ and } (b, d) \in \sigma \circ \theta \quad \text{for some } b$$
$$= \quad \langle \text{Definition of } \sigma \circ \theta \rangle$$
$$(a, b) \in \rho \text{ and } (b, c) \in \sigma \text{ and } (c, d) \in \theta \quad \text{for some } b, c$$
$$= \quad \langle \text{Definition of } \rho \circ \sigma \rangle$$
$$(a, c) \in \rho \circ \sigma \text{ and } (c, d) \in \theta \quad \text{for some } c$$
$$= \quad \langle \text{Definition of } (\rho \circ \sigma) \circ \theta \rangle$$
$$(a, d) \in (\rho \circ \sigma) \circ \theta$$

Figure 11.4: A calculational proof of associativity of relation composition

A calculational proof of the same theorem is given in Figure 11.4. It is shorter, and it shows directly the equivalence of $\rho \circ (\sigma \circ \theta)$ and $(\rho \circ \sigma) \circ \theta$. It is easier to internalize, since it follows a form that is common to many proofs of properties: replace a notation by its definition, manipulate, and reintroduce the notation.

In showing these examples of a calculational style of proof or development, I am attempting to convince that the style has broad application and that it results in crisper, shorter, and more precise work. I am not advocating the formal proof of correctness of all programs. I am simply arguing that acquiring calculational skill can produce a marked change in one's perception and use of formal methods.

In developing a calculational skill, one learns that formalization can lead to crisper and more precise descriptions. One learns that the form of the formalization can itself lend insight into developing a solution. One acquires the urge to clarify and simplify, to seek the right notation in which to express a problem. One acquires a frame of mind that encourages precision and rigor. This frame of mind can have a strikingly beneficial effect on whatever work one does later as a professional in computing.

11.4   We should be teaching discrimination

Generally speaking, our text books in computing, and hence our courses, teach facts. We teach a programming language. We teach sets, relations, functions, graphs, logic, Turing machines, automata, and formal languages. We teach a few data structures, compiler construction, operating systems, and so forth.

In few places in the undergraduate curriculum do we discuss judgement and discrimination. For example, rarely do we compare the advantages and disadvantages of two styles, or several different methods for performing a task. Or introduce different notations and discuss the contexts in which each is better, the reasons for their existence, and their history. Or ask students to compare two proofs. Rarely are formal and informal techniques for the same problem juxtaposed.

As a result, many students think they have learned the way the science is, has to be, and will be in the future. They haven't learned that the science is a living thing, which changes and grows. They haven't learned to question, to think for themselves, to discriminate.

Some students go on to graduate school and, through research, begin to think as scientists or engineers. The majority, however, do not, and the computing profession is poorer for it. We end up with professionals who are unable to make technical decisions on technical grounds. This is unfortunate, because judging and choosing based on technical merit seem to be important in computing, with its many different languages and styles — and particularly in software engineering.

Thus, in the introductory courses, I would place more emphasis on style, taste, making choices based on technical reasons, and comparing advantages and disadvantages. Here are examples of what I mean.

Three ways of proving an implication $X \Rightarrow Y$ are (0) transform it to *true* using equivalence transformations; (1) assume X true and, using its conjuncts as new axioms, transform Y to *true*; and (2) assume Y false and prove X false. A course may look at all three methods, but rarely is there any real discussion and comparison of them. The students are simply shown the three methods and given a *different* example of each, and are then expected automatically to be able to choose the appropriate one from then on.

Consider the problem of proving $\neg P \equiv P \equiv false$, given various axioms and theorems, among them being the following three:

Axiom 0 $(\neg P \equiv P) \equiv \neg(P \equiv P)$

Axiom 1 $P \equiv P \equiv true$

Axiom 2 $\neg true \equiv false$

Below are two proofs done by students in a course of mine, in which the majority of the students already had B.S. degrees in computer science. The left-hand proof was the predominant one, even though it is longer — it requires the copying of "$\equiv false$" on every formula except the last.

$$
\begin{array}{ll}
\neg P \equiv P \equiv false & \\
= \quad \langle \text{Axiom 0} \rangle & \\
\neg(P \equiv P) \equiv false & \\
= \quad \langle \text{Axiom 1} \rangle & \\
\neg true \equiv false & \\
= \quad \langle \text{Axiom 1} \rangle & \\
true &
\end{array}
\qquad
\begin{array}{ll}
\neg P \equiv P & \\
= \quad \langle \text{Axiom 0} \rangle & \\
\neg(P \equiv P) & \\
= \quad \langle \text{Axiom 1} \rangle & \\
\neg true & \\
= \quad \langle \text{Axiom 1} \rangle & \\
false &
\end{array}
$$

Do you think this example too trivial to dwell on? If we don't teach students to search for the simplest and shortest solutions on small problems, how will

Definition (Decreasing finite-chain property). Consider function $DCF.y$ defined by

$$DCF.y \equiv \text{'Every decreasing chain beginning with } y \text{ is finite'} \qquad (11.8)$$

$(U, <)$ has the decreasing finite-chain property iff $DCF.y$ holds for all y in U.

Lemma. $(U, <)$ is well founded iff the finite-chain property holds.

Proof: The proof of this lemma is trivial.

Theorem. $(U, <)$ admits induction iff if it is well founded.

Proof. We prove the two directions separately. First, we assume $(U, <)$ is well founded and prove

$$(\forall(y :: P.y \lor \exists(x : x < y : \neg P.x)) \Rightarrow (\forall(x :: P.x) \qquad (11.9)$$

Let P be a predicate on U that satisfies the antecedent of the implication in 11.9. Consider the set S defined as $\{x \mid \neg P.x\}$. Establishing that S is empty will prove one direction of the theorem.

Suppose that S is non-empty. Since $(U, <)$ is well founded, S has a minimal element u (say). We show a contradiction, which proves that the assumption that S is not empty is false. Since u is a minimal element of S, every element of U that is less than u cannot be in S; i.e. every such element satisfies P. Then, by our assumption about P, it follows that u satisfies P. In other words, u is not in S, which is the desired contradiction.

For the other direction, we assume that $(U, <)$ admits induction (i.e. 11.9 holds for all P) and show that it is well founded. We assert (without formal proof) that the following is a tautology: either $DCF.y$ holds or there exists an x such that $x < y$ and $\neg DCF.x$ holds:

$$\forall(y :: DCF.y \lor \exists(x : x < y : \neg DCF.x)) \qquad (11.10)$$

Using the induction principle, we conclude by mathematical induction that $\forall(x :: DCF.x)$ holds. By the lemma, $(U, <)$ is well founded.

Figure 11.5: Alternative proof of equivalence of induction and well foundedness

they learn to do it on larger ones? Through many exercises, discussions, and comparisons, we can get students to see that a choice can make a big difference, and that they should seek the best choice in each situation.

The conventional mathematical notation for function application is $f(x, y)$. We also use infix notation $x f y$ (for some functions), postfix notation $x y f$, the notation $(f\ x\ y)$ used in some functional languages, the notion of currying, and a newer notation $f.x.y$, with which some computing scientists are experimenting. These notations could be discussed and compared, and each one could be used in the context in which it is most appropriate.

For the ancient Greeks, numbering began with 2. In the modern world, most people think the numbers start with 1. However, there are good technical reasons for beginning with 0, and these can be discussed in detail.

In Figure 11.2, we provided a calculational proof of equivalence of the validity of mathematical induction in a universe $(U, <)$ and well foundedness of $(U, <)$. Some mathematicians and computer scientists would rather see a more English-style proof, with more "intuition". Such a proof, done by a colleague of mine, is given in Figure 11.5. In discussing the differences in the two proofs, the students will begin to develop their own sense of judgement and discrimination. (I am amazed at how many people like the proof in Figure 11.5 better, but they never have an answer to my argument that the proof in Figure 11.2 is shorter and, more importantly, *far* easier to internalize and then to repeat to others. Basically, one needs to know the definitions of well foundedness and mathematical induction and to be able to translate these definitions into logical formulae. Thereafter, simple manipulations are used to translate one into the other, and the shapes of the formulae help tremendously in this translation. Heuristics can be taught that help one gain skill in such manipulations.)

Compare two formulas for expressing mathematical induction: (11.9), in Figure 11.5 and (11.4). One uses an implication and the other an equivalence. Why the difference? Which is better? Does it matter? Which of the two proofs in Figures 11.2 and 11.5 proof is shorter? Which is easier to internalize, so that one can repeat it without having to read it again? Why is one longer than the other?

There will be other situations where the better technique or method is not so clear, and discussions with students will begin to build discrimination based on technical reasons.

One should also illustrate from time to time how our experiences and habits with syntactic formalisms can hurt or help. For example, is the following, in which x, y, and z are integers, true or false? After determining the answer, try it out on your friends; see how long it takes them to solve this problem and what techniques they use in doing so.

$$x > z \;\Rightarrow\; x > y \;\lor\; y > z$$

As another example, consider the following problem, due to Wim Feijen. Let $x \max y$ denote the maximum of x and y. Is the following true or false, and how do you prove it?

$$x + y \geq x \max y \;\equiv\; x \geq 0 \land y \geq 0 \tag{11.11}$$

Before looking at the solution given below, try to solve this problem yourself. Be conscious of the techniques you apply.

Often, one attempts to devise a proof by looking at examples, or by performing a case analysis of one sort or another. A better approach may be to depend on a formal definition of max, one that allows for calculation. We can define max by

$$z \geq x \max y \quad \equiv \quad z \geq x \ \wedge \ z \geq y \quad \text{for all } z.$$

Then we manipulate the left-hand side of (11.11) as follows:

$$\begin{aligned}
& x + y \geq x \max y \\
= \quad & \langle \text{Definition of max} \rangle \\
& x + y \geq x \ \wedge \ x + y \geq y \\
= \quad & \langle \text{Arithmetic} \rangle \\
& y \geq 0 \ \wedge \ x \geq 0
\end{aligned}$$

Thus, by relying on formal definitions and calculation, we see in an extremely simple manner that (11.11) is true.

11.5   Overhauling the beginning of the CS major

In many undergraduate computer science programs, a second programming course (the one beyond the remedial first course) is followed by a course in discrete mathematics. The second programming course teaches analysis of algorithms, recursion, abstract data types, a bit about correctness proofs, abstraction and design, and the like, sometimes using a functional approach (Abelson and Sussman, 1985; Bird and Wadler, 1988). The discrete-math course teaches logic, relations, sets, formal languages, automata theory, combinatorics, and graph theory. Much of the theory taught in discrete mathematics could be applied in the programming course, but the order in which the material is presented conveys the opposite impression! Rightly so, many students question the usefulness of the discrete mathematics courses they have to take. Rarely does either course teach skill in formal manipulation or attempt to convey a sense of judgement and discrimination.

I suggest merging the contents of the two courses into a two-semester course and, at each stage, teaching theory and then putting it into practice. My choice for the first topic would be five to six weeks worth of mathematical logic, taught so that the students acquire a *skill* in calculation. Completeness, nonstandard logics, and so forth would not be taught at this time; instead, the emphasis would be on the acquisition of skill in formal manipulation. This topic would form the basis for a calculational style of thinking that would permeate the whole two-course sequence. I would rely on references like Dijkstra and Scholten (1990) and van Gasteren (1988), which place importance on the form or shape of mathematical arguments in developing heuristics and techniques for shortening and simplifying proofs. They deal with method, rather than simply with facts.

Thereafter, the course could teach the conventional topics, but in a way that would rely on the calculational skill just acquired. The proof of equivalence of mathematical induction and well foundedness when dealing with mathematical induction is an example. Also, since the students would have a thorough knowledge of logic, it would be far easier to teach about specifications of a program, the theory of correctness of programs, and the like, and then to put it all into practice.

In such a two-semester course, I would teach both functional and imperative algorithmic styles, illustrating the advantages and disadvantages of each and pointing out similarities in developmental methods for the two. The functional style would probably come first, for it is a simple step from teaching mathematical induction to talking about and manipulating recursive functions. The imperative approach would enter the picture when talking about economy of space and time.

One of the key notions for computer science is *abstraction*. Abstraction seems to be more important to us than to mathematicians — at least we talk about it more. The functional approach seems more appropriate for conveying a sense abstraction, for building larger program units out of smaller ones. This, however, may be due more to the status of our current understanding of programming notations than to anything else.

There is the age-old problem of giving the students more experience with "real" languages and programming assignments. Where it makes sense, applications of theory should be backed up by computer-based assignments. However, we should not let the problems of our implemented languages, with all their idiosyncracies, dictate the concepts and their applications that we teach. In fact, it would not be so bad if the students began to feel frustrated with some of the languages and implementations that they are forced to use. Exposing the students to several different implemented programming notations within the two-semester course would help them to see the value of knowing several notations and the contexts in which each is useful.

One does have to be careful with the students' time. Too many instructors are insensitive to the fact that students take several courses and have limited time for each. They glory in giving a difficult and time-consuming course and pride themselves on the number of students who drop it. Programming assignments especially are often out of control, because instructors expect too much without giving the students the skill needed to do them effectively (a skill that the instructors often don't have themselves, because of their own poor education.)

This macho attitude endears the student neither to the instructor nor to the content of the course. It serves little purpose except to falsely boost the ego of the instructor. Instead, the aim should be to structure our teaching and homework so that the students can learn the maximum amount in the minimum amount of time.

11.6   On method and design

These days, the notion of an algorithm, as well as some skill in programming, is important in almost every scientific and engineering field. More and more research and practice deals with implementing ideas on the computer and requires the presentation of algorithms.

The computer science viewpoint has also affected some fields of mathematics. New research ideas have sprung from computer scientists' use of logic. Constructive logic has become an area of hot activity, due to its use in extracting programs from proofs. Computational complexity has excited many a mathematician. Category theory is finding applications in computing. All sorts of mathematical concepts are becoming more and more important in applications such as graphics and robotics, requiring mathematicians and computer scientists to work side by side.

In this context, it appears to me that the proposed two-semester course, which includes programming as well as mathematics from a computer-science viewpoint, would be of interest to both engineers and mathematicians.

However, there are even stronger reasons for students from mathematics and engineering to take the proposed course. Let us consider the mathematics student first.

It was the mathematician Morris Kline who said, "More than anything else, mathematics is Method." Yet, few courses in mathematics attempt to teach method, and many mathematicians don't even think it can be taught. Rather, they think that method is something one learns in a rather unconscious fashion over the years. (Pólya, of course, was interested in method and wrote several illuminating books on the subject.)

I believe that one *can* furnish the student with some idea of method quite early in the game and that this may give the student more of a sense of appreciation for mathematics and how it is done. The simple heuristics that we can teach concerning syntactic calculations in proofs and programs, along with a sense of discrimination, can be of tremendous help to the student. (Of course, we should not convey the idea that all proofs arise simply out of following a few heuristics.)

Computing, like most fields that have been shown to be amenable to mathematical treatment, has benefited greatly from that mathematical treatment. And, like those fields, computing has repaid the debt by enriching mathematics with new areas of concern and new problems to tackle. But another kind of enrichment stands out in my mind: the emphasis on method that is associated with calculational approach to proofs and programs. The calculational approach is not really new, of course, and many mathematical proofs have been given in it. What is new is the sense of its pervasiveness and its ability to simplify, which comes by treating the propositional and predicate calculi as calculational systems and using them throughout other areas of mathematics, wherever appropriate.

Now let us consider the proposed course as it relates to engineering. The main activity that is supposed to separate engineering from other fields is *design*: the actual activity of preparing plans for some object (a bridge, radio, electronic circuit, whatever). Within the engineering curriculum, design is viewed as a pervasive, pragmatic activity. During design, the student is particularly encouraged to learn to deal with issues of structure and to evaluate designs with regard to different measures, such as cost, time, complexity, reliability, and ease of production.

In this regard, I believe that the two-course sequence that I am proposing could be an important part of the engineering curriculum. First, it attempts to teach something about the design of (some form of) proofs, giving the students heuristics for their construction and a few ways of comparing them (e.g. with regard to simplicity, length, structure). It helps make the student more aware of choices and the need for discrimination. Second it attempts to teach about the design of programs, using principles and heuristics for algorithmic development that arise out of a theory of program correctess. The need for rigorous specifications before designing a program becomes clear. The use of different notations, each with its suitable domain of discourse, is discussed. The use of abstraction to help structure programs, as well as discussions of notations for expressing structuring, is expounded upon. Comparison of algorithms with regard to time and space requirements, structure, simplicity, and the like is an important activity. Laboratories, in which the students receive practical experience, are an integral part of the course.

Thus, aside from the obvious benefit of more (and useful) mathematical formalism in the engineering curriculum, the second benefit would come from the notion of design based on theoretical principles, which is so evident in the proposed course.

11.7 The effect on more advanced courses

Providing a solid mathematical foundation and a skill in manipulation can have a profound effect on later courses. The presentation of almost *any* algorithm becomes easier when the instructor and student share a common basis for the specification and presentation of programs in a rigorous and calculational manner —rather than the ineffective operational approach that is so prevalent today. The idea behind an algorithm can be conveyed more effectively and in less time, and often it is the idea rather than the whole algorithm that counts. Thus, the increased understanding of the students should allow us to cover more material and to compress some of the courses in our burgeoning curricula.

Courses that would be most directly affected by the proposed change in the introductory course are assembly language programming and machine architecture, data structures, algorithms, computational complexity, compiler construction, and operating systems, since they deal most directly with the development and presentation of algorithms.

11.8 In conclusion

Software engineering, and to some extent the rest of computing, suffers from a lack of rigor and professionalism, which stems partly from the belief that formal methods in algorithmic analysis, development, and presentation are useless. As long as computing is taught in a manner that conveys the impression that formal methods are useless, students will believe that formal methods are useless. The calculational methods that have been developed in the past fifteen years offer hope that the situation can be changed.

Thus far, there has been little experience in teaching this material to freshmen in the United States, so at this point my opinion that the suggested changes will help is more a matter of faith than fact. That faith, however, is based on the solid experiences of myself and others in using the calculational style in their own programming, in the presentation of programs, and in the teaching of programming.

Calculational techniques deserve to be given a fair chance, especially since nothing else has appeared on the horizon to solve the ills of the profession. Let us all learn more about calculational techniques and gain a skill with them, and then let us begin to teach computing using them. Then, the 1990's may see the drastic revisions of our texts and lower level courses that are needed to effect the change.

References

Abelson, H. and Sussman, G.J. (1985) *Structure and Interpretation of Computer Programs*, MIT Press, Cambridge, MA.

Bird, R. and Wadler, P. (1988) *Introduction to Functional Programming*, Prentice Hall International Series in Computer Science, Hemel Hempstead.

Chandy, K.M. and Misra, J (1988) *Parallel Program Design*, Addison-Wesley, Menlo Park, CA.

Cherniavsky, J.C. (1990) Software failures attract congressional attention. *Computing Research News*, **2**(1):4–5, January.

Computer Science and Technology Board (1990) Scaling up: a research agenda for software engineering, Report of the Computer Science and Technology Board, National Academy Press. Excerpted in *Communications of the ACM*, **33**(3):281–293, March.

Dijkstra, E.W. and Scholten, C.S. (1990) *Predicate Calculus and Program Semantics*, Springer Verlag, New York.

van Gasteren, A.J.M. (1988) *On the Shape of Mathematical Arguments*. Ph.D. thesis, Technical University Eindhoven, Eindhoven, The Netherlands.

Government Printing Office (1989) Bugs in the program — problems in federal government computer software development and regulation. GPO 052-070-06604-1, Superintendent of Documents, Government Printing Office, Washington, D.C. 20402.

Gries, D. (1981) *The Science of Programming*. Springer Verlag, New York.

Programming, proving, and calculation

12.1 Introduction

It has been recognized for a long time now that formalisms are indispensable for the design of reliable, i.e. correct, programs. It has been recognized also, however, that formalization in itself is not enough: we must see to it that both the formalisms and the way in which they are used are simple enough and clear enough to be useful and teachable. This, in a nutshell, has been the primary aim of most of our work over the years, and it constitutes the main theme of the present chapter.

Such use of formalism is, for instance, illustrated by the calculational style in which the predicate calculus is used throughout the chapter. After having used the calculational format for many years, both in teaching and otherwise, we are convinced that it is a primary means for combining clarity of exposition with economy of expression.

There are three sections to this chapter. The sections on sequential (imperative) programming and multiprogramming each contain a small collection of specimens of how we teach programming to our students to date. They exemplify how sequential and parallel programs can be derived from their specifications hand in hand with their proofs of correctness. Here, the austerity and simplicity of the formalisms used, viz. predicate calculus, Hoare-triple semantics and the theory of Owicki and Gries, are of decisive importance. The section on calculational mathematics is an illustration of how we think that students can be made familiar with the calculational style.

As a prerequisite we assume the reader to be more or less familiar with the predicate calculus and with Hoare triples and their use.

12.2 A little on calculational mathematics

12.2.1 What associativity is about

We all know what it means for a binary operator Δ to be associative:

$$(a \, \Delta \, b) \, \Delta \, c \; = \; a \, \Delta \, (b \, \Delta \, c).$$

Now, if you interview people, asking them what associativity is really about, one of the first answers you get is that it is allowed to omit the parentheses and write

$$a \,\Delta\, b \,\Delta\, c$$

without introducing ambiguity. And this is right!

Next you may get the answer that thanks to the associativity it does not matter whether the value of $a \,\Delta\, b \,\Delta\, c$ is computed from left to right or from right to left. And you may get several other answers, but hardly ever the one to be explained next.

For people that calculate, the property of associativity may offer very strong heuristic guidance in proof construction : if, in a calculation, the expression

$$a \,\Delta\, b \,\Delta\, c$$

enters the picture as

$$(a \,\Delta\, b) \,\Delta\, c,$$

then the advice for the next step(s) is to focus on the subexpression $b \,\Delta\, c$ in

$$a \,\Delta\, (b \,\Delta\, c).$$

In our experience, this heuristic rule has worked well in a tremendous number of cases. And if you come to think of it: of course, what else could associativity be about?

The proof of the pudding is in the eating, and we shall now present the proof of a FANTASTIC theorem that our colleague Paul F. Hoogendijk challenged us to prove one day. The theorem is FANTASTIC to the extent that we have absolutely no idea what the mathematics involved "means".

In what follows, constant Γ and dummies x and y are of type Thing. Further, Λ and E map Things to Things, and, last but not least, binary operator $\circ$, which maps two Things on a Thing, is associative. In short, in the ensuing expressions there is no type conflict.

Now, given (0) and (1)

(0)	$x = \Lambda.y \;\equiv\; \Gamma \circ x = y$	$(\forall x, y)$
(1)	$E.x = \Lambda.(x \circ \Gamma)$	$(\forall x)$

we have to prove

(2)	$E.x \circ \Lambda.y \;=\; \Lambda.(x \circ y)$	$(\forall x, y)$

Proof   Property (0) is a so-called *Galois connection* and the advice is that we then always write down the corresponding *cancellation rules* as well (Aarts, 1992). Here they are (instantiate (0) with $x := \Lambda.y$ and $y := \Gamma \circ x$, respectively, so as to make one side vacuously true) :

(3)	$\Gamma \circ \Lambda.y = y$	$(\forall y)$
(4)	$x = \Lambda.(\Gamma \circ x)$	$(\forall x)$

Now we tackle (2) and, for this occasion, we shall make the steps that appeal to the associativity of $\circ$ explicit.

$$E.x \circ \Lambda.y \;=\; \Lambda.(x \circ y)$$

$\equiv$ $\qquad$ { (0) from left to right }

$$\Gamma \circ (E.x \circ \Lambda.y) \;=\; x \circ y$$

$\equiv$ $\qquad$ { $\circ$ is associative }

$$(\Gamma \circ E.x) \circ \Lambda.y \;=\; x \circ y$$

$\equiv$ $\qquad$ { (1) to eliminate E }

$$(\Gamma \circ \Lambda.(x \circ \Gamma)) \circ \Lambda.y \;=\; x \circ y$$

$\equiv$ $\qquad$ { (3) with $y := x \circ \Gamma$ }

$$(x \circ \Gamma) \circ \Lambda.y \;=\; x \circ y$$

$\equiv$ $\qquad$ { $\circ$ is associative }

$$x \circ (\Gamma \circ \Lambda.y) \;=\; x \circ y$$

$\equiv$ $\qquad$ { (3) }

$$x \circ y = x \circ y$$

$\equiv$ $\qquad$ { }

$true.$

End Proof.

12.2.2 The very beginning of lattice theory

> Let's start at the very beginning.
> A very good place to start.
>
> Julie Andrews in *The Sound of Music*

For a large part, mathematics consists of exploring concepts and of investigating and proving their properties. The art of proving plays a major role in this game. Since the advent of modern computing science, it has become clear that in many branches of elementary mathematics, proofs can be beneficially rendered in a calculational format. The benefits comprise greater precision and lucidity — without loss of concision —, an enhanced view on how to separate one's concerns, and hence an improved economy of thought. Unfortunately, most textbooks on elementary mathematical issues have not (yet) adopted such a calculational style, so that yet another generation of young people will receive a mathematical education without having experienced the joy and usefulness of calculating. And this is a pity.

The purpose of this note is to transmit some of the flavour of calculation. We have selected a topic from the very beginning of lattice theory and we intend to present a treatment that can be read, understood, and hopefully enjoyed by a reasonable university freshman.

Our universe of discourse will be some fixed, anonymous set of things on which a binary relation $\leq$ (" at most") is defined. This relation we postulate to be

•	reflexive, i.c.	$x \leq x$	$(\forall x)$
•	antisymmetric, i.e.	$x \leq y \wedge y \leq x \Rightarrow x = y$	$(\forall x, y)$

Remark   In the standard literature we usually find the additional postulate that $\leq$ is

$$\text{transitive, i.e.} \qquad x \leq y \wedge y \leq z \Rightarrow x \leq z \qquad (\forall x, y, z)$$

For the time being though, we do not need the transitivity of $\leq$. Therefore, we do not introduce it now. And apart from that, it will — as we shall see — enter the picture in a totally different way.
End Remark .

Equality of things is a very important concept to have. It is as important as the notion of a function. Equality and functions are at the heart of mathematics, and they are beautifully related by the

Rule of Leibniz
For any function f,
End

The two postulates that we have of $\leq$ do not reveal very much about equality; only the antisymmetry mentions it. Therefore, the first thing to do is to collect some more facts concerning equality. The most common one is the

Rule of mutual inequality
$$x = y \; \equiv \; x \leq y \wedge y \leq x$$
End

It is an immediate restatement of $\leq$'s reflexivity and antisymmetry.

A very useful but less common statement about equality is the so-called

Rule of indirect equality
$$x = y \; \equiv \; \langle \forall z :: z \leq x \equiv z \leq y \rangle$$
End

Let us prove it. We prove it by mutual implication. (In our jargon we refer to the implication $LHS \Rightarrow RHS$ from left to right by "ping" and to $RHS \Rightarrow LHS$ by "pong".)

Proof of ping
$$x = y \Rightarrow \langle \forall z :: z \leq x \equiv z \leq y \rangle$$

$$\equiv \qquad \{ \ (P\Rightarrow) \text{ distributes over } \forall \ \}$$

$$\langle \forall z :: \ x = y \ \Rightarrow \ (z \leq x \equiv z \leq y) \rangle$$

$$\equiv \qquad \{ \text{ Rule of Leibniz, see below } \}$$

$$true$$

The function f involved in this application is the boolean function given by $f.a \equiv z \leq a$.

End Proof of ping .

Proof of pong We have to prove

$$\langle \forall z :: z \leq x \equiv z \leq y \rangle \ \Rightarrow \ x = y \ ,$$

and we do so by setting up a weakening chain of predicates that begins with the antecedent and ends with the consequent. Notice that in this chain we will quite likely have to refer to the antisymmetry of $\leq$ because this is the only property of $\leq$ that mentions the $=$symbol; and we have not used it in the ping part yet. (The latter remark is a very simple example of the kind of bookkeeping that has proved to be very useful in proof design.) Here is the chain

$$\langle \forall z :: \ z \leq x \ \equiv \ z \leq y \rangle$$

$$\Rightarrow \qquad \{ \text{ instantiate with } z := x \text{ and with } z := y \ \}$$

$$(x \leq x \equiv x \leq y) \ \wedge \ (y \leq x \equiv y \leq y)$$

$$\equiv \qquad \{ \text{ reflexivity of } \leq \ \}$$

$$x \leq y \ \wedge \ y \leq x$$

$$\Rightarrow \qquad \{ \text{ antisymmetry of } \leq \ \}$$

$$x = y$$

Notice that the first step — the instantiation — is not brilliant at all: the first line contains the symbol $\forall$ and the target line does not, so that somewhere along the way we must eliminate $\forall$. In fact, about the only rule from the predicate calculus with which one can eliminate the universal quantifier $\forall$, is the rule of instantiation. Once we are aware of this, the step is no longer a surprise. Furthermore, there is not much we can instantiate z with, viz. just x and y; and we did both in order to make the next line as strong as possible, which is beneficial if one has to construct a weakening chain.

End Proof of pong .

The rule of indirect equality has a companion, also called the rule of indirect equality. It reads

$$x = y \ \equiv \ \langle \forall z :: \ x \leq z \equiv y \leq z \rangle \ .$$

The difference is the side of the $\leq$ symbol at which x and y reside. Which of the two is to be used depends on the particular application.

So much for $\leq$ and for $=$ in our universe. We now enter lattice theory by postulating that in our universe the equation in p

$$p: \quad \langle \forall z :: \ p \leq z \ \equiv \ x \leq z \wedge y \leq z \rangle$$

has, for each x and y, at least one solution. (The inexperienced reader should not feel daunted here: in case our universe is just the universe of real numbers with the usual $\leq$ relation, the maximum of x and y may be recognized as a good candidate for p.)

The first thing we do is to show that the equation has at most one solution. This is done by showing $p = q$, for p and q solutions of the equation. Here, one of the rules of indirect equality comes in handy: for any z, we have

$$p \leq z$$

$\equiv \qquad \{\ p \ \text{is a solution}\ \}$

$$x \leq z \wedge y \leq z$$

$\equiv \qquad \{\ q \ \text{is a solution}\ \}$

$$q \leq z,$$

and, hence, $p = q$. So our equation has exactly one solution for each x and y. Therefore, that solution is a function of x and y, which we propose to denote by $x \uparrow y$ (x "up" y). In summary, we have the beautiful

(0) $\qquad x \uparrow y \leq z \ \equiv \ x \leq z \wedge y \leq z$ $\qquad\qquad (\forall x, y, z)$

(In the standard literature we find $\uparrow$ under entries like "sup" or "join" or "lub".)

Examples

♦ A well-known instance of (0) can be found in set theory. If we take set inclusion $\subseteq$ as an instance of $\leq$ — it is reflexive and antisymmetric! —, set union $\cup$ is the corresponding $\uparrow$. Indeed, we have for all sets x, y, and z,

$$x \cup y \subseteq z \ \equiv \ x \subseteq z \wedge y \subseteq z .$$

♦ Also, if we take set containment $\supseteq$ for $\leq$, set intersection is the corresponding $\uparrow$. Indeed,

$$x \cap y \supseteq z \ \equiv \ x \supseteq z \wedge y \supseteq z .$$

♦ Another well-known instance is in the predicate calculus where we have

$$[x \vee y \Rightarrow z] \ \equiv \ [x \Rightarrow z] \wedge [y \Rightarrow z] , \quad \text{and}$$
$$[x \wedge y \Leftarrow z] \ \equiv \ [x \Leftarrow z] \wedge [y \Leftarrow z] .$$

♦ From number theory we know the reflexive, antisymmetric relation denoted | ("divides"). Now, the least common multiple of x and y can see the light via

$$(x \text{ lcm } y) \mid z \;\equiv\; x \mid z \land y \mid z ,$$

and the greatest common divisor of x and y by

$$z \mid (x \text{ gcd } y) \;\equiv\; z \mid x \land z \mid y .$$

Both are instances of (0). (How?)

♦ But probably the best-known instance of (0) is when we take for $\leq$ the usual order between numbers. Then $\uparrow$ is the familiar maximum operator. We will return to this later.

End

Now let us investigate (0). We can rather straightforwardly deduce from it that

- $\uparrow$ is idempotent, i.e. $\qquad x \uparrow x = x$
- $\uparrow$ is symmetric, i.e. $\qquad x \uparrow y = y \uparrow x$
- $\uparrow$ is associative, i.e. $\qquad x \uparrow (y \uparrow z) = (x \uparrow y) \uparrow z .$

Let us prove the symmetry. We appeal to indirect equality :

$$x \uparrow y \leq z$$

$\equiv \qquad \{ (0) \}$

$$x \leq z \land y \leq z$$

$\equiv \qquad \{ \land \text{ is symmetric } \}$

$$y \leq z \land x \leq z$$

$\equiv \qquad \{ (0) \text{ with } x, y := y, x \}$

$$y \uparrow x \leq z,$$

and the conclusion follows. From this proof we see that $\uparrow$ inherits its symmetry from $\land$. The same holds for $\uparrow$'s idempotence and $\uparrow$'s associativity, as the reader may verify.

The next thing we do with (0) is to study it for some simple instantiations. For instantiation $z := y$ we find

$$x \uparrow y \leq y$$

$\equiv \qquad \{ (0) \}$

$$x \leq y \land y \leq y$$

$\equiv \qquad \{ \leq \text{ is reflexive } \}$

$$x \leq y .$$

Thus we have derived the

Rule of absorption

$$x{\uparrow}y \leq y \;\equiv\; x{\leq}y$$

End

Next, from (0) with $z := x{\uparrow}y$, we find the

Rule of expansion

$$y \leq x{\uparrow}y$$

End

Using mutual inequality, we can combine the rules of absorption and expansion into

(1) $\qquad\qquad x{\uparrow}y = y \;\equiv\; x{\leq}y$ $\hfill (\forall x, y)$

Remark   Almost every established treatment of lattice theory starts from (1), but that is not nearly as nice as the treatment given here, because the pleasing symmetry exhibited by (0) is completely hidden.
End

    So much for some simple instantiations of (0).
    Now the time has come to prove the beautiful[1].

Theorem   For reflexive and antisymmetric $\leq$, and for $\uparrow$ as defined by (0), we have that

    $\leq$ is transitive .

Proof   We have to prove that for all x, y, and z

$$x{\leq}y \wedge y{\leq}z \;\Rightarrow\; x{\leq}z .$$

Using (1), this we can rewrite as

$$x{\uparrow}y=y \wedge y{\uparrow}z=z \;\Rightarrow\; x{\uparrow}z=z ,$$

and we shall prove this latter by showing the consequent — $x{\uparrow}z=z$ — thereby using the antecedent — $x{\uparrow}y=x \wedge y{\uparrow}z=z$ —:

        $x{\uparrow}z$

=   { since $y{\uparrow}z=z$, from the antecedent }

        $x{\uparrow}(y{\uparrow}z)$

=   { $\uparrow$ is associative }

        $(x{\uparrow}y){\uparrow}z$

=   { since $x{\uparrow}y=y$, from the antecedent }

        $y{\uparrow}z$

=   { since $y{\uparrow}z=z$, from the antecedent }

        z .

And we are done. (We ask the reader to notice that each individual step in the above calculation is almost forced upon us. This is a very typical characteristic of many a calculation.)
End

Now that we have obtained the transitivity of $\leq$, we shall feel free to use it. For the sake of completeness we mention that a reflexive, antisymmetric, and transitive relation is commonly called a *partial order*, and that a universe equipped with a partial order is called a *partially ordered set* — a "poset" for short.

Definition (0) of $\uparrow$ tells us when $x \uparrow y \leq z$. We now may ask when $z \leq x \uparrow y$. We leave to the reader to verify that

(2) $\qquad z \leq x \uparrow y \;\Leftarrow\; z \leq x \;\vee\; z \leq y \;,$

and we investigate the converse :

$$z \leq x \uparrow y \;\Rightarrow\; z \leq x \;\vee\; z \leq y$$

$\equiv \qquad$ { predicate calculus }

$$(z \leq x \uparrow y \;\Rightarrow\; z \leq x) \;\vee\; (z \leq x \uparrow y \;\Rightarrow\; z \leq y)$$

$\Leftarrow \qquad$ { $\leq$ is transitive }

$$x \uparrow y \leq x \;\vee\; x \uparrow y \leq y$$

$\equiv \qquad$ { rule of absorption, twice }

$$y \leq x \;\vee\; x \leq y \;.$$

For this last line to be valid for any x and y, we require that $\leq$ be a so-called linear or total order: by definition a total order is a partial order with the additional property that, for all x and y, $x \leq y \;\vee\; y \leq x$.
So, in combination with (2) we find

(3) $\qquad$ for $\leq$ a total order,
$$z \leq x \uparrow y \;\equiv\; z \leq x \;\vee\; z \leq y \;.$$

Furthermore, we deduce from (1) that

(4) $\qquad$ for $\leq$ a total order, operator $\uparrow$ as defined by (0) satisfies
$$x \uparrow y = x \;\vee\; x \uparrow y = y \;.$$
(In words : $\uparrow$ is a selector.)

From here, we can proceed in many different directions. After all, lattice theory is a huge mathematical terrain, with many ins and outs. We conclude this introduction by confronting $\uparrow$ with other functions.

We consider functions from and to our anonymous universe. For f such a function we have, by definition,

♦ f is monotonic $\;\equiv\; \langle \forall x, y :: x \leq y \;\Rightarrow\; f.x \leq f.y \rangle$.

♦ f distributes over $\uparrow \;\equiv\; \langle \forall x, y :: f.(x \uparrow y) = f.x \uparrow f.y \rangle$.

We can now formulate the well-known, yet beautiful, theorem

(5) f distributes over $\uparrow$ $\Rightarrow$ f is monotonic .

Proof   For any x and y, we observe

$$f.x \leq f.y$$

$\equiv$ $\{\,(1)\,\}$

$$f.x \uparrow f.y = f.y$$

$\equiv$ $\{\,f$ distributes over $\uparrow\,\}$

$$f.(x \uparrow y) = f.y$$

$\Leftarrow$ $\{$ Leibniz's rule $\}$

$$x \uparrow y = y$$

$\equiv$ $\{\,(1)\,\}$

$$x \leq y \ ,$$

and the result follows from the outer two lines.
End

Small intermezzo   (on proof design)
We would like to draw the reader's attention to the fact that the above proof — no matter how simple it is — displays a great economy of thought. Let us analyze it in some detail. Given that f distributes over $\uparrow$, we have to construct a calculation of the form

$$f.x \leq f.y \ldots \Leftarrow \ldots x \leq y \ .$$

Right at the outset we can argue that such a calculation will require at least four steps, viz.

- a step to introduce symbol $\uparrow$, in order to be able to exploit the given about f

- a step in which the given about f is actually used

- a step to eliminate symbol $\uparrow$ again, because the target line $x \leq y$ does not mention it

- a step to eliminate symbol f , for which Leibniz's rule is our only means so far.

Our proof contains precisely (these) four steps, so it cannot be shortened. In fact, it was designed with these four considerations in mind. When we wrote above "no matter how simple it is", this may have sounded paradoxical, but it isn't. On the contrary, the proof derives its simplicity from the consciously considered shapes of the formulas and from the manipulative possibilities available. Nowadays, many more proofs can be and are being designed following such a procedure.
End Small Intermezzo .

A direct consequence of (5) concerns monotonicity properties of $\uparrow$. Because function f defined by $f.x = c \uparrow x$, for whatever c, distributes over $\uparrow$ — as the reader may verify —, theorem (5) tells us that $\uparrow$ is monotonic in its second argument. Since $\uparrow$ is symmetric, we therefore have

(6) $\uparrow$ is monotonic in both arguments.

What about the converse of (5)? Does it hold as well? In order to find out, we try to prove

$$f.(x \uparrow y) = f.x \uparrow f.y$$

on the assumption that f is monotonic. We do this by mutual inequality:

$\qquad$ $f.x \uparrow f.y \leq f.(x \uparrow y)$

$\equiv \qquad\qquad$ { definition of $\uparrow$, see (0) }

$\qquad$ $f.x \leq f.(x \uparrow y) \ \wedge \ f.y \leq f.(x \uparrow y)$

$\Leftarrow \qquad\qquad$ { monotonicity of f , twice }

$\qquad$ $x \leq x \uparrow y \ \wedge \ y \leq x \uparrow y$

$\equiv \qquad\qquad$ { rule of expansion, twice }

$\qquad$ *true* ,

$\qquad$ $f.(x \uparrow y) \leq f.x \uparrow f.y$

$\Leftarrow \qquad\qquad$ { (2) }

$\qquad$ $f.(x \uparrow y) \leq f.x \ \vee \ f.(x \uparrow y) \leq f.y$

$\Leftarrow \qquad\qquad$ { monotonicity of f , twice }

$\qquad$ $x \uparrow y \leq x \ \vee \ x \uparrow y \leq y$

$\equiv \qquad\qquad$ { rule of absorption, twice }

$\qquad$ $y \leq x \ \vee \ x \leq y$,

and the validity of this last line requires $\leq$ to be total. Thus, we have derived, in combination with (5),

(7)   for $\leq$ a total order,
$\qquad\qquad$ f is monotonic $\equiv$ f distributes over $\uparrow$.

In lattice theory, one always introduces a companion to $\uparrow$; it is $\downarrow$ ("down"). (In the standard literature we find $\downarrow$ under entries like "inf", or "meet", or "glb".) It sees the light via

(8) $z \leq x \downarrow y \ \equiv \ z \leq x \wedge z \leq y$ $(\forall x, y, z)$,

i.e. in a way that is very similar to (0). It has very similar dual properties to $\uparrow$. In fact, it has the same properties if we simply flip $\leq$ into $\geq$, and $\uparrow$ into $\downarrow$: just compare (0) and (8). With this symbol dynamics in mind the companion properties for $\downarrow$ come free. We mention

- ♦ $\downarrow$ is idempotent, symmetric, and associative

- ♦ $y \leq x \downarrow y \ \equiv \ y \leq x$ Absorption

- ♦ $x \downarrow y \leq y$ Contraction (= the dual of Expansion)

- ♦ $x \downarrow y = y \ \equiv \ y \leq x$

- ♦ $x \downarrow y \leq z \ \Leftarrow \ x \leq z \ \vee \ y \leq x$

- ♦ $\downarrow$ is monotonic in both arguments

- ♦ etc.

Of course, we can now also investigate formulae containing both $\uparrow$ and $\downarrow$. We mention

$$x \downarrow (x \uparrow y) = x \ , \ \ x \uparrow (x \downarrow y) = x \ , \ \ \text{and}$$

$$x \downarrow y = x \ \equiv \ x \uparrow y = y \ .$$

The proofs are left as exercises. We will not continue these investigations now.

In case we take for $\leq$ the usual order between real numbers, $\downarrow$ is the familiar minimum operator.

Let us, to conclude this story, consider the real numbers with the usual order $\leq$. This is a total order. The foregoing little theory now grants us quite a number of useful arithmetical results.

- ♦ In order to find out which part of the (x,y)-plane satisfies $x \uparrow y \leq x + y$, we simply calculate :

$$\begin{array}{ll} & x \uparrow y \ \leq \ x + y \\ \equiv & \quad \{ \text{ definition of } f \ \} \\ & x \leq x + y \ \wedge \ y \leq x + y \\ \equiv & \quad \{ \text{ arithmetic } \} \\ & 0 \leq y \ \wedge \ 0 \leq x \ . \end{array}$$

So the answer is: the first quadrant.
(Ask one of your colleagues or students to solve this little problem, and observe how he does it. This could be a very instructive experiment.)

- ♦ Since function f , defined by $f.x = c + x$, is monotonic, we infer from (7):

addition distributes over the maximum.

♦ Likewise, multiplication with a nonnegative number distributes over the maximum.

♦ And also

$$2^{x \uparrow y} = 2^x \uparrow 2^y \text{ , and}$$

$$(x \uparrow y)^2 = x^2 \uparrow y^2 \text{ (for } x, y \geq 0, 0) \text{ , and}$$

$$z \downarrow (x \uparrow y) = (z \downarrow x) \uparrow (z \downarrow y) \text{ .}$$

♦ And now the reader should prove — with a minimal amount of case analysis —

$$x^2 \downarrow y^2 \leq x * y \ \Leftarrow\ 0 \leq x * y \text{ .}$$

♦ Perhaps, we can also learn to handle absolute values more readily, because we have $\mid x \mid\ = x \uparrow -x$. Try to use it to prove the triangular inequality

$$\mid x+y \mid\ \leq\ \mid x \mid + \mid y \mid \text{ .}$$

♦ Etc.

This really was the beginning of lattice theory. Was it difficult? We hope that most of our readers will say: no! We believe that elementary lattice theory — which goes beyond this note — can and should be taught to reasonable freshmen or, in any case, to sophomores, of computing science and mathematics alike. Many of our colleagues, world-wide, especially computing science colleagues, will shudder at the thought, because lattice theory is regarded far too abstract to be useful or to be teachable to the average student. And abstract stands for frightening, doesn't it? We really must disagree with such a point of view, because — as we tried to show — the game is completely under control by the use of a modest repertoire of simple calculational rules. It is the peaceful calculational style which does away with the fear for abstract things. And also, it is the peaceful calculational style which lets the subject matter sink in much more profoundly than would have been the case otherwise. If still in doubt, remember Newton and Leibniz: they took away the deep difficulties attending the notions of limits and derivatives by ... proposing a symbolism to denote them and a set of formula rewrite rules to manipulate and ... to master them. By now these notions are high-school topics.

12.2.3 A high-tech calculation

As members of a high-tech society, we sometimes feel obliged to embark on high-tech calculations. Here is one.

When we have a tedious calculation of the form

$$x = y$$

$$\Rightarrow \quad \vdots$$

$$P.x.y \ ,$$

there is no need to redo all the work if we want to strengthen the last line with conjunct $P.y.x$. We exploit symmetry, and simply continue our calculation with a step indicated

$$\equiv \qquad \{ \text{ Symmetry } \}$$

$$P.x.y \ \wedge \ P.y.x \ .$$

The simplest application of the above principle is

$$x = y \qquad\qquad (0)$$

$$\Rightarrow \qquad \{ \text{ calculus } \}$$

$$x \leq y \qquad\qquad (1)$$

$$\equiv \qquad \{ \text{ Symmetry } \}$$

$$x \leq y \ \wedge \ y \leq x$$

$$\equiv \qquad \{ \text{ calculus } \}$$

$$x = y \qquad\qquad (2)$$

Comparing lines (0), (1), and (2) we have shown

$$x = y \ \equiv \ x \leq y \ .$$

And that is what we call high technology.

12.3   From sequential programming

12.3.1   Around Bresenham

We consider the task of plotting a curve in the Euclidean plane by marking pixels from a grid covering that plane. More specifically, given a real-valued function f on some finite interval, we wish to mark, for each integer x in that interval,, a pixel with integer coordinates (x, y) such that y is as close to $f.x$ as possible. This latter requirement can be formulated as

$$| y - f.x | \ \leq \tfrac{1}{2} \ ,$$

or, equivalently, as the conjunction of Qa and Qb, given by

Qa: $y \ \leq \ \tfrac{1}{2} + f.x$

Qb: $-\tfrac{1}{2} + f.x \ \leq \ y.$

We furthermore assume that f satisfies a kind of "smoothness" property on the interval, to wit

$$0 \leq f.(x+1) - f.x \leq 1,$$

which can also be formulated as the conjunction of Da and Db, given by

Da: $\qquad f.x \leq f.(x+1)$

Db: $\qquad f.(x+1) \leq 1 + f.x$.

It is this property that suggests that the curve be plotted in the order of increasing (or decreasing) value of x, because the pixel to be marked for $x+1$ is not too far away from the pixel to be marked for x (thus yielding the nicer picture). Thus, with the interval given by two integers A and B, $A \leq B$,we will consider a marking program of the form

$$x := A$$

$$; \text{do } x \neq B \rightarrow Mark\ (x,y)\ ;\ x := x+1 \text{ od}$$

and regard it as our task to extend this program with operations on y such that $Qa \wedge Qb$ is an invariant of the repetition.

The reader may recognize the above problem statement as one from the world of graphics. We wish to emphasize, however, that in this essay neither this specific problem nor its origin is of much concern to us here. We are concerned with the development of a program meeting the specification, by paying attention to uninterpreted formulae only, i.e. without further reference — mental or otherwise — to pixels, pictures, or whatever.

The program above requires two adaptations, one for the initialization of y and one for y's adjustment in the step. As for the initialization, we cannot say much without taking specificities of f into account. For the time being, we may record it as

$$x,y:\ \ x = A \wedge Qa \wedge Qb.$$

For the step, we consider an adaptation of the form $x,y\ :=\ x+1,y+\xi$, and try to find out for what integer values of ξ this maintains $Qa \wedge Qb$. We will deal with the invariances of Qa and Qb in turn.

Qa's invariance
The weakest precondition for $x,y\ :=\ x+1,y+\xi$ to establish Qa is

$G.\xi$: $\qquad y+\xi \leq \frac{1}{2} + f.(x+1).$

We now investigate for which (integer) values of ξ the required precondition $G.\xi$ is implied by the actual precondition, which is $Qa \wedge Qb \wedge Da \wedge Db$. To that end, we observe

$$y+\xi \leq \tfrac{1}{2} + f.(x+1)$$

$\Leftarrow \qquad \qquad$ { using Qa and the transitivity of $\leq$ }

$$\tfrac{1}{2} + f.x + \xi \leq \tfrac{1}{2} + f.(x+1)$$

$$\equiv \qquad \{ \text{ arithmetic } \}$$

$$f.x + \xi \;\leq\; f.(x+1)$$

$$\Leftarrow \qquad \{ \text{ using } Da \text{ and the transitivity of } \leq \}$$

$$f.x + \xi \;\leq\; f.x$$

$$\equiv \qquad \{ \text{ arithmetic } \}$$

$$\xi \leq 0.$$

As a result, statement $x,y \;:=\; x+1, y+\xi$ "automatically" maintains Qa for $\xi \leq 0$, but for other values of ξ the statement had better be guarded by $G.\xi$.

Now we expect that, in view of the properties D of f, we will never need to consider increments of y — i.e. values for ξ — outside the range $0,1$. This expectation will turn out to be true, and, anticipating that, we can summarize the above analysis as

$$\{ Qa \} \{ Da \}$$

$$\text{if } G.1 \rightarrow x,y \;:=\; x+1, y+1$$

$$[\!] \;\; true \rightarrow x \;:=\; x+1 \quad (\text{i.e. } x,y \;:=\; x+1, y+0)$$

fi

$$\{ Qa \}.$$

End Qa's invariance .

$Qb's$ **invariance**

The weakest precondition for $x,y \;:=\; x+1, y+\xi$ to establish Qb is

$$H.\xi : \qquad -\tfrac{1}{2} + f.(x+1) \;\leq\; y+\xi.$$

As before, we investigate for which values of ξ this is implied by the actual precondition:

$$-\tfrac{1}{2} + f.(x+1) \;\leq\; y+\xi$$

$$\Leftarrow \qquad \{ \text{ using } Qb \text{ and the transitivity of } \leq \}$$

$$-\tfrac{1}{2} + f.(x+1) \;\leq\; -\tfrac{1}{2} + f.x + \xi$$

$$\equiv \qquad \{ \text{ arithmetic } \}$$

$$f.(x+1) \;\leq\; f.x + \xi$$

$$\Leftarrow \qquad \{ \text{ using } Db \text{ and the transitivity of } \leq \}$$

$$1 + f.x \;\leq\; f.x + \xi$$

$$\equiv \qquad \{ \text{ arithmetic } \}$$

$$1 \leq \xi.$$

In summary, we derived

$\{Qb\}\{Db\}$

if $true \rightarrow x,y := x+1,y+1$

$[\!]\ H.0 \rightarrow x := x+1$

fi

$\{Qb\}$.

End $Qb's$ invariance .

Now we combine the two fragments above into a single program fragment maintaining both Qa and Qb :

$\{Qa \wedge Qb\}\{Da \wedge Db\}$

if $G.1 \rightarrow x,y := x+1,y+1$

$[\!]\ H.0 \rightarrow x := x+1$

fi

$\{Qa \wedge Qb\}$.

The only remaining proof obligation is to verify that this program fragment does not suffer from the danger of abortion, i.e. we have to check that the disjunction of the guards is implied by the precondition of the if-statement. In order to examine this we expand the guards (while simplifying them):

$G.1$: $\qquad y+\frac{1}{2} \le f.(x+1)$

$H.0$: $\qquad f.(x+1) \le y+\frac{1}{2},$

and, lo and behold, we have $G.1 \vee H.0$, so that there is no danger of abortion. (At the same time, this also confirms our expectation that we need not consider increments of y beyond 0 or 1 .)

Collecting the pieces, we have derived that the program depicted in Figure 12.1 below plots the curve as demanded.

So much for the development of this algorithm.

There is, however, a little bit more to be said. The evaluation of the guards $G.1$ and $H.0$ will, in general, demand floating-point arithmetic, and for many functions f there is no escaping it. But for some classes of curves — most notoriously the conic sections — there is an opportunity to transform the algorithm so that its execution will require integer arithmetic only. And this is sometimes considered an advantage. We next show such a transformation for the case of a (specific) hyperbola.

Consider the curve given by

$$0 \le f.x \ \wedge \ (f.x)^2 - x^2 = C,$$

for some (large) positive integer constant C. It is the "positive branch" of a hyperbola. We wish to plot it on the interval $[A,B)$, with A and B integers satisfying $0 \le A \le B$. The reader may verify that, on this interval, f satisfies

$\{Da \wedge Db\}\{A \leq B\}$

$x, y:\ x = A \wedge Qa \wedge Qb$

$\{\text{inv. } Qa \wedge Qb\}$

; do $x \neq B \rightarrow$

    $Mark\,(x, y)$

    ; if $G.1 \rightarrow x, y := x+1, y+1$

    ▯ $H.0 \rightarrow x := x+1$

    fi

od .

Figure 12.1: The curve-plotting program

properties Da and Db.

We first expand guard $G.1$, seeking to express it with integer subexpressions only:

$$
\begin{array}{ll}
 & G.1 \\
\equiv & \quad \{ \text{ definition of } G \ \} \\
 & y{+}1 \ \leq \ \tfrac{1}{2} + f.(x{+}1) \\
\equiv & \quad \{ \text{ arithmetic } \} \\
 & y{+}\tfrac{1}{2} \leq f.(x{+}1) \\
\equiv & \quad \{ \text{ both sides are nonnegative; for } y{+}\tfrac{1}{2} \text{ this is so by } Qb \ \} \\
 & (y{+}\tfrac{1}{2})^2 \leq (f.(x{+}1))^2 \\
\equiv & \quad \{ \text{ arithmetic and definition of } f \ \} \\
 & y^2{+}y{+}\tfrac{1}{4} \leq (x{+}1)^2{+}C \\
\equiv & \quad \{ \text{ arithmetic } \} \\
 & \tfrac{1}{4} \ \leq \ x^2 + 2{*}x - y^2 - y + C + 1 \\
\equiv & \quad \{ \bullet \text{ by } P \text{ given below } \} \\
 & \tfrac{1}{4} \leq h \quad .
\end{array}
$$

For the "complementary" guard $H.0$, we find

$$H.0 \ \equiv \ \tfrac{1}{4} \geq h \quad .$$

The reason for introducing the additional invariant

$$P: \qquad h \ = \ x^2 + 2{*}x - y^2 - y + C + 1 \ ,$$

is that the repeated updating of h is assumed to be less costly than the repeated evaluation of P's right-hand side for the successive values of x and y. Furthermore note that h is an integer — as demanded.

Now we have almost succeeded in expressing $G.1$ and $H.0$ in terms of integer expressions only, except for the occurrence of that $\frac{1}{4}$. Because h is an integer, we can eliminate this $\frac{1}{4}$ painlessly because of

$$\tfrac{1}{4} \le h \equiv 1 \le h$$

and

$$\tfrac{1}{4} \ge h \equiv 0 \ge h.$$

Thus, we find

$$G.1 \equiv 1 \le h \quad \text{and} \quad H.0 \equiv 0 \ge h.$$

We now give the final program at once, leaving the standard proof of the invariance of P to the reader. (All that is needed for this is the axiom of assignment.)

$$x,y := A, round.(sqrt.(A^2 + C))$$
$$; h := x^2 + 2{*}x - y^2 - y + C + 1$$
$$; \text{do } x{\neq}B \rightarrow$$
$$\qquad Mark\,(x,y)$$
$$\qquad ; \text{if } 1{\le}h \rightarrow x,y,h := x{+}1, y{+}1, h + 2{*}x - 2{*}y + 1$$
$$\qquad [\!] \; 0{\ge}h \rightarrow x,h := x{+}1, h + 2{*}x + 3$$
$$\qquad \text{fi}$$
$$\quad \text{od}.$$

The program text can be further embellished, but we leave it at this. For some interesting details concerning the marking we refer to, for instance, van der Sommen (1993).

The reader that feels like constructing a plotting algorithm himself, may try to do so for, say, a straight line segment in the "first octant" of the plane. The exercise can be quite rewarding, since he will find himself *designing* the famous algorithm that was *invented* by J.E. Bresenham (van de Snepscheut, 1993).

Acknowledgement

We thank Rob Hoogerwoord and Anne Kaldewaij for their comments.

Postscript

This note was written in 1990, because we felt intrigued but not satisfied by Wirth (1990).

12.3.2   How to bound in "branch and bound"

"Branch and bound", in particular "bound", refers to a technique to remove some of the inefficiency that almost inevitably attends most "backtracking algorithms". Before dealing with that technique, we first spend a few words on backtracking.

Backtracking algorithms usually enter the picture if a huge class of things has to be explored in order to identify a subclass with certain properties. Typical examples of such huge classes are: all subsets of a given set, all permutations of a number of objects, all partitions of a natural number, all walks through a graph, all tic-tac-toe games, etc. If certain members of such a class have to be identified, a safe procedure is to generate *all* members and to check, for each of them individually, whether they have the desired properties. The procedure is safe but its time complexity may grow gigantically, and in many cases there is no cure.

As a typical example, let us investigate the set V of all bitstrings of length N, and let us assume that each bitstring x — of whatever length — has a cost $c.x$ associated with it. The problem we consider is to compute the minimal cost of a bitstring in V, i.e. the value of

$$\langle \downarrow x : x \in V : c.x \rangle .$$

The backtracking strategy boils down to the introduction of a function f on the set $prefV$ of all bitstrings of length at most N, defined by

$$f.u = \langle \downarrow x : u \# x \in V : c.(u \# x) \rangle , u \in prefV$$

(Symbol $\#$ denotes concatenation.)

Then the desired answer is the value of $f.[\ ]$. (Symbol $[\ ]$ denotes the empty string.)

The recursive scheme governing the computation of f is (proof omitted)

♦ for $\#u = N$, $f.u = c.u$

♦ for $\#u < N$, $f.u = f.(u \# [0]) \downarrow f.(u \# [1])$.

($\#u$ stands for the length of u, and $[b]$ is the singleton list containing element b.)

For the actual computation of f we introduce a function $F(u : \text{list}) : \text{int}$ with specification

precondition : $u \in prefV$

postcondition : $F = f.u$.

The code for a program to print target value $f.[\ ]$ is now straightforward. It reads func $F(u : \text{list}) : \text{int}$;

$\qquad \{\,\text{pre}: \quad u \in prefV\,\}$

$\qquad \{\,\text{post}: \quad F = f.u\,\}$

$\qquad$ if $\#u = N \rightarrow F := c.u$

$\qquad [\!] \ \#u < N \rightarrow F := F(u \mathbin{+\!\!+} [0]) \downarrow F(u \mathbin{+\!\!+} [1])$

$\qquad$ fi

cnuf

; print $(F([\,]))$.

As can be seen from the function definition, the recursion only comes to an end when $\#u = N$, i.e. when a bitstring of full length has been generated. In fact, the above program will generate all 2^N elements of V exactly once, and compute the cost of each of them. And if function c is of a whimsical nature, there is nothing we can do to improve on the program's efficiency.

In many practical circumstances, however, cost function c is not whimsical at all. A very frequent situation is that we have

(0) $\qquad c.u \leq c.(u \mathbin{+\!\!+} x),$

a case that we shall now further investigate. The traditional jargon exploits (0) by a remark like : "there is no need to extend string u if $c.u$ is at least as big as the c-value of any bitstring of length N that the program has computed so far". We will illustrate how to exploit (0) in a non-operational manner.

We generalize function f into a function g defined by

$\qquad g.r.u = r \downarrow f.u \qquad (r \in \text{Int}, \ u \in prefV)$

Here, parameter r is called the "bound". In terms of g, the desired answer — which was $f.[\,]$ — is

$\qquad g.r.[\,] \qquad$ for any r satisfying $f.[\,] \leq r$

The great advantage of g over f is that now the value of $g.r.u$ can sometimes be computed without recourse to a "laborious" calculation of $f.u$, viz. when $r \downarrow f.u = r$, in which case $g.r.u = r$. Let us investigate this condition :

$\qquad r \downarrow f.u = r$

$\equiv \qquad\qquad \{\text{ property of } f \ \}$

$\qquad r \leq f.u$

$\equiv \qquad\qquad \{\text{ definition of } f \ \}$

$\qquad r \leq \langle \downarrow x: u \mathbin{+\!\!+} x \in V: c.(u \mathbin{+\!\!+} x) \rangle$

$\equiv \qquad\qquad \{\text{ property of } f \ \}$

$\qquad \langle \forall x: u \mathbin{+\!\!+} x \in V: r \leq c.(u \mathbin{+\!\!+} x) \rangle$

$\Leftarrow \qquad\qquad \{\ (0)\ \}$

$$\langle \forall x: u \mathbin{+\!\!+} x \in V: r \le c.u \rangle$$

$\Leftarrow \qquad$ { predicate calculus }

$$r \le c.u \ .$$

As a result we find

- $\qquad$ for $r \le c.u$, $g.r.u = r$.

For the remaining case, viz. $c.u < r$, we resort to the recursive scheme for f:

- $\qquad$ for $c.u < r \ \wedge \ \#u = N$,

$\qquad g.r.u$

$= \qquad$ { definition of g }

$\qquad r \!\downarrow\! f.u$

$= \qquad$ { $\#u = N$ } { scheme for f }

$\qquad r \!\downarrow\! c.u$

$= \qquad$ { $c.u < r$ }

$\qquad c.u$.

- $\qquad$ for $c.u < r \ \wedge \ \#u < N$,

$\qquad g.r.u$

$= \qquad$ { definition of g }

$\qquad r \!\downarrow\! f.u$

$= \qquad$ { $\#u < N$ } { scheme for f }

$\qquad r \downarrow (f.(u \mathbin{+\!\!+} [0]) \downarrow f.(u \mathbin{+\!\!+} [1]))$

$= \qquad$ { $\downarrow$ is associative }

$\qquad (r \downarrow f.(u \mathbin{+\!\!+} [0])) \downarrow f.(u \mathbin{+\!\!+} [1])$

$= \qquad$ { definition of g }

$\qquad g.r.(u \mathbin{+\!\!+} [0]) \downarrow f.(u \mathbin{+\!\!+} [1])$

$= \qquad$ { definition of g }

$\qquad g.(g.r.(u \mathbin{+\!\!+} [0])).(u \mathbin{+\!\!+} [1])$

or, equivalently,

with $\quad t = g.s.(u \mathbin{+\!\!+} [1])$

and $\quad s = g.r.(u \mathbin{+\!\!+} [0])$

$$g.r.u = t \ .$$

In summary, the recursive scheme governing the computation of g is

- for $r \leq c.u$, $\qquad\qquad\qquad g.r.u = r$
- for $c.u < r \land \#u = N$, $\qquad g.r.u = c.u$
- for $c.u < r \land \#u < N$, $\qquad g.r.u = t$

$$\text{where} \quad t = g.s.(u + [1])$$
$$\text{and} \quad s = g.r.(u + [0]) \ .$$

The corresponding program text that prints the target value reads

```
func G(r : int, u : string) : int ;
    { pre :    u ∈ prefV }
    { post :   G = g.r.u }
    if r ≤ c.u → G := r
    [] c.u < r ∧ #u = N → G := c.u
    [] c.u < r ∧ #u < N →
        |[ s, t : int ;
            s := G(r, u + [0])
          ; t := G(s, u + [1])
          ; G := t
        ]|
    fi
cnuf
; "for some r such that f.[ ] ≤ r, print(G(r, [ ]))" .
```

Remark   The difference between F and G is that the recursion in G also comes to an end when $r \leq c.u$, i.e. when $c.u$ has become too large or r has become small enough. Therefore, it is beneficial — even considerably so — for the efficiency of the program, if the initial value for r in the main call can be chosen as small as possible. And in many applications one can indeed without too much effort find an initial estimate for r that is quite close to target value $f.[\ ]$. **End** Remark .

In practice, one usually wishes to compute a witness for the cheapest solution as well. We shall now show how to do this for our program above.

In order to compute a cheapest bitstring in V, we introduce a global variable z of type string, and strengthen the postcondition of G with the conjunct

$$z \in V \land c.z = G.$$

Because $G(r, [\ ])$ as it occurs in the main call, is the desired minimal value, the string z satisfying this additional postcondition is an appropriate witness indeed.

Now we investigate how the three alternatives of function G can establish this new postcondition

- $$r \leq c.u \rightarrow G := r :$$

$$(z \in V \ \wedge \ c.z = G)\,(G := r)$$

$\equiv$ { substitution }

$$z \in V \ \wedge \ c.z = r,$$

and because this does not follow from the guard $r \leq c.u$ nor from G's precondition $u \in pref V$, we decide that

(∗) $z \in V \ \wedge \ c.z = r$

        be a precondition of G as well.

- $$c.u < r \ \wedge \ \#u = N \rightarrow G := c.u :$$

$$(z \in V \ \wedge \ c.z = G)\,(G := c.u)$$

$\equiv$ { substitution }

$$z \in V \ \wedge \ c.z = c.u$$

$\Leftarrow$ { Leibniz }

$$z \in V \ \wedge \ z = u \ .$$

Because $u \in pref V$ (from pre of G) and because $\#u = N$ (from the guard) we conclude that $u \in V$, so that the above calculated precondition $z \in V \ \wedge \ z = u$ of $G := c.u$ is readily established by prefixing $G := c.u$ with statement $z := u$.

-    $c.u < r \ \wedge \ \#u < N \rightarrow$ block :

For the block in the third alternative we need no further adjustments of G, as may follow from the annotation given below. Please observe that the preassertion of each call of G exactly matches the required additional precondition (∗) of G.

$$|[\ s,t : \text{int} \ ;$$

$$\{ z \in V \ \wedge \ c.z = r \ , \ \text{ from precondition } (∗) \}$$

$$s := G(r, u + [0])$$

$$; \ \{ z \in V \ \wedge \ c.z = s \ , \ \text{ from added postcondition of } G \}$$

$$t := G(s, u + [1])$$

$$; \ \{ z \in V \ \wedge \ c.z = t \ , \ \text{ from added postcondition of } G \}$$

$$G := t$$

$$\{ z \in V \ \wedge \ c.z = G , \ \text{ as required} \}$$

$$]|$$

End •

Thus, our final program which computes a witness as well, has become

func $G(r : \text{int}, u : \text{string}) : \text{int}$;

$\quad\quad\quad$ { pre : $\ u \in prefV \ \wedge \ z \in V \ \wedge \ c.z = r$ }

$\quad\quad\quad$ { post : $\ G = g.r.u \ \wedge \ z \in V \ \wedge \ c.z = G$ }

$\quad\quad\quad$ if $r \leq c.u \rightarrow G := r$

$\quad\quad\quad$ [] $c.u < r \ \wedge \ \#u = N \rightarrow z := u$; $G := c.u$

$\quad\quad\quad$ [] $c.u < r \ \wedge \ \#u < N \ \rightarrow$

$\quad\quad\quad\quad$ |[$s, t : \text{int}$;

$\quad\quad\quad\quad\quad$ $s := G(r, u +\!\!+ [0])$

$\quad\quad\quad\quad$; $t := G(s, u +\!\!+ [1])$

$\quad\quad\quad\quad$; $G := t$

$\quad\quad\quad\quad$]|

$\quad\quad\quad$ fi

$\quad\quad$ cnuf

$\quad$; "for some r and z such that $z \in V$, $c.z = r$, and $f.[\,] \leq r$,

$\quad\quad$ print($G(r, [\,])$) ; print(z) " .

Branch and bound, and backtracking, belong to what the field has called "combinatorial algorithms". Those algorithms are usually presented in a very operational manner. Backtracking is explained as tree traversal and bounding as some sort of pruning. And the algorithms are presented in terms of pictures rather than with formulae. We do not really like such explanations, in particular if one realizes that the mathematical crux of bounding, viz. the transition from function

$\quad\quad$ $f.u$

to $\quad\quad\quad$ $r \!\downarrow\! f.u$

is so beautifully simple.

$\quad$ We learned this technique from our colleagues Anne Kaldewaij and Rob Hoogerwoord. Kaldewaij in his book (Kaldewaij, 1993) has considerably raised the standards for dealing with Combinatorial Algorithms, and it should be pointed out (for methodological reasons) that this rise in standard has become possible due to the emergence of nice calculational styles of functional programming as, for instance, the one laid down in Hoogerwoord (1989).

12.3.3   The binary search revisited

The binary search is a beautiful, simple, efficient, and hence well-known little algorithm for searching. Most computing scientists and programmers will be familiar with it. Unfortunately, there are two observations that cast some doubt on the level of familiarity. First, many programmers still have a relatively hard time writing down correct program code for it, this in spite of the fact that it concerns an algorithm of just a few lines. Second, most programmers believe that the algorithm only works for searching in sorted arrays, which reveals a misunderstanding. (A long time ago, we ourselves, too, used to sell the binary search to our students by first drawing an analogy with searching for a word in a dictionary. Afterwards, we learned to judge this as an educational blunder.) The purpose of this note is to remedy the situation.

Our starting point is that we are given a function or an array $f[a..b]$, $a < b$, of elements of some kind, such that the two outer elements $f.a$ and $f.b$ are in some relation Z to each other, a fact that we denote by aZb . The problem is to find a pair of neighbouring elements of f that are in the relation Z . (Of course, such a pair need not exist; we will address this problem later on.) More precisely, we wish to construct a program with postcondition

R: $a \leq x \land x < b \land x Z (x+1)$

on the premise that the precondition implies

$$a < b \land aZb .$$

The procedure for constructing such a program is quite standard. In view of the shapes of the pre- and the postcondition we try to establish R by means of a repetition with invariants $P0$ and $P1$, given by

$P0$: $a \leq x \land x < y \land y \leq b$

$P1$: xZy ,

and with bound function $y-x$. Our program thus gets the form

$\{ a < b \land aZb \}$

$x,y := a,b$

$\{ \text{inv } P0 \land P1 \} \{ \text{bnd } y-x \}$

$; \text{do } y \neq x+1 \rightarrow \quad \text{shrink } y-x \text{ under invariance of } P0 \land P1 \text{ od}$

$\{ R \}$.

And indeed, by construction, $P0 \land P1 \land y = x+1 \Rightarrow R$.

For the shrinking of $y-x$ in the body of the repetition we investigate an increase of x and a decrease of y. (We do so since our problem is highly symmetric in x and y.) On the assumption that $x < h$, for some h still to be determined, assignment $x := h$ increases x. We now find out under what circumstances this assignment maintains $P0 \land P1$. As for the invariance of $P0$, we observe

$P0 \ (x := h)$

$\equiv$ { definition of $P0$ }

$a \leq h \ \wedge \ h < y \ \wedge \ y \leq b$

$\equiv$ { $P0$ and $x < h$ are preconditions to $x := h$,

hence $a < h \ \wedge \ y \leq b$ }

$h < y$.

So we require h to satisfy not just $x < h$ but also $h < y$, and hence

$x < h \ \wedge \ h < y$.

Note   Fortunately, such an h exists because from $P0$ and the guard $y \neq x+1$ of the repetition we conclude that $x+2 \leq y$.
End

Having settled the invariance of $P0$ under $x := h$, we now turn our attention to $P1$. We observe

$P1 \ (x := h)$

$\equiv$ { definition of $P1$ }

hZy .

Since this latter condition does not in general follow from $P1$ or $P0$, we plug it in as a guard to $x := h$.

We next address a decrease of y . Because we already have an h such that $h < y$, we propose $y := h$. By the problem's symmetry in x and y, our program now becomes as shown in Figure 12.2.

$\{ a < b \ \wedge \ aZb \}$

$x, y := a, b$

$\{ \text{inv } P0 \wedge P1 \ \} \ \{ \text{ bnd } y - x \}$

$; \ \textbf{do } y \neq x+1 \ \rightarrow$

$\{ x+2 \leq y \}$

"h such that $x < h \wedge h < y$ "

$; \ \textbf{if } hZy \rightarrow x := h$

$[] \ xZh \rightarrow y := h$

$\textbf{fi}$

$\textbf{od}$

$\{ R \}$

Figure 12.2: The binary search program

The question of termination of this program remains. It does terminate if we can ensure that at least one of the guards of the if statement evaluates to *true*. This will in general not be the case, but it is if relation Z satisfies

(0) $xZy \;\Rightarrow\; hZy \lor xZh$ $(\forall x, y, h)$

(The antecedent is the valid precondition $P1$; the consequent is the disjunction of the guards.)

While adopting this condition on Z, we can even ensure very fast termination by choosing h to be equal to $(x+y) \underline{\text{div}}\, 2$, which thanks to precondition $x+2 \leq y$ indeed establishes $x < h \land h < y$. And thus, binary search is born!

Our program computes an x satisfying postcondition R. Of course, there may be many x's satisfying R. And here we arrive at what we think is a distinguishing feature of the binary search, namely that

> it is beyond our control which x
> satisfying the postcondition
> will be generated.

(This is in sharp contrast to linear searches where a fully specified value is computed.)

In order to substantiate this feature we consider the instantiation $a, b := 0, 100$ and $Z := true$, meeting Prog0's precondition and (0). We then obtain

$$x, y := 0, 100$$
$$; \,\text{do } y \neq x+1 \;\rightarrow$$
$$h := (x+y) \underline{\text{div}}\, 2$$
$$; \,\text{if } true \rightarrow x := h$$
$$[\!]\; true \rightarrow y := h$$
$$\text{fi}$$
$$\text{od}$$
$$\{\, 0 \leq x \land x < 100 \,\},$$

which is a highly nondeterministic program. And the reader may check, in whatever way comes to mind, that, indeed, it can generate *any* value x such that $0 \leq x \land x < 100$.

We will return to this distinguishing feature at a later stage.

Meanwhile, some readers may have been puzzled by the "weird" condition (0). But it is not weird at all; when taking the contrapositive of (0), we get

(0') $x(\neg Z)h \,\land\, h(\neg Z)y \;\Rightarrow\; x(\neg Z)y,$

and this just expresses that Z's complement relation $\neg Z$ is transitive.

Here are some of such relations Z (for array f of the appropriate type):
$xZy \equiv$

♦ $f.x \neq f.y$

- $f.x < f.y$
- $f.x \leq A \;\wedge\; A \leq f.y$
- $f.x * f.y \leq 0$
- $f.x \vee f.y$
- $\neg Q.x \wedge Q.y,$ for any Q.

The reader can easily verify that they all satisfy (0) (or (0')).

Hint   The first example, $f.x \neq f.y$, is a very appropriate choice when novices are to be introduced to the binary search.
End Hint .

The last example in the above list, $\neg Q.x \wedge Q.y$, is a frequently occurring one, and we shall now deal in more detail with its probably best-known instance, viz. $Q.i \equiv C < f.i$. That is, given

- integer array $f[a..b]$ with $a < b$

- integer constant C satisfying $f.a \leq C \wedge C < f.b$,

our binary search becomes (see remark below)

$$\{a < b\} \; \{f.a \leq C \wedge C < f.b\}$$

$$x, y := a, b$$

$$\{\,\text{inv } P0: \; a \leq x \;\wedge\; x < y \;\wedge\; y \leq b$$

$$P1: \; f.x \leq C \;\wedge\; C < f.y \,\} \; \{\,\text{bnd } y - x\}$$

$$; \; \text{do } y \neq x + 1 \;\rightarrow$$

$$h := (x + y) \,\underline{\text{div}}\, 2 \; \{a \leq x < h < y \leq b\}$$

$$; \; \text{if } f.h \leq C \rightarrow x := h$$

$$[\!] \; C < f.h \rightarrow y := h$$

$$\text{fi}$$

$$\text{od}$$

$$\{a \leq x \wedge x < b\} \; \{f.x \leq C \;\wedge\; C < f.(x+1)\}$$

Remark   Actually, we arrived at the above program not by instantiating our original program scheme (Figure 12.2), but by just rederiving it for the current relation $f.x \leq C \wedge C < f.y$. That derivation is so simple that it can be done mentally: guided by the invariants $P0$ and $P1$, the program can be written down at once.
End Remark .

Note that the precondition of the program in Figure 12.2 (and hence of the program given above) is the *only* property of f used in the derivation. Thus we hope to have shown that the binary search has a right of existence outside the realm of sorted arrays.

However, if f *is* sorted in ascending order, the program above comes in very handy to record the presence of C in $f[a..b]$, namely by postfixing the program with the assignment

$$present := (f.x = C) \ .$$

And, in fact, it is only for the conclusion that C is absent from f ($present \equiv false$) that we use f's ascending property.

We have derived these programs under a precondition $(a < b \wedge a\,Z\,b)$. In many practical situations, however, this condition need not be satisfied. There are two general ways out. The first way out is to try to solve the problem separately for the case in which the precondition does not hold.

The more elegant way out is based on the observation that Prog1 does not inspect the array elements $f.a$ or $f.b$ at all — see precondition $a < h \wedge h < b$ to the inspection of $f.h$. This implies that their actual values are completely irrelevant to the (outcome of the) computation : they are thought variables mainly.

We exploit this observation in the following way. Suppose all we know about $f[a..b]$ is that it is ascending and that $a \leq b+1$ (the array may be empty). We define thought values $f.(a-1)$ and $f.(b+1)$ in such a way that

♦ $f[a-1 .. b+1]$ is ascending, and

♦ $f.(a-1) \leq C \ \wedge \ C < f.(b+1)$

and since in addition $a-1 < b+1$ holds, we have thus laid down precisely the required precondition of the last program, but with the instantiation $a,b :=$ $a-1, b+1$. The solution to our problem to record the presence of C in array $f[a..b]$ now reads

$$x,y := a-1, b+1$$

$; \text{do } y \neq x+1 \ \rightarrow$

$\qquad h := (x+y) \underline{\text{div}} \ 2$

$\qquad \{ a \leq h \wedge h \leq b \text{, hence } f.h \text{ is defined} \}$

$\qquad ; \text{if } f.h \leq C \rightarrow x := h$

$\qquad [\!] \ C < f.h \rightarrow y := h$

$\qquad \text{fi}$

od

$\{ a-1 \leq x \ \wedge \ x < b+1 \ \} \ \{ \ f.x \leq C \wedge C < f.(x+1) \}$

$; \text{if } a-1 = x \rightarrow \ \{ C < f.a \} \ present := false$

$[\!] \ a-1 < x \rightarrow \{ a \leq x \wedge x \leq b \text{, hence } f.x \text{ is defined} \}$

$\qquad present := (f.x = C)$

      fi

The technique applied — adding thought values so as to establish a required precondition — is suitable in many other examples as well.

We conclude this note on the binary search with two exercises and a question. The exercises are

(*i*)   Given that integer array $f[a..b]$, $a \leq b$, is the concatenation of an increasing and a decreasing sequence, find the top (maximum). More precisely, design a program that computes a value M such that

$$a \leq M \wedge M \leq b$$

$\wedge$ $f[a .. M]$ is increasing

$\wedge$ $f[M .. b]$ is decreasing

(Note : $f[a .. M]$ is increasing $\equiv \langle \forall i: a \leq i < M: f.i < f.(i+1) \rangle$) .

(*ii*) Given that integer array $f[a .. b]$, $a < b$,

     $\Diamond$ is the concatenation of two increasing sequences

     $\Diamond$ contains a dip, i.e.

$$\langle \exists i: a \leq i < b: f.i > f.(i+1) \rangle \; , \quad \text{and}$$

     $\Diamond$ satisfies $f.a > f.b$,

     design a program to compute a dip .

Both exercises can be solved using a binary search.

If, however, in exercise (*ii*) the given $f.a > f.b$ is dropped, we no longer know of a way to solve this problem with the binary search technique, not even if we introduce a thought value $f.(a-1)$ such that $f.(a-1) > f.b$. The reason why the introduction of such a thought value does not help here is that it may introduce a second dip at $a-1$, and as we said before, it is now beyond our control which dip will be computed by the binary search: it could be the required one, but it could also be the thought dip that we ourselves introduced.

The as yet unsolved problem that remains is to identify the *precise* conditions for a binary search to be applicable.

12.4   On multiprogramming

12.4.1 A preamble

If there is one branch of computer programming where the guideline "keep it simple, please" is to be taken highly seriously, it certainly is the branch called "parallel programming" or "multiprogramming". Why is multiprogramming so difficult? There are many reasons, and just one of them is exemplified by the following.

Consider the simple, meaningless, random program

$$x := y+1$$
$$; \ x := y^2$$
$$; \ x := x-y \ .$$

It consists of just three assignment statements. If we start it in an initial state such that $x=7 \wedge y=3$, it will deliver $x=6 \wedge y=3$ as final answer. This is easily checked.

Also consider the equally simple and meaningless program

$$y := x+1$$
$$; \ y := x^2$$
$$; \ y := y-x \ .$$

When started in $x=7 \wedge y=3$, it yields $x=7 \wedge y=42$.

Now let us run these two programs in parallel. Such a parallel execution boils down to selecting an arbitrary interleaving of the three statements of the x-program and the three statements of the y-program, and then executing the six statements in the order selected. Because there are 20 possible interleavings, the parallel execution of the two programs can give rise to 20 different computations. Here are the possible final values for x and y.

x	y
-4032	8128
-3968	4032
-600	1225
-575	600
-72	153
-63	72
-1	2
2	-1
6	30
20	380
56	3080
132	12
240	-224
496	-240
1722	42
2352	-2303
4753	-2352
5112	72
6480	-6399

13041   -6480

The moral of the example is clear: by the parallel composition, the two extremely simple programs have turned into a horrendous monster. The number of possible computations has exploded. If more component programs or less simple ones join the game, the phenomenon becomes much more pronounced. As a result, any attempt to come to grips with a multiprogram by considering all the individual computations that can be evoked by it is far beyond what we can imagine or grasp, and is — in practice and in principle — doomed to fail. In short, operational reasoning should be out!

If operational reasoning is to be out, we have to resort to formalism. From sequential programming we have learned that the Hoare-triple semantics (Hoare, 1969) and the predicate transformer semantics (Dijkstra, 1976) do away with individual computations in a highly effective manner. Moreover, these — very similar — semantics have created eminent opportunity for the formal *derivation* of programs. The formalism that faithfully imports these virtues into the area of multiprogramming is the theory of Owicki and Gries (1976; Dijkstra, 1982), which we shall explain next.

Remark   The theory of Owicki and Gries, said the computing community, has been designed for the *a posteriori* verification of multiprograms, and is of no use for the *derivation* of such programs. The only thing we can say to this is that this is not true. The main reason for us to write this note is to show how the Owicki–Gries theory can support a method for the formal derivation of multiprograms. Of course, in a short note like this we can show only some of the flavour of such a method. Reasonable introductory accounts can be found in Moerland (1993) and in van der Sommen (1994), treatises of former students of ours.
End Remark .

12.4.2   The theory of Owicki and Gries

We consider a system of ordinary sequential programs. We call it a multiprogram. The constituent sequential programs we call the (multiprogram's) components. The multiprogram as a whole has a precondition (describing an initial state from which the component programs can start their execution). If all components terminate, the multiprogram has a postcondition as well (describing the combined final states of the components).

We now consider the components to be annotated with assertions, in the way we are used to for sequential programs. The intended operational interpretation of the annotation is the following: if execution of a component has reached an assertion P, then the state of the system as a whole satisfies P. With this in mind, the subsequent proof rules for the correctness of an annotation may sound "sweetly reasonable".

By definition, the annotation is correct whenever for *every* assertion in *every* component, it holds that

(*i*) that assertion is "locally correct", and

(*ii*) that assertion is "globally correct".

Re (*i*)   For proving the local correctness of an assertion P in a component program, we just follow the rules of sequential programming. We can proceed as if this program were to be dealt with in isolation. There are two cases.

• If P is the preassertion of the component program, we have to ensure that it is implied by the precondition of the entire multiprogram.

• If P is the postassertion of a statement S with preassertion Q, we have to ensure the validity of Hoare-triple

$$\{Q\}S\{P\}.$$

End

Re (*ii*)   For proving the global correctness of an assertion P in a component program, we have to do more work, because now all other components have to be taken into account. Namely, we have to prove for *each* $\{Q\}S$ — i.e. a statement S with preassertion Q — taken from a *different* component, the validity of the Hoare-triple

$$\{P \wedge Q\}S\{P\}.$$

In words, this boils down to showing that assertion P in the one component cannot be falsified by the statements of the other components. In the jargon we can often hear P's global correctness phrased as "P is stable".
End

Finally, if the multiprogram has a postcondition, we have to show that all components terminate and that the postcondition is implied by the conjunction of the postassertions of the individual components.

And this, in fact, is all there is to be said about the theory of Owicki and Gries. We can summarize it quite succinctly by

the annotation is correct

$\equiv$

each assertion is established by the component in which it occurs, and
it is maintained by the statements of all other components.

There is another notion that is very important for discussing multiprograms, viz. the notion of a system invariant. A relation P is a system invariant whenever

♦ it is implied by the precondition of the multiprogram (P holds initially), and

♦ for each $\{Q\}S$ in each component, we have

$$\{P \wedge Q\} S \{P\}$$

(P is not falsified by any statement from any component).

As a result, an invariant can be added as a conjunct to *each* assertion, and therefore we can afford the freedom of writing it *nowhere* in our annotation. This is of great importance for the clarity of exposition and for the economy of reading and writing.

Example and Exercise
We return to the example at the beginning of this section on multiprogramming :

Pre: $x = 7 \wedge y = 3$

$Compx$: $x := y+1$ $Compy$: $y := x+1$
         $; x := y^2$ $; y := x^2$
         $; x := x-y$ $; y := y-x$

$Post?$: $\langle \exists i :: x+y = i^2 \rangle$

Certainly, both components terminate. The exercise is to prove that

$Post$: $\langle \exists i :: x+y = i^2 \rangle$

is a correct postcondition. This, most definitely, is not an easy exercise. (Giving *a posteriori* proofs usually isn't easy; designing programs and their correctness proofs — hand in hand — is much more do-able, and far more rewarding.) The problem is that we have to invent, or at best develop, annotation that enables us to draw the desired conclusion. At this point of presentation, we simply reveal an adequate annotation, and then embark on a proof of its correctness. Unfortunately, the exercise is already that complicated that we need to introduce auxiliary variables (thought variables) to carry out the proof. The annotated multiprogram, extended with the thought variables, is — see explanation below —

Pre: $x = 7 \wedge y = 3 \wedge \neg p \wedge \neg q$

$Inv?$: $p \wedge q \Rightarrow \langle \exists i :: x+y = i^2 \rangle$

$Compx$: $\{\neg p\} x := y+1$ $Compy$: $y := x+1$
         $; \{\neg p\} x := y^2$ $; y := x^2$
         $; \{\langle \exists i :: x = i^2 \rangle\}$ $; y,q := y-x, true$
            $x,p := x-y, true$ $\{q\}$
            $\{p\}$

$Post?$: $\langle \exists i :: x+y = i^2 \rangle$

For reasons of symmetry between the components we have annotated $Compy$ less lavishly than $Compx$. We laid down a post-assertion p to $Compx$ and a post-assertion q to $Compy$, with the intent that their conjunction $p \wedge q$ imply

Post. That is how the need for invariant Inv arose. We leave it as an exercise to the reader to check the correctness of the annotation — which is not difficult. By way of example, we shall demonstrate the invariance of Inv, i.e. of

$$p \wedge q \Rightarrow \langle \exists i :: x+y=i^2 \rangle .$$

We have to show that it holds initially — which it vacuously does — , and that no statement of the multiprogram violates it. By the symmetry in Inv and in the components, we can confine our attention to the statements of $Compx$:

Re $\{\neg p\} x := y+1$
Our proof obligation is

$$\{ Inv \wedge \neg p \} x := y+1 \{ Inv \} ,$$

the correctness of which follows from the following calculation:

$$Inv(x := y+1)$$

$\equiv$ { definition of Inv }

$$p \wedge q \Rightarrow \langle \exists i :: y+1+y=i^2 \rangle$$

$\equiv$ { $\neg p$, from precondition $Inv \wedge \neg p$ }

$true$.

End

Re $\{\neg p\} x := y^2$
     Similarly.
End

Re $\{ \langle \exists i :: x=i^2 \rangle \} x,p := x-y, true$
Our proof obligation is

$$\{ Inv \wedge \langle \exists i :: x=i^2 \rangle \} x,p := x-y, true \{ Inv \} ,$$

the correctness of which follows from

$$Inv(x,p := x-y, true)$$

$\equiv$ { definition of Inv }

$$true \wedge q \Rightarrow \langle \exists i :: x-y+y = i^2 \rangle$$

$\equiv$ { simplification }

$$q \Rightarrow \langle \exists i :: x=i^2 \rangle$$

$\equiv$ { $\langle \exists i :: x=i^2 \rangle$, from the precondition of the statement }

$true$.

End

Finally, we have to spend a word on our program notation. We write down our sequential programs just the way we are used to, viz. in the guarded command notation. There is one point, though, that needs extra emphasis, namely that an alternative construct like

if B → skip fi

is our main tool for achieving synchronization. To all intents and purposes, it is equivalent to

do ¬B → skip od ,

i.e. "waiting until B is true". In the literature, we often find it denoted as await B . Its semantics, in Hoare-triple format, is given by

$\{ B \Rightarrow R \}$ if B → skip fi $\{ R \}$.

12.4.3 Total deadlock and the multibound

In most multiprogramming problems, the component programs have to cooperate on a task. Correctness of the cooperation usually requires some sort of synchronization among the components. The synchronization becomes manifest by the occurrence of statements like if B → skip fi (or await B) in the program texts. The effect of their execution is that the normal computational "progress" of a component is blocked until guard B is "found" to be true. However, with the incorporation of these "blocking" statements, a new and very serious complication has entered the game.

While, on the one hand, these statements are necessary for a temporary blocking of a component's progress, they introduce the danger of infinite blocking on the other hand. As a consequence, a new kind of proof obligation is imposed on us, namely to show that each individual blocking statement that we introduce into a component program will not lead to an infinite blocking of that component. This proof obligation is of a completely different nature from the proof obligation we had for the correctness of annotation. In fact, showing what the jargon has called "individual progress" or "liveness", is, in full generality, so difficult that computing science has not yet succeeded in making this problem technically feasible.

However, there are some special circumstances in which individual progress can be shown quite easily. One of these circumstances is when we have the following scenario. Consider, as an example, a three-component multiprogram that, projected on the variables x, y, and z, has the form

$* [x := x+1]$ $\qquad * [y := y+1]$ $\qquad * [z := z+1]$

($* [S]$ is short for do $true$ → S od .)

The rest of the code of these components is such that it satisfies some synchronization requirement, the precise nature of which does not concern us here. Now suppose that it so happens that this multiprogram maintains as a system invariant

MB: $x \leq y+K \ \wedge \ y \leq z+L \ \wedge \ z \leq x+M$,

for some constants K, L, and M. We then observe that if, due to the (unknown) synchronization protocol, one of the components comes to a definitive halt in one of its blocking statements, so will the others. As a result, the multiprogram as a whole can exhibit only two scenarios as far as progress is concerned, to wit

> either *all* components get stuck forever
> — this is called "total deadlock" —
>
> or *each* individual component makes progress.

So, in the presence of a "multibound" like MB, individual progress can be demonstrated by showing the absence of the danger of total deadlock. And the nice thing about this is that the latter can be done using the theory of Owicki and Gries. (We do not need to go into this for the purpose of this note.)

So much for these notational and conceptual issues. We now turn our attention to some examples of multiprogram derivation.

12.4.4   The parallel linear search

The problem of the parallel linear search is a nice little paradigm which was first communicated to us in the mid 1980s by Ernst-Rüdiger Olderog. It serves as a running example in Apt and Olderog (1991). In Knapp (1992), we can find a first formal derivation of the algorithm, a derivation which is carried out in terms of the UNITY-formalism (Chandy and Misra, 1988).

The problem is as follows. Given is a boolean function f on the integers, such that

(0) $\langle \exists i :: f.i \rangle$.

Our goal is to design a terminating multiprogram with two components that "finds" an integer with a true f-value. The idea is that one component "searches" through the nonnegative integers and the other component through the nonpositive ones. More precisely, we have to design a terminating multiprogram with the following specification

Pre: $x = 0 \ \wedge \ y = 0$

Inv: $0 \leq x \ \wedge \ y \leq 0$

$Post$: $f.x \ \vee \ f.y$

$CompA$:   do $\dots \to x := x+1$ od $\{ RA \}$

$CompB$:   do $\dots \to y := y+1$ od $\{ RB \}$.

At this point, there are two immediate concerns. One is that we have to choose (correct!) assertions RA and RB such that

(1) $\qquad RA \wedge RB \;\Rightarrow\; f.x \vee f.y$.

The other is that we have to ensure termination for both components.

In order to satisfy (1) we choose both RA and RB equal to $f.x \vee f.y$.

Remark   In view of the symmetry between the components, this choice for RA and RB is quite reasonable. Besides, it is a good heuristic to choose the annotation as weak as possible, if there is a choice. The reason for this is that the annotation can always be strengthened later on, should the need arise — see Moerland (1993) or Feijen (1990). In our example, these heuristics rule out the stronger choice $f.x$ for RA, and $f.y$ for RB .
End Remark .

In order to ensure the local correctness of RA, i.e. of $f.x \vee f.y$, we can choose $\neg f.x$ as a guard of the repetition of $CompA$, but this one is too weak to ensure termination of $CompA$: given (0) does not guarantee the existence of a nonnegative x for which $f.x$ holds. Therefore, we *must* resort to a stronger guard. Let it be $\neg f.x \wedge \neg d$.

We thus arrive at the first approximation of the multiprogram to be designed.

Pre: $x=0 \wedge y=0$

Inv: $0 \leq x \wedge y \leq 0$

$Post$: $f.x \vee f.y$

$CompA$:   do $\neg f.x \wedge \neg d \;\rightarrow$
$\qquad\qquad$ { $\neg f.x$, see later in Note 1 }
$\qquad\qquad$ $x := x{+}1$
$\qquad$ od
$\qquad$ { $f.x \vee f.y$ }

$CompB$:   do $\neg f.y \wedge \neg c \;\rightarrow$
$\qquad\qquad$ { $\neg f.y$ }
$\qquad\qquad$ $y := y{-}1$
$\qquad$ od
$\qquad$ { $f.x \vee f.y$, see Note 0 below }

In Note 0 we now examine the — local and global — correctness of assertion $f.x \vee f.y$ in $CompB$. (The correctness of $f.x \vee f.y$ in $CompA$ follows by symmetry.)

Note 0   "$f.x \vee f.y$ in $CompB$"

L: For $f.x \vee f.y$ in $CompB$ to be locally correct it suffices that

$$\neg(\neg f.y \wedge \neg c) \;\Rightarrow\; f.x \vee f.y$$

which — by predicate calculus — is equivalent to

$$c \Rightarrow f.x \lor f.y \ .$$

We shall meet this condition by adopting

PA: $c \Rightarrow f.x \lor f.y$

as a system invariant, and — by symmetry — also

PB: $d \Rightarrow f.x \lor f.y \ .$

We will address the invariance of PA and PB in a moment.

G: For $f.x \lor f.y$ in $CompB$ to be globally correct we have to show the correctness of the Hoare-triple

$$\{f.x \lor f.y\}\, x := x+1 \,\{f.x \lor f.y\} \ .$$

To that end we observe

$$f.x \lor f.y \Rightarrow (f.x \lor f.y)(x := x+1)$$

$\equiv$ { substitution }

$$f.x \lor f.y \Rightarrow f.(x+1) \lor f.y$$

$\Leftarrow$ { nothing is known about $f.(x+1)$ }

$$f.x \lor f.y \Rightarrow f.y$$

$\Leftarrow$ { predicate calculus }

$$\neg f.x \ .$$

And here we encounter the reason why it is pleasant to have $\neg f.x$ as a valid precondition to $x := x+1$. That is why we add it .

End Note 0 .

Note 1   "$\neg f.x$ in $CompA$"

L: The local correctness follows from the guard

G: The global correctness follows, because $CompB$ changes neither x nor f .

End Note 1 .

At this point we are left with the care for the invariance of PA and PB, and with the care for termination of both components. The two concerns largely coincide. We first observe that

$$\langle \forall i:\, 0 \le i < x:\, \neg f.i \rangle \ \land \ \langle \forall i:\, y < i \le 0:\, \neg f.i \rangle$$

is a system invariant: this is easily checked. With the given (0), i.e.

$$\langle \exists i::f.i \rangle \ ,$$

we therefore conclude that at least one of the two components terminates. If $CompA$ terminates, it has established $f.x \lor f.y$ — see the annotation — and it can now enforce termination of $CompB$ as well by falsifying the latter's guard $\neg f.y \land \neg c$, which can be done by just $c := true$. Fortunately this does not interfere with the requirement that

PA: $c \Rightarrow f.x \lor f.y$

be an invariant, thanks to the validity of $f.x \lor f.y$. Thus we arrive at our next (and last) approximation of the multiprogram to be designed. We give the fully annotated program text, and leave to the reader the formal proof of the invariance of PA (and of PB).

Pre: $x=0 \land y=0 \land \neg c \land \neg d \land \langle \exists i :: f.i \rangle$

Inv: $0 \leq x \land y \leq 0 \land PA \land PB$

$Post$: $f.x \lor f.y$

$CompA$:

      do $\neg f.x \land \neg d \rightarrow \{ \neg f.x \} \, x := x{+}1$ od
      $\{ f.x \lor f.y \}$
    ; $c := true$
      $\{ c \land PA$, hence $f.x \lor f.y \}$

$CompB$:

      do $\neg f.y \land \neg c \rightarrow \{ \neg f.y \} \, y := y{-}1$ od
      $\{ f.x \lor f.y \}$
    ; $d := true$
      $\{ f.x \lor f.y \}$

12.4.5   A problem of phase synchronization

The problem of phase synchronization for two machines is one of the simplest problems enabling us to get across some of the flavour of a method for the formal derivation of multiprograms. (For many more examples, we refer to Moerland (1993) and van der Sommen (1994).) An interesting by-product of the problem is that it can serve to illustrate how "parallelism" can be traded for storage space. Namely, we shall present two solutions, one of which allows "more parallelism" than the other, be it at the expense of more storage space. We also illustrate how one can consciously choose between the two options.

    We consider the two-component multiprogram given by

    $Comp0$: $* [\, S \,]$ $Comp1$: $* [\, T \,]$

(Notation $*[\,S\,]$ is short for $\mathbf{do}\,true \rightarrow S\,\mathbf{od}$.)

*Comp*0 and *Comp*1 are given "to run in parallel". Moreover, each individual execution of S and each individual execution of T are guaranteed to terminate. The synchronization task ahead of us is to see to it that the number of completed S's and the number of completed T's are "never too far apart".

In order to make the synchronization requirement precise, we introduce two *fresh* auxiliary integer variables x and y, and adjust the multiprogram proper in the following way:

Pre: $x = 0 \wedge y = 0$

*Comp*0: $*[\,\{\,x \leq y, ?\,\}\,S \;\; ; \;\; x := x{+}1\,]$

*Comp*1: $*[\,\{\,y \leq x, ?\,\}\,T \;\; ; \;\; y := y{+}1\,]$

This, now, is our formal specification, to the extent that we are now supposed to understand that it is our task to superimpose on these program texts additional code so as to accomplish that

♦ in *Comp*0, $x \leq y$ is a valid precondition to S,
  and, similarly,

♦ in *Comp*1, $y \leq x$ is a valid precondition to T.

Remark   Variables x and y, and the operations on them, have been introduced to specify the synchronization problem. It goes without saying that in the further development of the multiprogram, no further changes of x or y are allowed, because they would defeat the purpose for which these variables and the operations on them were introduced in the first place. Inspections of them are, however, harmless.

End Remark .

Before we embark on a derivation, we observe that no matter which solution we end up with, relation $x \leq y{+}1$ will be a system invariant. This is so because

♦ it holds initially

♦ increments of y in *Comp*1 do not falsify it

♦ assignment $x := x{+}1$ will have precondition $x \leq y$. (Here we use that no other assignments to x are allowed in the further development.)

By symmetry, also $y \leq x{+}1$ will be an invariant, and hence

MB: $x \leq y{+}1 \wedge y \leq x{+}1$.

This is a perfect multibound for our multiprogram, and as a result our only proof obligation with respect to individual progress will be to show the absence of total deadlock, *no matter* what will be our ultimate solution.

Now let us start our derivation. We have to ensure the correctness of assertion $x \leq y$ in *Comp*0. Its global correctness is for free: $y := y{+}1$ does not falsify it.

As for its local correctness, we observe that it is implied by the precondition Pre of the multiprogram. So it suffices to make $x \leq y$ a *loop* invariant of $Comp0$. $Comp1$ is dealt with symmetrically. Thus we arrive at an approximation:

Pre: $x = 0 \wedge y = 0$

$Comp0$: $* [\{ x \leq y \} S ; \ x := x+1 \{ x \leq y, ? \}]$

$Comp1$: $* [\{ y \leq x \} T ; \ y := y+1 \{ y \leq x, ? \}]$

Remark   By design, this approximation satisfies our original formal specification. But moreover, it acts as the formal specification for what follows. The approximation above is the precise interface between the past and the future in the design process, and it is noteworthy that that interface is quite thin.
End Remark .

From here, there are two essentially different ways in which to proceed. They result in two different solutions.
Solution A
Again, the global correctness of $x \leq y$ in $Comp0$ is for free. We ensure its local correctness by "testing", i.e. by prefixing assertion $x \leq y$ with if $x \leq y \rightarrow$ skip fi . $Comp1$ is dealt with in a symmetric fashion, and thus we arrive at the following approximation:

$$Pre: \quad x = 0 \wedge y = 0$$

$Comp0$:* [$\{ x \leq y \} S$
      ; $x := x+1$
      ; if $x \leq y \rightarrow$ skip fi
      $\{ x \leq y \}$
      ]

$Comp1$:* [$\{ y \leq x \} T$
      ; $y := y+1$
      ; if $y \leq x \rightarrow$ skip fi
      $\{ y \leq x \}$
      ] .

There is no danger of total deadlock because the disjunction of the guards is true. So, in a way we are done. We wish to observe, though, that by the invariance of

MB: $x \leq y+1 \wedge y \leq x+1$,

the difference $y - x$ is just three-valued, so that we can eliminate the ever-growing integers x and y at the expense of, say, just two booleans. We will, however, not carry out such a coordinate transformation here.
End Solution A .

Solution B
Starting from Approximation 0 again, we now destroy the symmetry between the components. We ensure the local correctness of assertion $x \leq y$ in $Comp0$ by requiring that the precondition of $x := x+1$ implies $x+1 \leq y$. For $Comp1$ we do *not* carry out such a move. We thus obtain the approximation:

$$Pre: \quad x=0 \land y=0$$

$Comp0:* [\{x \le y\} S$
$\quad ; \{x+1 \le y, ?\}$
$\quad x := x+1$
$\quad \{x \le y\}$
$]$

$Comp1:* [\{y \le x\} T$
$\quad ; y := y+1$
$\quad \{y \le x, ?\}$
$]$

Along with the transition from the first approximation to the last, two things happened.

(*i*) The last approximation has a *stronger* annotation: preassertion $x+1 \le y$ to $x := x+1$ has crept in. Now, let us recall the operational interpretation of an assertion. If a component is "at" an assertion, the state of the system as a whole satisfies that assertion. The stronger the assertion, the smaller the space in which the rest of the system can maneuver, i.e. the lesser the degree of parallelism that can be exhibited.

(*ii*) No matter how we proceed from the last approximation, relation

$Q: \qquad x \le y \land y \le x+1$

will be a system invariant. This is easily checked. As a result, the difference $y-x$ is just two-valued, instead of three-valued as in Solution A. We therefore can represent in by a single boolean.

And here we see in a nutshell how "parallelism" can be traded for storage space, a phenomenon that we have alluded to before.

Remark   We can push the phenomenon to a limit by restoring the symmetry between the components and performing the same transformation for *Comp1*. Then the ensuing invariant will be $x \le y \land y \le x$, i.e. $x=y$. As a result, total deadlock will become unavoidable. And indeed, total deadlock can be implemented with zero variables, for instance by means of constructs like if $false \to$ skip fi .
End Remark .

Now we proceed from the final approximation, above, in a straightforward manner so as to arrive at:

$$Pre: \quad x=0 \land y=0$$

$$Inv: \quad x \le y \land y \le x+1$$

$Comp0:* [\{x \le y\} S$
$\quad ; \text{if } x+1 \le y \to \text{skip fi}$
$\quad \{x+1 \le y\}$
$\quad ; x := x+1$
$\quad \{x \le y\}$
$]$

$Comp1:* [\{y \le x\} T$
$\quad ; y := y+1$
$\quad ; \text{if } y \le x \to \text{skip fi}$
$\quad \{y \le x\}$
$] .$

And again, there is no danger of total deadlock, so that individual progress is guaranteed.

As a last step in our development we this time *do* perform the coordinate transformation towards a single boolean. We introduce boolean variable c, coupled to x and y by

$$c \equiv (x=y) .$$

Then, by the invariant $x \leq y \wedge y \leq x+1$,

$$x+1 \leq y \equiv \neg c \quad \text{and} \quad y \leq x \equiv c$$

$$\{x+1 \leq y\} x := x+1 \quad \leftrightarrow \quad \{\neg c\} c := true$$

$$\{y \leq x\} y := y+1 \quad \leftrightarrow \quad \{c\} c := false .$$

And thus we arrive at our final solution, for which the raw code reads

$$Pre: \quad c$$

$Comp0{:}^* \ [\ S$
    $; \ \text{if} \ \neg c \rightarrow \text{skip fi}$
    $; \ c := true$
    $]$

$Comp1{:}^* \ [\ T$
    $; \ c := false$
    $; \ \text{if} \ c \rightarrow \text{skip fi}$
    $]$

End Solution B .

12.4.6 A case of intuitive reasoning

Mathematical intuition is a very dangerous and unreliable compass, even more so in the case of multiprogramming. Recently we showed a very small multiprogram to our class, namely the following

$A: \quad y := false$
    $; \ \text{if} \ y \rightarrow skip \text{fi}$

$B: \quad x := false$
    $; \ \text{if} \ x \rightarrow skip \text{fi}$

These are just two straight-line programs, each consisting of just two simple statements. Hardly anything simpler can be conceived, can it?

Now, for the sake of letting both components terminate, we granted the class the possibility to add statements "$x := true$" to component A, as many as they wanted and wherever they wanted. And similarly, statements "$y := true$" were allowed to be added to B.

The class did not hesitate very long. Because component B is "waiting" for x to become true, termination of B becomes most likely if A performs "$x := true$" as often as possible. And symmetrically so for "$y := true$". So, here is the solution:

$$A: \quad x := true$$
$$; \ y := false$$
$$; \ x := true$$
$$; \ \text{if } y \to skip \text{ fi}$$
$$; \ x := true$$

$$B: \quad y := true$$
$$; \ x := false$$
$$; \ y := true$$
$$; \ \text{if } x \to skip \text{ fi}$$
$$; \ y := true$$

But, alas, each effort to give a genuine termination proof failed. And indeed, there is no guarantee that both components terminate. (Let A proceed to its if-statement. Then $x \wedge \neg y$ holds. Next, let B perform its first "$y := true$". Then $x \wedge y$ holds. Now let A terminate. Then B gets stuck.)

The nice thing is that, if we remove the first line from each component, i.e. if we consider

$$A: \quad y := false$$
$$; \ x := true$$
$$; \ \text{if } y \to \text{skip fi}$$
$$; \ x := true$$

$$B: \quad x := false$$
$$; \ y := true$$
$$; \ \text{if } x \to \text{skip fi}$$
$$; \ y := true$$

then everything is fine (proof omitted here — see Feijen, 1992).

To us, the above is a very nice example to demonstrate the intricacies of multiprogramming to a novice audience, and to warn them to never lean on "intuition", but on rigorous formal proofs instead.

Notes

1. We owe this theorem to Edsger W. Dijkstra. It seems to be not generally known to lattice theorists.

References

Aarts, C.J. (1992) *Galois Connections Presented Calculationally*, Masters Thesis, Department of Computing Science, Eindhoven University of Technology.

Apt, K.R. and Olderog, E.-R. (1991) *Verification of Sequential and Concurrent Programs*, Springer Verlag, Berlin.

Bresenham, J.E. (1965) Algorithm for computer control of a digital plotter, *IBM Systems Journal*, **4**(1):25–30.

Chandy, K.M. and Misra, J. (1988) *Parallel Program Design: A Foundation*, Addison-Wesley, Amsterdam.

Dijkstra, E.W. (1976) *A Discipline of Programming*, Prentice Hall, Englewood Cliffs, NJ.

Dijkstra, E.W. (1982) A personal summary of the Gries–Owicki theory. In *Selected Writings on Computing: A Personal Perspective*, Springer Verlag, New York.

Feijen, W.H.J. (1990) A little exercise in deriving multiprograms. In W.H.J. Feijen, A.J.M. van Gasteren, D. Gries and J. Misra, editors, *Beauty is our Business: A Birthday Salute to Edsger W. Dijkstra*, pp 119–127, Springer Verlag, New York.

Feijen, W.H.J. (1992) Phase synchronization for two machines. In M. Broy, editor, *Programming and Mathematical Method, Proceedings of the NATO Advanced Study Institute on Programming and Mathematical Method*, pp 27–32, Springer Verlag, Berlin.

Hoare, C.A.R. (1969) An axiomatic basis for computer programming, *Communications of the ACM*, **12**(10):576–583, October.

Hoogerwoord, R.R. (1989) *The Design of Functional Programs: A Calculational Approach*, Ph.D. thesis, Eindhoven University of Technology.

Kaldewaij, A. (1993) *Programmeren, Deel 3: Datastructuren en standaardalgoritmen*, Bohn Stafleu Van Loghem, Houten/Zaventem.

Knapp, E. (1992) Derivation of concurrent programs: two examples, *Science of Computer Programming*, **19**:1–23.

Moerland, P.D. (1993) *Exercises in Multiprogramming*, Computing Science Notes 93/07, Department of Computing Science, Eindhoven University of Technology.

Owicki, S. and Gries, D. (1976) An axiomatic proof technique for parallel programs I, *Acta Informatica*, **6**:319–340.

van de Snepscheut, J.L.A. (1993) *What Computing is All About*, Springer Verlag, New York.

van der Sommen, F.W. (1994) *Multiprogram Derivations*, Masters Thesis, Department of Computing Science, Eindhoven University of Technology.

Wirth, N. (1990) Drawing lines, circles and ellipses in a raster. In W.H.J. Feijen, A.J.M. van Gasteren, D. Gries and J. Misra, editors, *Beauty is our Business: A Birthday Salute to Edsger W. Dijkstra*, pp 427–434, Springer Verlag, New York.

Teaching hardware and software verification in a uniform framework

13.1 Introduction

Formal verification is a rapidly evolving area. There are many theories and notations in development and use (e.g. program logics, modal logics, process algebras, semantic theories, specification notations). Furthermore, tools are emerging that promise to allow formal theories to be applied to industrial scale problems. A challenge in teaching this material at the undergraduate level is to present an elementary and coherent story that will not immediately become obsolete as knowledge and technology advances.

This chapter describes a 24-lecture course for third year undergraduates reading Computer Science at the University of Cambridge. The aim of this course is to provide an elementary introduction to formal verification methods for both software and hardware. Although a number of fairly different topics are covered, an attempt is made to give a smooth presentation by drawing comparisons between the various areas and, as far as possible, placing them in a uniform framework. Section 13.2 is an overview of the goals and content of the course. The subsequent sections contain material to illustrate the way the varous topics are presented in a uniform manner.

13.2 Overview

The approach taken in the computer science course at the University of Cambridge is to concentrate on key ideas, with the hope of providing a foundation for understanding and evaluating particular formalisms and tools that may be met in practice. This is not unusual: many university courses share this goal.

The verification course at Cambridge is designed (i) to mesh with other courses in the undergraduate degree programme; (ii) to provide a coherent introduction to core ideas; (iii) to minimize the required mathematical prerequisites whilst still being rigorous; (iv) to introduce both theories and the principles underlying tools that use them; and (v) to minimize inessential distinctions between hardware and software.

Software courses at Cambridge include functional and logic programming. Each of these contains (or is linked to courses containing) material on foundational topics such as λ-calculus, structural induction, types, first-order logic etc. There is also a course on the theory of concurrency, which includes introductory material on the π-calculus. To avoid duplication, the software part of the course discussed here concentrates on traditional verification methods for sequential imperative programs.

The course starts with an elementary introduction to the use of programming logic — specifically Floyd–Hoare logic (Floyd, 1967; Hoare, 1969) — for establishing both partial and total correctness. The traditional Hilbert style of proof from axioms via rules of inference to theorems is presented first. This defines a formal notion of proof of correctness. Axioms and rules for assignments, sequencing, blocks with local variables, conditionals and while-commands are given and illustrated with numerous examples. To counter any false impression of simplicity, axioms and rules for for-commands and array access and assignment are also presented.

A careful, but informal, account of the notions of soundness and completeness is sketched, including the statement of Clarke's results on the impossibility of having relatively complete Hoare logics for certain combinations of constructs (Clarke, 1985). This is used to discuss the limitations of "axiomatics semantics".

Using Floyd–Hoare logic as a foundation, the "calculation" of programs from specifications is introduced. The refinement relation and the laws refinement are defined on top of Floyd–Hoare logic. This enforces the view that Floyd-Hoare logic is an application-neutral foundation, rather than just a calculus for *post hoc* verification. Refinement is shown to be an applied methodology built on this foundation.

Another methodology built on the same foundation is the *post hoc* verification of already completed programs. Such verification can either be based on traditional "forward proof", or via "backward reasoning" using verification conditions (Igarishi *et al.*, 1975; Good, 1985) (which is closely related to weakest preconditions (Dijkstra, 1976)). The architecture of a traditional verification-condition-based program verifier is described and its operation is justified with respect to Floyd–Hoare logic.

Partial correctness is treated first. It is then shown how total correctness can be handled using well-foundedness arguments (i.e. "variants").

The software part of the course concludes with an introduction to Floyd–Hoare logic viewed as a syntactically sugared subset of higher-order predicate calculus. Students are assumed to be familiar with first-order logic (via the prerequisite course "Logic and Proof"). Higher-order logic is introduced as an extension to first-order logic by allowing variables to range over functions and relations. Types are introduced as a device to preserve consistency (which is what they were originally invented for by Bertrand Russell).

A discussion of deep versus shallow embedding provides a context for discussing the treatment of Floyd–Hoare logic as syntactic sugar (i.e. as a set of macros") for a subset of higher-order logic. Embedding is first illustrated with a little propositional language. Floyd–Hoare logic is then given a shallow embedding and its axioms and rules are shown thereby to become derived rules of higher-order logic.

The second part of the course focuses on hardware. Hardware design at Cambridge is taught using the Verilog hardware description language (Verilog HDL). This includes the usual constructs of imperative programming (assignments, conditionals, while-commands etc) though with a very different semantics (Gordon, 1995). By comparing imperative programs to compute arithmetical functions with similar programs in Verilog (n-bit addition and multiplication are used as examples) it is possible to give an interesting comparison between imperative programming and behavioral specification (see Section 13.6). This contributes to a unified treatment of hardware and software.

A fairly detailed (but informal) description of Verilog HDL's discrete event simulation semantics is covered, with an emphasis on the differences from the semantics of conventional programming languages. It is shown how programming logic can be plausibly applied to behavioral models of hardware designs (though the soundness of Hoare-like rules with respect to simulation semantics is a current research problem).

The relational model of hardware is then introduced (a hardware device is modelled as a relation between the sequences of values on its inputs and outputs) and some standard combinational and sequential examples worked through. The combinational examples include the specification and verification of an n-bit ripple carry adder. The inductive proof of this in higher-order logic makes a nice contrast with a proof using invariants in Floyd–Hoare logic. The verification of devices with sequential behavior is also considered, including an elementary introduction to temporal abstraction. This is illustrated by abstracting between a pure sequential machine (register transfer) level in which the sequential primitive is the unit delay and a more concrete level in which there are explicit clocks and the sequential primitive is an edge triggered d-type register. The treatment follows the approach developed by Herbert (1988) and Melham (1993). A simple parity checker is used as an example.

Various crude transistor-level models are covered, including the simple switch model and a variation due to Mike Fourman that better reflects the role of voltage thresholds when using transitors as switches. Sequential models of transistors are also discussed, and some examples using charge-storage are worked through. The various formal models are compared with simulation models (e.g. the use of high impedance "z" values to model tri-state buses and charge storage). The main point made here is that none of the models suitable for use with formal verification adequately reflect all the electrical properties that at are at play in the working of circuits, but that nevertheless it is possible to perform a useful analysis (e.g. tricky CMOS switching circuits can be verified), though there are dangers due to the inaccuracy of the models. It is emphasized that "engineering compromises" are needed to get models that are simple enough to be tractable, yet still accurate enough to produce useful results.

The next topic covered is temporal logic. A CPU-memory handshake protocol is used as an example (the particular details are due to Joyce, 1988). This is specified (i) directly in higher-order logic using explicit time variables and (ii) in linear-time temporal logic. This illustrates the compactness and readability of temporal logic. A fragment of the implementation of a receiver circuit is then verified directly in predicate calculus. The proof is also sketched using temporal laws, to illustrate how proofs at the temporal logic level can be more compact.

Exhaustive enumeration methods are considered next. Ordered binary decision diagrams (OBDDs) are considered abstractly in the prerequisite course "Logic and Proof". Their use for automatic tautology checking (e.g. the verification of combinational circuits) is outlined. Automatic methods for sequential behavior are also covered, currently rather superficially. Clarke and Emerson's logic CTL is used to illustrate the key ideas of model checking. The presentation in Chapter 2 of McMillan's book (1993) is followed. Control of state explosion by using OBDDs to represent state-transition relations is mentioned (McMillan, 1993, Chapter 3). The property of the handshake receiver circuit that was verified manually corresponds to a formula in CTL*. This is equivalent, via some double-negation trickery, to a formula in CTL. This illustrates the general point that properties sometimes need to be reformulated to fit inside decidable logics. Both linear time and the branching-time (CTL) temporal logic are then shallowly embedded in higher-order logic. Some rules for linear time temporal logic are derived, including the main principle used to verify the receiver circuit at the temporal level. The reformulation of this property in CTL is discussed.

A unifying theme in the course is the use of higher order logic. The advantages and disadvantages of regarding specialized notations (e.g. Floyd–Hoare logic and temporal logic) as syntactic sugar for subsets of predicate calculus are discussed.

Finally, the course ends with a general discussion of the dangers of over-enthusiasm for formal methods. The Viper example is used as an illustration (Cohn, 1989).

The rest of this paper consists of technical outlines of the material in the course that I think readers will find most interesting.

♦ **Section 13.3:** The notion of semantic embedding in higher-order logic and the distinction between deep and shallow embedding.

♦ **Section 13.4:** The shallow embedding of Floyd–Hoare logic in higher-order logic.

♦ **Section 13.5:** A simple theory of operation refinement built on top of Floyd–Hoare logic.

♦ **Section 13.6:** Making the transition from software to hardware via a comparison of programming languages with hardware description languages.

♦ **Section 13.7:** The direct description of hardware structure and behavior in higher-order logic.

♦ **Section 13.8:** The comparison of "raw logic" with temporal logic for specifying a handshake protocol. Embedding of both linear time and branching
time temporal logic in higher-order logic.

This material is mostly condensed from the course notes, which are derived
from writings by myself, Paul Curzon, John Herbert, Jeff Joyce and Tom Melham.
An early version of the software part of the course appeared in a now out-of-print
textbook (Gordon, 1988).

13.3   Semantic embedding

Table 13.1 shows the notations used for higher-order logic, which extends first-
order logic by allowing higher-order variables (i.e. variables whose values are
functions) and higher-order functions.

Table 13.1: Predicate calculus notation

Notation	meaning
T	truth
F	falsity
$P(x)$ (or $P\,x$)	x has property P
$\neg t$	not t
$t_1 \vee t_2$	t_1 or t_2
$t_1 \wedge t_2$	t_1 and t_2
$t_1 \Rightarrow t_2$	t_1 implies t_2
$t_1 \equiv t_2$	t_1 if and only if t_2
$t_1 = t_2$	t_1 equals t_2
$\forall x.\ t[x]$	for all x it is the case that $t[x]$
$\exists x.\ t[x]$	for some x it is the case that $t[x]$
$(t \rightarrow t_1 \mid t_2)$	if t is true then t_1 else t_2

To avoid inconsistency (Russell's paradox) higher order logic must be typed.
Church's simple type system is used (Church, 1960), augmented with Milner-style
polymorphism. This is very similar to the type system of the ML programming
language, which the students are already familiar with.

Types are either *atomic* or *compound*. Examples of atomic types are *bool*, *ind*,
num and *real*, which denote the types of booleans, individuals, natural numbers
and real numbers respectively. Compound types are built from atomic types (or
other compound types) using *type operators*. For example, if σ, σ_1 and σ_2 are
types then so are σ *list*, $\sigma_1 \rightarrow \sigma_2$ and $\sigma_1 \times \sigma_2$, where *list* is a unary type operator

and $\rightarrow$ and $\times$ are an infixed binary type operators. Writing $t : \sigma$ means term t has type σ.

To illustrate semantic embedding consider the propositional language:

$$wff ::= \text{True} \mid \text{N}\,wff \mid \text{C}\,wff\,wff \mid \text{D}\,wff\,wff$$

One approach to embedding, called deep embedding[1], is to represent *wffs* *inside* the host logic (higher order logic in this example) by values of some type, *wff* say, and then define *in the host logic* a semantic function, $\mathcal{M}$ say, by recursion:

$$
\begin{aligned}
\mathcal{M}(\text{True}) &= \text{T} \\
\mathcal{M}(\text{N}\,w) &= \neg\mathcal{M}(w) \\
\mathcal{M}(\text{C}\,w_1\,w_2) &= \mathcal{M}(w_1) \wedge \mathcal{M}(w_2) \\
\mathcal{M}(\text{D}\,w_1\,w_2) &= \mathcal{M}(w_1) \vee \mathcal{M}(w_2)
\end{aligned}
$$

Here $\mathcal{M}$ is a constant of higher order logic of type *wff*$\rightarrow$*bool*.

Another approach, called shallow embedding, is to set up notational conventions for translating *wffs* into host logic terms. Suppose $[\![w]\!]$ is the translation of w into higher order logic. The operation $w \mapsto [\![w]\!]$ is not defined "inside" the host logic, but corresponds to meta-level "syntactic sugar" (or "macros", in programming jargon). The translation of w into logic is defined (recursively) by:

$$
\begin{aligned}
[\![\text{True}]\!] &\equiv \text{``}T\text{''} \\
[\![\text{N}\,w]\!] &\equiv \text{``}\neg\text{''} \frown [\![w]\!] \\
[\![\text{C}\,w_1\,w_2]\!] &\equiv [\![w_1]\!] \frown \text{``}\wedge\text{''} \frown [\![w_2]\!] \\
[\![\text{D}\,w_1\,w_2]\!] &\equiv [\![w_1]\!] \frown \text{``}\vee\text{''} \frown [\![w_2]\!]
\end{aligned}
$$

Deep and shallow embedding are really two ends of a spectrum. At intermediate points of this spectrum some aspects of the semantics would be formalized inside the host logic and others as informal notational conventions.

The advantage of deep embedding is that theorems about the embedded language can be proved. For example:

$$\forall w_1\,w_2 \in wff.\ \mathcal{M}(\text{C}w_1w_2) = \mathcal{M}(\text{NDN}w_1\text{N}w_2)$$

Deep embedding formalizes more of the embedding, but also requires a host logic expressive enough to accommodate this formalization.

With shallow embedding only theorems in the embedded language are provable. In the example above, quantification over *wffs* is not expressible. There is less in the logic, and hence the embedding is less demanding on it and so it is often easier to support complex notations.

13.4   A shallow embedding of Floyd–Hoare logic

The little imperative programming language specified by the grammar given below is a subset of that used in the course. In this specification, the variable N ranges over the *numerals* 0, 1, 2 etc, the variable V ranges over *program variables*[2] X, Y, Z etc, the variables E, E_1, E_2 etc. range over *integer expressions*, the variables B, B_1, B_2 etc. range over *boolean expressions* and the variables C, C_1, C_2 etc. range over *commands*.

$$E \quad ::= \quad N \mid V \mid E_1 + E_2 \mid E_1 - E_2 \mid E_1 \times E_2 \mid \ldots$$

$$B \quad ::= \quad E_1{=}E_2 \mid E_1 \leq E_2 \mid \ldots$$

$$
\begin{aligned}
C \quad ::= \quad & \text{SKIP} \\
\mid \quad & V := E \\
\mid \quad & C_1 \,;\, C_2 \\
\mid \quad & \text{IF } B \text{ THEN } C_1 \text{ ELSE } C_2 \\
\mid \quad & \text{WHILE } B \text{ DO } C
\end{aligned}
$$

13.4.1 Axioms and rules of Hoare logic

$\vdash \{P\}\, C\, \{Q\}$ means $\{P\}\, C\, \{Q\}$ is either an instance of one of the axiom schemes A1 or A2 below, or can be deduced by a sequence of applications of the rules R1, R2, R3, R4, or R5 below from such instances. If P is a formula of predicate logic, then $\vdash P$ means that P can be deduced from the laws of logic and arithmetic.

A1: the SKIP-axiom. For any formula P:

$$\vdash \{P\}\ \text{SKIP}\ \{P\}$$

A2: the assignment-axiom. For any formula P, program variable V and integer expression E:

$$\vdash \{P[E/V]\}\ V := E\ \{P\}$$

where $P[E/V]$ denotes the result of substituting E for all free occurrences of V in P (and free variables are renamed, if necessary, to avoid capture).

R1: the rule of precondition strengthening. For any formulae P, P' and Q, and command C:

$$\frac{\vdash P' \Rightarrow P \qquad \vdash \{P\}\, C\, \{Q\}}{\vdash \{P'\}\, C\, \{Q\}}$$

R2: the rule of postcondition weakening. For any formulae P, Q and Q', and command C:

$$\frac{\vdash \{P\}\, C\, \{Q\} \qquad \vdash Q \Rightarrow Q'}{\vdash \{P\}\, C\, \{Q'\}}$$

R3: the sequencing rule. For any formulae P, Q and R, and commands C_1 and C_2:

$$\frac{\vdash \{P\}\, C_1\, \{Q\} \qquad \vdash \{Q\}\, C_2\, \{R\}}{\vdash \{P\}\, C_1\,;\, C_2\, \{R\}}$$

R4: the IF-rule. For any formulae P, Q and B, and commands C_1 and C_2:

$$\frac{\vdash \{P \wedge B\}\, C_1\, \{Q\} \qquad \vdash \{P \wedge \neg B\}\, C_2\, \{Q\}}{\vdash \{P\}\ \text{IF } B \text{ THEN } C_1 \text{ ELSE } C_2\, \{Q\}}$$

Notice that in this rule (and also in R5 below) it is assumed that B is both a boolean expression of the programming language and a formula of predicate logic.

R5: the WHILE-rule. For any formulae P and B, and command C:

$$\frac{\vdash \{P \wedge B\}\, C\, \{P\}}{\vdash \{P\}\ \text{WHILE } B \text{ DO } C\, \{P \wedge \neg B\}}$$

A formula P such that $\vdash \{P \wedge B\}\, C\, \{P\}$ is called an *invariant* of C for B.

13.4.2   Semantics of commands

The traditional denotation of a command C is a function, $\mathsf{Meaning}(C)$ say, from machine states to machine states. The idea is:

$$\mathsf{Meaning}(C)(s) \ = \ \text{“the state resulting from executing } C \text{ in state } s\text{”}$$

Since WHILE-commands need not terminate, the functions denoted by commands are *partial*. For example, for any s and C $\mathsf{Meaning}(\text{WHILE T DO } C)(s)$ will be undefined. Since functions in conventional predicate calculus are total, they cannot be used as command denotations. Instead, the meaning of commands are predicates on pairs of states (s_1, s_2); the idea being that if C denotes c then:

$$c(s_1, s_2) \ \equiv \ (\mathsf{Meaning}(C)(s_1) \ = \ s_2)$$

i.e.

$$c(s_1, s_2) = \begin{cases} \mathsf{T} & \text{if executing } C \text{ in state } s_1 \text{ results in state } s_2 \\ \\ \mathsf{F} & \text{otherwise} \end{cases}$$

If c_{WHILE} is the predicate denoted by WHILE T DO C, then:

$$\forall s_1\ s_2 .\ c_{WHILE}(s_1, s_2) = \mathsf{F}$$

Formally, the type *state* of states is defined by: *state* $=$ *string*$\rightarrow$*num*. The notation "*XYZ*" will be used for the string consisting of the three characters X, Y

and Z; thus "XYZ" has type *string*. A state s in which the strings "X", "Y" and "Z" are bound to 1, 2 and 3 respectively, and all other strings are bound to 0, is defined by:

$$s \;=\; \lambda x. \, (x = \text{``}X\text{''} \to 1 \mid (x = \text{``}Y\text{''} \to 2 \mid (x = \text{``}Z\text{''} \to 3 \mid 0)))$$

If e, b and c are the denotations of E, B and C respectively, then:

$$
\begin{aligned}
e &: \; state \to num \\
b &: \; state \to bool \\
c &: \; state \times state \to bool
\end{aligned}
$$

For example, the denotation of $X + 1$ would be $\lambda s. \, s\text{``}X\text{''} + 1$ and the denotation of $(X + Y) > 10$ would be $\lambda s. \, (s\text{``}X\text{''} + s\text{``}Y\text{''}) > 10$.

It is convenient to introduce the notations $[\![E]\!]$ and $[\![B]\!]$ for the logic terms representing the denotations of E and B. For example:

$$
\begin{aligned}
[\![X + 1]\!] &= \lambda s. \, s\text{``}X\text{''} + 1 \\
[\![(X + Y) > 10]\!] &= \lambda s. \, (s\text{``}X\text{''} + s\text{``}Y\text{''}) > 10
\end{aligned}
$$

Note that $[\![E]\!]$ and $[\![B]\!]$ are terms, i.e. syntactic objects.

Sometimes it is necessary for pre- and postconditions to contain logical variables that are not program variables. An example is:

$$\{X = x \land Y = y\} \; Z := X; \; X := Y; \; Y := Z \; \{X = y \land Y = x\}$$

Here x and y are logical variables whereas X and Y (and Z) are program variables. The formulae representing the correct semantics of the pre- and postconditions of this specification are:

$$
\begin{aligned}
[\![X = x \land Y = y]\!] &= \lambda s. \, s\text{``}X\text{''} = x \land s\text{``}Y\text{''} = y \\
[\![X = y \land Y = x]\!] &= \lambda s. \, s\text{``}X\text{''} = y \land s\text{``}Y\text{''} = x
\end{aligned}
$$

The convention adopted here is that upper case variables are program variables and lower case variables are logical variables (as in the example just given).

13.4.3   Embedding of commands

Predicates in higher-order logic that correspond to the five kinds of commands are defined. For each command C, a term $[\![C]\!]$ of type *state* $\times$ *state* $\to$ *bool* is defined as follows:

1. $[\![\text{SKIP}]\!] = \text{Skip}$

   where the constant Skip is defined by:

$$\text{Skip}(s_1, s_2) \;=\; (s_1 = s_2)$$

2. $[\![V := E]\!] = \mathsf{Assign}(``V", [\![E]\!])$

   where the constant Assign is defined by:

   $$\mathsf{Assign}(v, e)(s_1, s_2) = (s_2 = \mathsf{Bnd}(e, v, s_1))$$

   where:

   $$\mathsf{Bnd}(e, v, s) = \lambda x.\, (x = v \to e\, s \mid s\, x)$$

3. $[\![C_1 ; C_2]\!] = \mathsf{Seq}([\![C_1]\!], [\![C_2]\!])$

   where the constant Seq is defined by:

   $$\mathsf{Seq}(c_1, c_2)(s_1, s_2) = \exists s.\, c_1(s_1, s) \wedge c_2(s, s_2)$$

4. $[\![\mathrm{IF}\ B\ \mathrm{THEN}\ C_1\ \mathrm{ELSE}\ C_2]\!] = \mathsf{If}([\![B]\!], [\![C_1]\!], [\![C_2]\!])$

   where the constant If is defined by:

   $$\mathsf{If}(b, c_1, c_2)(s_1, s_2) = (b\, s_1 \to c_1(s_1, s_2) \mid c_2(s_1, s_2))$$

5. $[\![\mathrm{WHILE}\ B\ \mathrm{DO}\ C]\!] = \mathsf{While}([\![B]\!], [\![C]\!])$

   where the constant While is defined by:

   $$\mathsf{While}(b, c)(s_1, s_2) = \exists n.\, \mathsf{Iter}(n)(b, c)(s_1, s_2)$$

   where $\mathsf{Iter}(n)$ is defined by primitive recursion as follows:

   $$\begin{aligned} \mathsf{Iter}(0)(b, c)(s_1, s_2) &= \mathsf{F} \\ \mathsf{Iter}(n{+}1)(b, c)(s_1, s_2) &= \mathsf{If}(b, \mathsf{Seq}(c, \mathsf{Iter}(n)(b, c)), \mathsf{Skip})(s_1, s_2) \end{aligned}$$

13.4.4   Embedding partial correctness specifications

A partial correctness specification $\{P\}\, C\, \{Q\}$ denotes:

$$\forall s_1\ s_2.\ [\![P]\!]\, s_1 \wedge [\![C]\!](s_1, s_2) \Rightarrow [\![Q]\!]\, s_2$$

To abbreviate this formula, define a constant Spec by:

$$\mathsf{Spec}(p, c, q) = \forall s_1\ s_2.\, p\, s_1 \wedge c(s_1, s_2) \Rightarrow q\, s_2$$

Note that the denotation of pre- and postconditions P and Q are not just the logical formulae themselves, but are $[\![P]\!]$ and $[\![Q]\!]$. For example, in the specification $\{X = 1\}\, C\, \{Q\}$, the precondition $X = 1$ asserts that the value of the string "X" in the initial state is 1, hence the precondition denotes $\lambda s.\, s``X" = 1$. Thus:

$$\{X = 1\}\ X := X + 1\ \{X = 2\}$$

denotes

$$\mathsf{Spec}([\![X = 1]\!], \mathsf{Assign}(``X", [\![X + 1]\!]), [\![X = 2]\!])$$

i.e.

$$\mathsf{Spec}((\lambda s.\ s``X" = 1),\ \mathsf{Assign}(``X", \lambda s.\ s``X" + 1),\ \lambda s.\ s``X" = 2)$$

Example: In the specification below, x and y are logical variables whereas X and Y (and Z) are program variables.

$$\{X = x \wedge Y = y\}\ Z := X;\ X := Y;\ Y := Z\ \{X = y \wedge Y = x\}$$

The semantics of this is thus represented by the term:

$$\mathsf{Spec}([\![X = x \wedge Y = y]\!],$$
$$\mathsf{Seq}(\mathsf{Assign}(``Z", [\![X]\!]),$$
$$\mathsf{Seq}(\mathsf{Assign}(``X", [\![Y]\!]), \mathsf{Assign}(``Y", [\![Z]\!]))),$$
$$[\![X = y \wedge Y = x]\!])$$

which abbreviates:

$$\mathsf{Spec}((\lambda s.\ s``X" = x \wedge s``Y" = y),$$
$$\mathsf{Seq}(\mathsf{Assign}(``Z", \lambda s.\ s``X"),$$
$$\mathsf{Seq}(\mathsf{Assign}(``X", \lambda s.\ s``Y"), \mathsf{Assign}(``Y", \lambda s.\ s``Z"))),$$
$$\lambda s.\ s``X" = y \wedge s``Y" = x)$$

13.4.5 Embedding Floyd–Hoare logic

Floyd–Hoare logic can be embedded in higher-order logic simply by regarding the concrete syntax as an abbreviation for the corresponding semantic formulae described in Section 13.4.2. For example:

$$\{X = x\}\ X := X + 1\ \{X = x + 1\}$$

can be interpreted as abbreviating:

$$\mathsf{Spec}([\![X = x]\!], \mathsf{Assign}(``X", [\![X + 1]\!]), [\![X = x + 1]\!])$$

i.e.

$$\mathsf{Spec}((\lambda s.\ s``X" = x),\ \mathsf{Assign}(``X", \lambda s.\ s``X" + 1),\ \lambda s.\ s``X" = x + 1)$$

If partial correctness specifications are interpreted this way then the axioms and rules of Hoare logic become derived rules of higher-order logic. For example, to derive the SKIP-axiom it must be shown for arbitrary P that:

$$\vdash \{P\}\ \mathsf{SKIP}\ \{P\}$$

which abbreviates:

$$\vdash \mathsf{Spec}([\![P]\!], \mathsf{Skip}, [\![P]\!])$$

This follows from the definition of Spec and Skip.

13.5 Refinement as derived Hoare logic

The approach to refinement presented in the course[3] follows the style of refinement developed by Morgan (1990), but is semantically founded on Floyd–Hoare logic, rather than on Dijkstra's theory of weakest preconditions. This foundation is a bit more concrete and syntactical than the traditional one: a specification is identified with its set of possible implementations and refinement is represented as manipulations on sets of ordinary commands. This approach aims to convey the "look and feel" of (Morgan style) refinement using the notational and conceptual ingredients introduced in other parts of the course.

The notation $[P, Q]$ will be used for specifications, and thus:

$$[P, Q] = \{\, C \mid \vdash [P]\, C\, [Q] \,\}$$

The process of refinement will then consist of a sequence of steps that make systematic design decisions to narrow down the sets of possible implementations until a unique implementation is reached. Thus a refinement of a specification S to an implementation C has the form:

$$S \supseteq S_1 \supseteq S_2 \supseteq \cdots \supseteq S_n \supseteq \{C\}$$

The initial specification S has the form $[P, Q]$ and each intermediate specification S_i is obtained from its predecessor S_{i-1} by the application of a *refinement law*.

In the literature $S \supseteq S'$ is normally written $S \sqsubseteq S'$. The use of "$\supseteq$" here, instead of the more abstract "$\sqsubseteq$", reflects the concrete interpretation of refinement as the narrowing down of sets of implementations.

13.5.1 Refinement laws

The refinement laws are derived from the axioms and rules of Floyd–Hoare logic. In order to state these laws, the usual notation for commands is extended to sets of commands as follows ($\mathcal{C}, \mathcal{C}_1, \mathcal{C}_2$ etc. range over *sets* of commands):

$\mathcal{C}_1; \cdots ; \mathcal{C}_n$	$= \{\, C_1; \cdots ; C_n \mid C_1 \in \mathcal{C}_1 \wedge \cdots \wedge C_n \in \mathcal{C}_n \,\}$
BEGIN VAR $V_1; \cdots$ VAR $V_n; C$ END	$= \{\, \text{BEGIN VAR } V_1; \cdots \text{VAR } V_n; C \text{ END} \mid C \in \mathcal{C} \,\}$
IF S THEN $\mathcal{C}$	$= \{\, \text{IF } S \text{ THEN } C \mid C \in \mathcal{C} \,\}$
IF S THEN $\mathcal{C}_1$ ELSE $\mathcal{C}_2$	$= \{\, \text{IF } S \text{ THEN } C_1 \text{ ELSE } C_2 \mid C_1 \in \mathcal{C}_1 \wedge C_2 \in \mathcal{C}_2 \,\}$
WHILE S DO $\mathcal{C}$	$= \{\, \text{WHILE } S \text{ DO } C \mid C \in \mathcal{C} \,\}$

This notation for sets of commands can be viewed as constituting a wide spectrum language.

Note that such sets of commands are *monotonic* with respect to refinement (i.e. inclusion). If $\mathcal{C} \supseteq \mathcal{C}', \mathcal{C}_1 \supseteq \mathcal{C}'_1, \ldots, \mathcal{C}_n \supseteq \mathcal{C}'_n$ then:

$\mathcal{C}_1; \cdots; \mathcal{C}_n$	$\supseteq \mathcal{C}'_1; \cdots; \mathcal{C}'_n$
BEGIN VAR $V_1; \cdots$ VAR $V_n; \mathcal{C}$ END	$\supseteq$ BEGIN VAR $V_1; \cdots$ VAR $V_n; \mathcal{C}'$ END
IF S THEN $\mathcal{C}$	$\supseteq$ IF S THEN $\mathcal{C}'$
IF S THEN $\mathcal{C}_1$ ELSE $\mathcal{C}_2$	$\supseteq$ IF S THEN $\mathcal{C}'_1$ ELSE $\mathcal{C}'_2$
WHILE S DO $\mathcal{C}$	$\supseteq$ WHILE S DO $\mathcal{C}'$

This monotonicity shows that a command can be refined by separately refining its constituents.

The following "laws" follow directly from the definitions above and the axioms and rules of Floyd–Hoare logic.

The skip law
$[P, P] \supseteq \{\text{SKIP}\}$

The assignment law
$[P[E/V], P] \supseteq \{V := E\}$

Derived assignment law
$[P, Q] \supseteq \{V := E\}$
provided $\vdash P \Rightarrow Q[E/V]$

Precondition weakening
$[P, Q] \supseteq [R, Q]$
provided $\vdash P \Rightarrow R$

Postcondition strengthening
$[P, Q] \supseteq [P, R]$
provided $\vdash R \Rightarrow Q$

The sequencing law
$[P, Q] \supseteq [P, R]; [R, Q]$

The block law
$[P, Q] \supseteq$ BEGIN VAR $V; [P, Q]$ END
where V does not occur in P or Q

The one-armed conditional law
$[P, Q] \supseteq$ IF S THEN $[P \wedge S, Q]$
provided $\vdash P \wedge \neg S \Rightarrow Q$

The two-armed conditional law

$[P, Q] \supseteq$ IF S THEN $[P \wedge S, Q]$ ELSE $[P \wedge \neg S, Q]$

The while law

$[P, P \wedge \neg S] \supseteq$ WHILE S DO $[P \wedge S \wedge (E{=}n), P \wedge (E{<}n)]$

provided $\vdash P \wedge S \Rightarrow E \geq 0$ and where E is an integer-valued expression and n is an identifier not occurring in P, S or E.

13.5.2   An example

$[P_1, P_2, P_3, \ldots, P_{n-1}, P_n]$ abbreviates $[P_1, P_2]$; $[P_2, P_3]$; $\ldots$; $[P_{n-1}, P_n]$. The brackets around fully refined specifications of the form $\{C\}$ will be omitted. Let $\mathcal{I}$ stand for the invariant $X = R + (Y \times Q)$. In the refinement that follows, the comments in brackets after the symbol "$\supseteq$" indicate the refinement law used for the step.

$[Y > 0, \mathcal{I} \wedge R \leq Y]$
$\supseteq$ (Sequencing)
$[Y > 0, R = X \wedge Y > 0, \mathcal{I} \wedge R \leq Y]$
$\supseteq$ (Assignment)
$R := X$; $[R = X \wedge Y > 0, \mathcal{I} \wedge R \leq Y]$.
$\supseteq$ (Sequencing)
$R := X$; $[R = X \wedge Y > 0, R = X \wedge Y > 0 \wedge Q = 0, \mathcal{I} \wedge R \leq Y]$
$\supseteq$ (Assignment)
$R := X$; $Q := 0$; $[R = X \wedge Y > 0 \wedge Q = 0, \mathcal{I} \wedge R \leq Y]$
$\supseteq$ (Precondition weakening)
$R := X$; $Q := 0$; $[\mathcal{I} \wedge Y > 0, \mathcal{I} \wedge R \leq Y]$
$\supseteq$ (Postcondition strengthening)
$R := X$; $Q := 0$; $[\mathcal{I} \wedge Y > 0, \mathcal{I} \wedge Y > 0 \neg (Y \leq R)]$
$\supseteq$ (While)
$R := X$; $Q := 0$;
WHILE $Y \leq R$ DO $[\mathcal{I} \wedge Y > 0 \wedge Y \leq R \wedge R = n]$
$\qquad\qquad\qquad [\mathcal{I} \wedge Y > 0 \wedge R < n]$
$\supseteq$ (Sequencing)
$R := X$; $Q := 0$;
WHILE $Y \leq R$ DO $[\mathcal{I} \wedge Y > 0 \wedge Y \leq R \wedge R = n]$
$\qquad\qquad\qquad [X = (R - Y) + (Y \times Q) \wedge Y > 0 \wedge (R - Y) < n]$
$\qquad\qquad\qquad [\mathcal{I} \wedge Y > 0 \wedge R < n]$
$\supseteq$ (Derived assignment)
$R := X$; $Q := 0$;
WHILE $Y \leq R$ DO $[\mathcal{I} \wedge Y > 0 \wedge Y \leq R \wedge R = n]$
$\qquad\qquad\qquad [X = (R - Y) + (Y \times Q) \wedge Y > 0 \wedge (R - Y) < n]$
$\qquad\qquad\qquad R := R - Y$
$\supseteq$ (Derived assignment)
$R := X$; $Q := 0$;
WHILE $Y \leq R$ DO $Q := Q + 1$; $R := R - Y$

The "Morgan style of refinement" illustrated here provides laws for systematically introducing structure with the aim of eventually getting rid of specification statements.

The "Back style" (Back, 1989) is less rigidly top-down and provides a more flexible (but maybe also less disciplined) program development framework. It also emphasizes and supports transformations that distribute control (e.g. going from sequential to parallel programs). General algebraic laws not specifically involving specification statements are used, for example: $C = $ IF S THEN C ELSE C, which can be used both to introduce and eliminate conditionals.

Both styles of refinement include large-scale transformations (data refinement and superposition) where a refinement step actually is a much larger change than a simple IF or WHILE introduction. However, this is not covered in the course.

13.6   From software to hardware

Hardware verification by formal proof has had more industrial success than formal software verification. This is for several reasons: the high cost and visibility of hardware design errors, the relative tractability of hardware compared with software (many useful hardware correctness properties can be automatically verified using decision procedures) and the fact that the use of formal methods (e.g. Boolean algebra) to reason about hardware designs is a well-established practice in electrical engineering, but not in software engineering.

There are both similarities and differences between software and hardware. Here, for example, is a description of a simple add-and-shift multiplier in the Verilog hardware description language:

```
while (i < n)
  begin SUM = P + A[0]*B;
        CARRY = SUM[n];
        P = SUM[(n-1):0];
        A = {P[0],A} >> 1;
        P = {CARRY,P} >> 1;
        i = i + 1;
  end
```

Even if one doesn't know Verilog, it is clear that this hardware specification is a kind of program. However, from a programming point of view code like that shown above is an implementation, whereas from a hardware point of view it is a relatively abstract "behavioral specification". An implementation is something like that shown in Figure 13.1.

A major part of the hardware part of the course concerns methods for representing diagrams like this in higher-order logic to enable the proof of various kinds of correctness properties (see Section 13.7). As a prelude to this, and to smooth the transition from software to hardware, the hardware part of the course starts with a comparison between imperative programs and hardware specifications using hardware description languages.

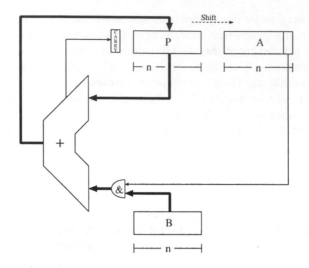

Figure 13.1: A shift-and-add multiplier

13.6.1 Behavioral specification of hardware

A ripple carry adder is a simple example that can be used to compare various styles of software and hardware specification.

Treating words as arrays of bits, the "ripple carry" binary addition algorithm can thus be represented by the following program for adding two words A and B of size N and putting the result in SUM ($a \oplus b \oplus c$ computes the sum bit, where $\oplus$ is "exclusive-or", and $(a \wedge b) \vee (c \wedge (a \oplus b))$ the carry bit of the sum of a, b and c).

```
I := 0; CARRY := F; SUM := W N 0;
WHILE I < N DO
 BEGIN
  SUM[I] := A[I] ⊕ B[I] ⊕ CARRY;
  CARRY := (A[I] ∧ B[I]) ∨ (CARRY ∧ (A[I] ⊕ B[I]));
  I := I+1
 END
```

This is a behavioral specification written in a programming language. The corresponding behavioral specification in Verilog HDL is:

```
I=0; CARRY=0; SUM=0;
   while (I < N)
     begin SUM[I] = A[I] ^ B[I] ^ CARRY;
           CARRY = (A[I] & B[I]) | (CARRY & (A[I] ^ B[I]));
           I = I+1;
     end
```

In Verilog ^ is exclusive-or, | is disjunction and & is conjunction.

The Verilog program is superficially very similar to the simple imperative program, but whereas the latter constitutes an implementation (i.e. is "code"), the Verilog represents an abstract behavioural model. Compilers from behavioral HDLs to hardware implementations (i.e. circuits) are still at a relatively early stage of development — only advanced hardware compilers could handle the example above.

A yet more abstract Verilog specification of the adder that just does addition without giving any particular algorithm would simply be:

```
{CARRY,SUM} = A + B + CARRY
```

Here {CARRY,SUM} is the concatenation of the one-bit CARRY and the n-bit SUM. Paradoxically, this is easier to compile to hardware: just generate a standard adder cell.

The semantics of HDLs like Verilog and VHDL are based on discrete event simulation. This is a different model of computation than that normally used for imperative programming languages. However, as the adder example illustrates, the two kinds of semantics can be used to get similar results.

13.6.2 Structural specification of hardware

The standard hardware structure for implementing a ripple carry adder is shown in Figure 13.2

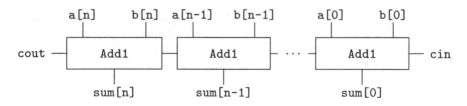

Figure 13.2: A ripple carry adder

A simple structural HDL is MODEL. Here is the description of the above adder in it:

```
PART Adder_Imp (n) [a(0:n),b(0:n),cin] -> sum(0:n),cout
  SIGNAL c(0:n+1)
  INTEGER i
  cin -> c(0)
  FOR i = 0:n CYCLE
   Add1[a(i),b(i),c(i)] -> sum(i),c(i+1)
  REPEAT
```

```
    c(n+1) -> cout
END
```

Another European HDL is Ella. An iterative structural specification of the same circuit in Ella is:

```
MAC N_BIT_ADDER = ([INT n]bit: a b, bit: cin) -> ([n]bit, bit):
    BEGIN
        MAKE [n]Add1: fulladd.
        LET carry = cin CONC ([INT k=1..n-1]fulladd[k][2]).
        FOR INT k=1..n JOIN (a[k], b[k], carry[k]) -> fulladd[k].
        OUTPUT ([INT k=1..n]fulladd[k][1], fulladd[n][2])
    END
```

The constructs of Ella won't be explained here, beyond noting that the MAKE construct generates an array of n one-bit adders, and the FOR construct connects them up. Structural specifications can also be written recursively in a functional style:

```
MAC Adder_Imp {INT n} = ([n]bit: a b, bit: cin) -> ([n]bit, bit):
    (LET oneadd = Add1(a[1], b[1], cin).
     OUTPUT IF n=1
            THEN ([1]oneadd[1], oneadd[2])
            ELSE (LET recadder =
                    Adder_Imp{n-1}(a[2..n], b[2..n], oneadd[2]).
                  OUTPUT (oneadd[1] CONC recadder[1], recadder[2]))
          FI)
```

Ella, unlike MODEL, also allows behavioral specifications. These are functional programs operating on sequences of values (representing signals).

Parameterized structures cannot be expressed in currently used versions of structural Verilog[4]. A structural specification of a four-bit version of the adder in Verilog (with a behavioural specification of Add1) is:

```
module AdderImp (a, b, sum, cout);
  input[3:0] a, b;
  output[3:0] sum;
  output cout;
  wire[3:0]carry;

  function [1:0] Add1;
    input a, b, c;
    Add1 = {(a&b)|(c&(a^b)), a^b^c};
  endfunction

  assign {carry[0],sum[0]} = Add1(a[0],b[0],0);
  assign {carry[1],sum[1]} = Add1(a[1],b[1],carry[0]);
  assign {carry[2],sum[2]} = Add1(a[2],b[2],carry[1]);
  assign {carry[3],sum[3]} = Add1(a[3],b[3],carry[2]);

  assign cout = carry[3];

endmodule
```

If Verilog allowed structural iteration then one could write something like the following, instead of the four assignments above:

```
for(n=0;n<=N;n=n+1)
  assign {carry[n],sum[n]} = Add1(a[n],b[n],(n=0)?0:carry[n-1]]);
```

Unfortunately Verilog 1.0 does not allow this (though some form of structural iteration is available in Verilog 2.0).

Structural HDLs can be directly translated into higher-order logic. This is discussed in the course. For example, the translation of the MODEL specification of the adder into logic is:

$$\text{Adder\_Imp}(n)(a, b, cin, sum, cout) \equiv$$
$$\exists c.$$
$$cin = c(0) \ \wedge$$
$$\text{Iterate } (0, n) \ (\lambda i. \ \text{Add1}(a(i), b(i), c(i), sum(i), c(i+1))) \ \wedge$$
$$c(n+1) = cout$$

13.6.3   Sequential examples

The ripple carry adder is a combinational example, i.e. it is just a combination of gates; there is no clocked logic, or other kinds of sequencing. The behavioral specifications of it used standard programming idioms (iteration and sequencing) to characterize the desired function, but these idioms were not meant to reflect any hardware implementation.

With sequential devices, a state held in registers is modified on successive clock cycles. There is a more direct correspondence between program and hardware execution. Consider, for example, the add-and-shift multiplier example whose schematic is given above.

Hennessey and Patterson (1990) describe the algorithm based on this architecture as follows:

> The numbers to be multiplied are $a_{n-1}a_{n-2}\cdots a_0$ and $b_{n-1}b_{n-2}\cdots b_0$, and they are placed in registers A and B, respectively. Register P is initially zero. There are two parts to each multiply step.
>
> 1. If the least significant bit of A is 1, then register B, containing $b_{n-1}b_{n-2}\cdots b_0$, is added to P; otherwise $00\cdots00$ is added to P. The sum is placed back in P.
>
> 2. Registers P and A are shifted right, with the low-order bit of P being moved into register A and the rightmost bit of A, which is not used in the rest of the algorithm, being shifted out.
>
> After n steps, the product appears in registers P and A, with A holding the lower-order bits.

A Verilog representation of this algorithm is:

```
while (i < n)
  begin SUM = P + A[0]*B;
        CARRY = SUM[n];    P = SUM[(n-1):0];
```

```
        A = {P[0],A} >> 1; P = {CARRY,P} >> 1;
        i = i + 1;
  end
```

In the course, Floyd–Hoare logic is used to verify the imperative programs mimicking the Verilog specifications for ripple carry addition and multiplication. This shows that Floyd–Hoare logic is applicable to behavioral HDLs (to the extent that the little language of commands can be considered to be such an HDL). It also provides an interesting point of comparison with the direct verifications of hardware structures in higher-order logic.

13.7   Direct specification of hardware in logic

Consider a device Dev with external lines a1, a2, ... , am, b1, b2, ... , bn (as shown in Figure 13.3).

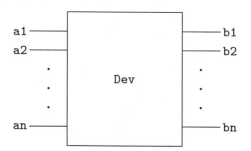

Figure 13.3: The device Dev

When the device is in operation each line has a value drawn from some set of possible values. Different kinds of device are modeled with different sets of values. The behavior of device Dev is specified by defining a predicate Dev (with $m+n$ arguments) such that $\mathsf{Dev}(a_1, a_2, \ldots, a_m, b_1, b_2, \ldots, b_n)$ holds if and only if $a_1, a_2, \ldots, a_m, b_1, b_2, \ldots, b_n$ are allowable values on the corresponding lines of Dev.

Here are two examples that illustrate the use of predicates to specify behaviour. In the first of these examples the values on lines are modelled with truth-values. In the second example the values on lines are modelled with functions, and consequently the predicate used to specify the behaviour of the device is higher-order.

13.7.1   A delayless switch

Zero-delay combinational devices can be modelled by taking the boolean values T
and F as the allowed values on their lines. An example is a switch (see Figure 13.4).

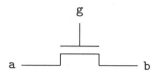

g

a ———⌐___⌐——— b

Figure 13.4: A switch

The intended behaviour of this is that a is connected to b if g has the value T and
a and b are not connected if g has the value F. This behavior can be represented
by the predicate Switch defined by:

$$\text{Switch}(g, a, b) \equiv (g \Rightarrow (a = b))$$

The condition Switch(g, a, b) holds if and only if whenever g is true then a and b
are equal. For example, Switch(T, F, F) holds because T $\Rightarrow$ (F=F) is true, and
Switch(F, T, F) holds because F $\Rightarrow$ (T=F) is true, but Switch(T, T, F) does not
hold because T $\Rightarrow$ (T=F) is false.

In the course other switch models are considered, including ones that better
reflect the physical behavior of transistors and can model aspects of charge storage. The inadequacy of existing models is discussed and the need to make an
"engineering compromise" between tractability and accuracy is stressed.

13.7.2   An inverter with delay

The values occurring on the lines of devices may vary over time. When this happens, their behavior must be represented by predicates whose arguments are "time
varying values". Such values correspond to "waveforms" and can be modeled by
functions of time. For example, the behavior of an inverter with a delay of δ units
of time can be specified with a predicate Invert defined by:

$$\text{Invert}(i, o) \equiv \forall t.\ o(t+\delta) = \neg i(t)$$

Here the values on lines i and o are functions i and o which map times (represented
by numbers) to values (represented by booleans). These functions are in the Invert
relation if and only if for all times t, the value of o at time $t+\delta$ equals the value of
i at time t.

Many other sequential examples are considered in the course. In the past, I have
attempted to cover the basic ideas underlying the specification and verification

of simple microprocessors. However, I found it hard to present the material convincingly in the time available and recently have only considered smaller-scale examples. The specification and formal verification of microprocessors would make a good follow-on course to this one.

13.7.3   Representing circuit structure with predicates

Consider the structure shown in Figure 13.5 (called D).

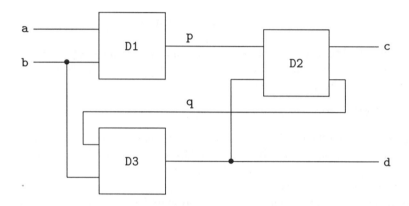

Figure 13.5: The structure D

This device is built by connecting together three component devices D1, D2 and D3. The external lines of D are a, b, c and d. The lines p and q are internal and are not connected to the "outside world". (External lines might correspond to the pins of an integrated circuit, and internal lines to tracks.)

Suppose the behaviors of D1, D2 and D3 are specified by predicates D_1, D_2 and D_3 respectively. How can the behaviour of the system D shown above be derived? Each device constrains the values on its lines. If a, b and p denote the values on the lines a, b and p, then D1 constrains these values so that $D_1(a,b,p)$ holds. To get the constraint imposed by the whole device D, just conjoin (i.e. $\wedge$-together) the constraints imposed by D1, D2 and D3; the combined constraint is thus:

$$D_1(a,b,p) \ \wedge \ D_2(p,d,c) \ \wedge \ D_3(q,b,d)$$

This expression constrains the values on both the external lines a, b, c and d and the internal lines p and q. If D is a "black box" with the internal lines invisible, then what constraints are imposed on its external lines? The variables a, b, c and d will denote possible values at the external lines a, b, c and d if and only if the conjunction above holds *for some* values p and q. A predicate D representing the behavior of D can thus be defined by:

$$D(a,b,c,d) \equiv \exists p\, q.\, D_1(a,b,p) \wedge D_2(p,d,c) \wedge D_3(q,b,d)$$

Thus the behavior corresponding to a circuit is got by conjoining the constraints corresponding to the components, and then existentially quantifying the variables corresponding to the internal lines. This technique of representing circuit diagrams in logic is fairly well known. Other ways of representing structure in logic are also possible.

The examples given in the course aim to demonstrate that higher-order logic is a formalism in which a wide variety of behavior and structure can be directly specified.

Hardware verification requires various kinds of reasoning including mathematical induction (to deal with iterated structures and for proving arithmetic lemmas), temporal concepts (see Section 13.8) and reasoning about abstractions between different time scales. All these can be done using the standard inference rules of logic. In the course, a collection of derived rules of predicate calculus are given that enable proofs of correctness of devices to be written down fairly easily. The exact formulation of correctness is also discussed in some detail.

13.8 Temporal Logic

Temporal logic is useful for expressing requirements for various kinds of protocols. Standard temporal operators are:

- □ "henceforth"
- ◇ "eventually"
- ○ "next"
- U "unless"

and logical connectives (not, ⟶, and) that are "lifted" versions of propositional logic operators.

Figure 13.6 shows a timing diagram for a four-phase handshaking sequence. A request at time t1 by the sender is acknowledged at time t2 by the receiver. A request to end the interaction is signaled at time t3 and eventually acknowledged at time t4.

The handshaking protocol is formally specified by a number of constraints imposed on both the sender and receiver.

A handshaking interaction is initiated whenever dreq becomes true. dreq must continue to be true until this is acknowledged. This constraint is expressed by:

dreq ⟶ (dreq U dack)

A request must be eventually be acknowledged. Furthermore, once dack becomes true, it must remain true until dreq becomes false.

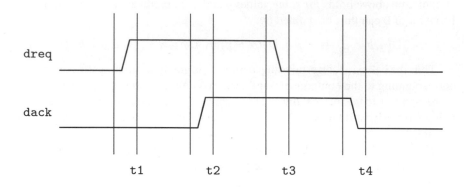

Figure 13.6: A timing diagram for a four-phase handshaking sequence

    dreq $\longrightarrow$ ($\diamond$ dack)
    dack $\longrightarrow$ (dack U (not dreq))

Once a request has been acknowledged, dreq must eventually become false again to signal the end of the interaction. The next request cannot be signaled until dack also returns to false.

    dack $\longrightarrow$ ($\diamond$ (not dreq))
    (not dreq) $\longrightarrow$ ((not dreq) U (not dack))

When dreq becomes false, dack must also becomes false and stay false until the next request.

    (not dreq) $\longrightarrow$ ($\diamond$ (not dack))
    (not dack) $\longrightarrow$ ((not dack) U dreq)

Upon completion of the handshaking interaction, the protocol requires another request to be initiated sometime in the future. This final constraint is usually included in the handshaking protocol specification to obtain the property that system activity never ceases.

    (not dack) $\longrightarrow$ ($\diamond$ dreq)

The use of temporal logic operators to specify the relative order of events in a handshaking protocol has been developed by Bochman (1982), Dill, Clarke, Fujita and others.

13.8.1 Embedding temporal logic in higher-order logic

Temporal logic is often treated as primitive. However, like Floyd–Hoare logic, it can be regarded as syntactic sugar for subsets of higher-order logic. The following defines operators for linear temporal logic.

```
□ P = λt. ∀n.P (t+n)
◇ P = λt. ∃n. P (t+n)
○ P = λt. P(t+1)
P ∪ Q = λt. ∀n. (∀m. m < n ⇒ ¬(Q(t+m))) ⇒ P(t+n)
not P = λt. ¬(P t)
P ⟶ Q = λt. P t ⇒ Q t
P and Q = λt. P t ∧ Q t
true = λt. T
false = λt. F
```

An assertion in temporal logic such as,

$$P \longrightarrow \Diamond(Q \cup R)$$

is only true or false relative to a particular instant of time. A temporal logic formula can be asserted to hold for all times with the function ⊨:

```
(⊨ P)  =  ∀t. P t
```

Inferences rules for direct manipulation of temporal logic assertions can be derived. Many such rules effectively "package up" what would otherwise be tedious and repetitive patterns of inference. For instance, the following theorem provides a particularly useful rule that achieves in a single step, an inference which would otherwise involve a proof by mathematical induction.

```
⊢ ∀P Q. ⊨ ((P and (not Q)) ⟶ (○ P)) ⇒ ⊨ (P ⟶ (P ∪ Q))
```

Note this this is similar to the `while`-rule of Floyd-Hoare logic: P is the invariant and `not` Q the test. Other temporal logic rules include:

```
⊢ ⊨ ((P ⟶ (◇ Q)) and (Q ⟶ R)) ==> ⊨ (P ⟶ (◇ R))
⊢ ⊨ ((not(□ P)) ⟶ (◇(not P)))
⊢ P or (not P) = true
⊢ P and false = false
⊢ P and true = P
```

Earlier the formal specification of the handshaking protocol was given in terms of constraints expressed by a set of temporal logic assertions. One can distinguish

between *functional constraints* on outputs which must be satisfied by a process
and *domain constraints* which are allowable assumptions about inputs. In the
handshaking protocol, constraints imposed on dreq are functional constraints for
the sender process and domain constraints for the receiver process. Constraints
imposed on dack are functional constraints for the receiver process and domain
constraints for the sender process.

It turns out that only some of the domain constraints are actually needed in
each case. Furthermore, these domain constraints are only needed to establish
specific functional constraints. For example, the domain constraint,

$$\text{dreq} \longrightarrow (\text{dreq} \cup \text{dack})$$

that dreq, once true, must remain true can be assumed in showing that the receiver
satisfies the functional constraint,

$$\text{dreq} \longrightarrow (\Diamond \text{ dack})$$

that it will eventually detect and acknowledge the request.

The following definitions give the functional constraints for the sender and
receiver respectively and, where required, the domain constraints which can be
assumed in showing that a process satisfies a particular functional constraint.

```
Sender (dreq,dack) =
  |= ((dreq ⟶ (dreq ∪ dack)) and
      ((not dreq) ⟶ ((not dreq) ∪ (not dack))) and
      ((dack ⟶ (dack ∪ (not dreq))) ⟶
       (dack ⟶ (◇ (not dreq)))) and
      (((not dack) ⟶ ((not dack) ∪ dreq)) ⟶
       ((not dack) ⟶ (◇ dreq))))

Receiver (dreq,dack) =
  |= ((dack ⟶ (dack ∪ (not dreq))) and
      ((not dack) ⟶ ((not dack) ∪ dreq)) and
      ((dreq ⟶ (dreq ∪ dack)) ⟶
       (dreq ⟶ (◇ dack))) and
      (((not dreq) ⟶ ((not dreq) ∪ (not dack))) ⟶
       ((not dreq) ⟶ (◇ (not dack)))))
```

When the sender and receiver parts of the handshaking protocol specification
are both satisfied, this results in the set of constraint mentioned at the beginning
of this section for the system as a whole. This is shown by the following theorem.

```
⊢ Sender(dreq,dack) and
  Receiver(dreq,dack)
  ⇒
  |= ((dreq ⟶ (dreq ∪ dack)) and
      (dreq ⟶ (◇ dack)) and
```

```
(dack ⟶ (dack ∪ (not dreq))) and
(dack ⟶ (◇ (not dreq))) and
((not dreq) ⟶ ((not dreq) ∪ (not dack))) and
((not dreq) ⟶ (◇ (not dack))) and
((not dack) ⟶ ((not dack) ∪ dreq)) and
((not dack) ⟶ (◇ dreq)))
```

13.8.2   An example implementation

An implementation of the receiver is shown in Figure 13.7.

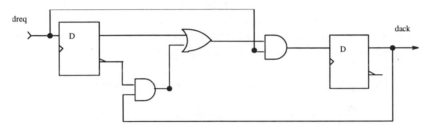

Figure 13.7: An implementation of the receiver

Using the methods sketched in Section 13.7, this is represented by a formula like:

```
⊢ ∀dreq dack.
    Receiver_cct(dreq,dack) =
    (∃q0 qbar0 a0 or0 a1.
      Dtype_bar(dreq,q0,qbar0) ∧
      And_gate(qbar0,dack,a0) ∧
      Or_gate(q0,a0,or0) ∧
      And_gate(dreq,or0,a1) ∧
      Dtype(a1,dack))
```

which simplifies to:

```
⊢ ∀dreq dack.
    Receiver_cct(dreq,dack) =
    (∃q0.
      (∀t. q0(t+1) = dreq t) ∧
      (∀t. dack(t+1) =
            dreq t ∧ (q0 t ∨ (¬q0 t ∧ dack t)))))
```

The implementation is correct if:

$$\text{Receiver\_cct}(dreq, dack) \Rightarrow \text{Receiver}(dreq, dack)$$

This can be proved by straightforward logical methods.

When temporal logic operators are simply abbreviations for higher-order functions, anything which can done with the temporal logic operators can also be done without them using explicit time variables. The flexibility to mix temporal operators and explicit time variables enables the advantages of both styles to be combined. This is illustrated here: the receiver implementation written in higher-order logic is verified against a specification written in temporal logic.

For some temporal logics there are efficient algorithms for automatically checking whether a temporal formula holds for a transition system. The use of such algorithms is called *model checking*, and is a very active and rapidly-changing research area. Model checking is probably provides the most successful application of formal methods for hardware to real world problems.

A common approach to model checking is to represent models (i.e. implementation) by a state transition system. For example, if the state of the receiver implementation is represented by a pair (q0,dack) consisting of the values stored in the two registers, then the implementation defines a *transition system*:

$$(\text{q0, dack}) \quad \text{--->} \quad (\text{dreq, dreq} \land (\text{q0} \lor (\neg\text{q0} \land \text{dack})))$$

A popular model checking system is SMV (McMillan, 1993). Transition systems (models) are expressed in a concurrent imperative programming language and properties are expressed in a branching time logic called computation tree logic (CTL). CTL, which is a subset of a more general logic called CTL*, is a logic for making assertions about transition systems. Branching time logics like CTL* have two kinds of formulas: *state formulas*, which are true in a particular state, and *path formulas*, which are true along a specific path in the transition graph.

A transition system can be represented in higher-order logic by a relation between states: $R(s,s')$ means s' is a possible successor state to s[5].

A path can be represented as a function from natural numbers to states. Such a function p is a path starting from state s in the state transition graph defined by R if and only if Path p (R,s), where:

$$\text{Path p (R,s)} \quad = \quad (\text{p 0 = s}) \land \forall n.\ R(p(n),\ p(n+1))$$

If g is a path formula (i.e. a predicate on paths), then A g is the state formula that is true of (R,s) if and only if g is true of all paths starting from s in the state transition graph defined by R. E g is the dual.

$$\mathsf{A}\ g \ = \ \lambda(R,s).\ \forall p.\ \text{PATH R p s} \Rightarrow g\ p$$
$$\mathsf{E}\ g \ = \ \lambda(R,s).\ \exists p.\ \text{PATH R p s} \land g\ p$$

If f is a state formula then PF f is a path formula that is true of a path p if f is true of the first state in the path.

$$\mathsf{PF}\ f \ = \ \lambda p.\ f(p\ 0)$$

To define the path formulas of CTL*, it is convenient to first define an auxiliary function that chops off m elements of a path (i.e. gives the path suffix starting at the m-th element).

Chop p m = λn. p(m+n)

The path formulas of CTL* are then defined by:

X g = λp. g(Chop p 1)

F g = λp. $\exists$n. g(Chop p n)

G g = λp. $\forall$n. g(Chop p n)

g1 U g2 = λp. $\exists$n. g2(Chop p n) $\land$ $\forall$m. (m<n) $\Rightarrow$ g1(Chop p m)

Notice that the "until" operator of CTL* is subtly different to the linear time "unless" operator introduced earlier: the difference is that U does not require its first argument ever to be true, whereas U does (Manna and Pnueli, 1992, page 189). Consider the first property required of the receiver circuit:

dack $\longrightarrow$ (dack U (not dreq))

This corresponds to the CTL* formula:

A ((p U q) or (G p))

Unfortunately, this is not in CTL, the subset of CTL* handled by SMV, but fortunately it is equivalent to the following formula, which is in CTL[6].

not(E ((p and (not q)) U ((not p) and (not q))))

which is. The former formula could be shown to hold of the receiver circuit by laborious interactive proof using a theorem-proving tool. The latter could be shown automatically using a model checker. This illustrates how sometimes a property needs to be reformulated to get it into the subset handled by an automatic tool.

13.9   Conclusions

The course described here aims to present a diverse collection of specification and verification topics in a coherent way. The two main ideas used to give a uniform approach are:

♦ Treating the various logics as syntactically sugared subsets of higher-order logic.

♦ Making the transition from software to hardware via a comparison of programming languages and hardware description languages.

Two weaknesses of the course are: (i) the semantics of discrete event simulation HDLs are not treated formally and (ii) model checking and other automatic methods are not covered in enough detail. It is hoped to remedy these in the future.

The course in the form described here has been given only once, and at the time of writing has not been examined. It is thus hard to say how well students coped. However, much of the material has been presented in earlier incarnations of the course, and students have generally done well. The little feedback that has been received is generally favourable, though one student commented that the software/hardware transition was a bit forced and artificial. My own feeling is that the course was reasonably successful and I plan to continue with it for several years. I expect the contents will evolve to relect developments in the field (e.g. to cover the principles underlying verification tools that turn out to be useful in practice).

Acknowledgements

In 1994 this course was taught jointly by Paul Cuzon (software) and John Herbert (hardware). They were responsible for introducing the sections on refinement and temporal logic, respectively. Richard Boulton provided the examples of Ella.

Notes

1. The terms "deep" and "shallow" embedding are due to Boulton *et al.* (1992).
2. To distinguish program variables from logical variables, the convention is adopted here that the former are upper case and the latter are lower case. The need for such a convention is explained in Section 13.4.2.
3. The approach described here is due to Paul Curzon. Mark Staples and Joakim Von Wright provided feedback.
4. Parameterized structures can be expressed in the next version of Verilog and in VHDL using "Generate statements".
5. An important implementation technique in model checking is to use BDDs to compactly represent state transition systems. For example, the transition system for the receiver can be represented by the BDD of the Boolean formula:

   $(q0' \Leftrightarrow dreq) \wedge (dack' \Leftrightarrow dreq \wedge (q0 \vee (\neg q0 \wedge dack)))$

   The pair of primed variables $(q0', dack')$ representing the "next state".
6. This encoding was told to me by David Long of AT&T Bell Laboratories.

References

Back, R.J.R. (1981) On correct refinement of programs. *Journal of Computer and Systems Sciences*, **23**(1):49–68, August.

Bochman, G. (1982) Hardware specification with temporal logic, *IEEE Transactions on Computers*, **31**(3):223–231, March.

Boulton, R.J., Gordon, A.D., Gordon, M.J.C., Harrison, J.R., Herbert, J.M.J. and Van Tassel, J. (1992) Experience with embedding hardware description languages in HOL. In V. Stavridou, T.F. Melham and T. Boute, editors, *Theorem Provers in Circuit Design: Theory, Practice and Experience*, Proceedings of the IFIP TC10/WG 10.2 International Conference, Nijmegen, June, IFIP Transactions A-10, pp 129–156, North-Holland.

Clarke, E.M. Jr. (1985) The characterization problem for Hoare logics. In C.A.R. Hoare and J.C. Shepherdson, editors, *Mathematical Logic and Programming Languages*, Prentice Hall International Series in Computer Science, Hemel Hempstead.

Cohn, A.J. (1989) The notion of proof in hardware verification, *Journal of Automated Reasoning*.

Church, A. (1940) A formulation of the simple theory of types, *The Journal of Symbolic Logic*, **5**:56–68.

Dijkstra, E.W. (1976) A Discipline of Programming, Prentice Hall, Englewood Cliffs.

Floyd, R.W. (1967) Assigning meanings to programs. In J.T. Schwartz, editor, *Mathematical Aspects of Computer Science*, Proceedings of Symposia in Applied Mathematics **19**:19–32, American Mathematical Society, Providence, RI.

Good, D.I. (1985) Mechanical proofs about computer programs. In C.A.R. Hoare and J.C. Shepherdson, editors, *Mathematical Logic and Programming Languages*, Prentice Hall International Series in Computer Science, Hemel Hempstead.

Gordon, M.J.C. (1995) The semantic challenge of Verilog HDL. In Proceedings of the *10th Annual IEEE Symposium on Logic in Computer Science*, San Diego, California, 26–29 June.

Gordon, M.J.C. (1988) *Programming Language Theory and its Implementation*, Prentice Hall, Hemel Hempstead.

Hennessey, J.L. and Patterson, D.A. (1990) *Computer Architecture: A Quantitative Approach*, Morgan Kaufman, San Francisco, CA.

Herbert, J.M.J. (1988) Temporal abstraction of digital designs. In G.J. Milne, editor, *The Fusion of Hardware Design and Verification*, North-Holland, Amsterdam.

Hoare, C.A.R. (1969) An axiomatic basis for computer programming, *Communications of the ACM*, **12**(10):576–583, October.

Igarashi, S., London, R.L. and Luckham, D.C. (1975) Automatic program verification I: logical basis and its implementation, *Acta Informatica*, **4**:145–182.

Joyce, J.J. (1988) *Formal Specification and Verification of Asynchronous Processes in Higher Order Logic*, Technical Report No. 136, University of Cambridge Computer Laboratory, June.

McMillan, K.L. (1993) *Symbolic Model Checking*, Kluwer Academic Publishers, Boston.

Manna Z. and Pnueli, A. (1992) *The Temporal Logic of Reactive and Concurrent Systems: Specification*, Springer Verlag, New York.

Melham, T.F. (1993) *Higher Order Logic and Hardware Verification*, Cambridge Tracts in Theoretical Computer Science **31**, Cambridge University Press, Cambridge.

Morgan, C.C. (1990) *Programming from Specifications*, Prentice Hall International Series in Computer Science, Hemel Hempstead.